The Path to a Modern Economics

Henning Schwardt

The Path to a Modern Economics

Dealing with the Complexity of Economic Systems

palgrave
macmillan

Henning Schwardt
Denver, CO, USA

ISBN 978-3-319-52784-0 ISBN 978-3-319-52785-7 (eBook)
DOI 10.1007/978-3-319-52785-7

Library of Congress Control Number: 2017937052

Cover design by Samantha Johnson

Printed on acid-free paper

This Palgrave Macmillan imprint is published by Springer Nature
The registered company is Springer International Publishing AG
The registered company address is: Gewerbestrasse 11, 6330 Cham, Switzerland

Preface

This book offers an overview of different approaches to economic analyses. How we deal with the complexity of real-world economic systems in the formulation of the analytical framework we draw on for our understanding influences how we perceive our economic environment. Our approach shapes how we view a situation, what we believe needs to be addressed to change that situation, and how we think we may be able to accomplish this.

These frameworks have been developed over longer periods of time. The oldest ones have their roots in concepts formulated a couple of centuries ago, while newer ones have developed out of the advances in other sciences over the last decades. It is, however, interesting to reread older economics texts, because not everything the authors observed and developed has been integrated into more formal frameworks that rely on their writings. The ability to translate thoughts into the acceptable methodological tools of the time has partly determined what was adopted, what was nominally integrated, and what was left aside and eventually forgotten, at least by most. Advances in our ability to formulate formal analyses have made earlier ideas more accessible in ways that has been deemed acceptable by many economists, and led to a rediscovery, or reintegration, of concepts that have been around for a long time, and had been ignored for a good period of that time.

Not only social and political interests and interest groups' influence shape our economic analyses, our ability to communicate in and adapt ideas to the specific form that is considered proper economic analyses at a time matters as well. Advances in our ability to grasp more and more intricate aspects of complex systems have opened a number of doors for theoretical economics. As a consequence of these developments, we are also reminded that our formal abilities in the discipline always pose limitations to our analytical understanding.

As stated, we see very different pictures of economies emerge in different analytical frameworks. To leave simpler ones does not merely offer a more involved route to the same result. On the contrary, we may find different, and at times radically different, perspectives for our interpretations of economic issues. Therefore, we will likely be neglecting the richness of different perspectives on economies at our own peril. None is inherently right or wrong. However, how far we go in our avoidance of the complications that an integration of aspects of the complexity of our economic environments presents may well be a first criterion in our decision what frameworks to draw on for addressing economic problems.

Where we find the same or similar results in simple frameworks as in more complicated, and complex ones, we may rely on the simpler ones, especially for communication and teaching. Their shortcomings will have to be remembered though, and while they may be felt to be suitable for communicating certain aspects of our analytical findings, they may also shape a rather simplistic view on an economic environment, and thus do more harm than good in the longer run. When we find different results, brushing the more complicated analyses aside for ease of communication and an anchor to our positions will be difficult to justify in any case.

The results of our analyses not only inform our interpretation of economic environments, they inform our economic policies. Where analyses are inadequate, policies cannot succeed in any structured manner. An awareness of the fact that analyses can only focus on partial aspects of a situation, and that their foundation may be inadequate for the situation in hand, has to be expected from policy advisors and policy makers at all times. When we choose a framework for our policies, we accept the emphases and valuations in that framework. The damage that misguided policies can do is too large not to demand such an awareness. We should be open and honest about the choices we have made.

The potential for misguided decisions, for whatever reason, does not mean that we should ignore the potential for improvements that we may believe to exist, on the other hand. Which framework we draw on for coming to a decision in the policy arena also shapes our evaluation of developments. The pronounced differences in perspectives, and the close relation with political ideologies into which they may be drawn, cannot be avoided. A better understanding of their basic structure may help us address issues and concerns raised better.

In a complex system, we cannot assume a neutral reference point to exist, on which to orient our evaluations. Changes in the structure of an economic system will always result in changes in the distribution of benefits, costs, and risks attributable to economic activities. Likewise, changes in the rules and norms required to structure and stabilize transactions will allow different interests to assert themselves differently. Where a public sector cannot adequately perform its tasks, it is unlikely that it can provide the framework for private agents to take that task on themselves. Differences in the ability to exert influence over others, where not exercised through distorting public sector decisions, can as well, or better, make themselves be felt where no corrective is in place. A solid understanding of economic environments, and policy potential, is all the more important as a consequence.

The overview this book offers, aims to provide a stronger foundation for identifying the different vantage points from which economic analyses are formulated. Insofar, it is a rather basic text. I believe it is not necessary to rely on formal mathematical representations of the concepts discussed. These concepts are accessible in their internal logic, and we can verbally trace how assumptions we make affect the outcomes of our analyses. This holds for the general frameworks, as well as for more detailed analyses of specific situations, and concurrent adaptations in detailed assumptions.

For organizing our discussions, we will introduce a distinction between two families of economic perspectives, as top-down frameworks and bottom-up frameworks. The top-down frameworks formulate assumptions about the economic system, and then populate that system with agents showing certain behavior patterns. There is a certain degree of openness to what behaviors can be accommodated, as long as results do not interfere with the assumptions about the economic system itself. In the bottom-up family, economists ask how individuals act, and then determine the characteristics of the economic arena that results. The formulations in this second group can generally address aspects of complex economic environments more easily, as they do not have to pay attention to a preset structure into which an analysis has to fit.

As in a regular textbook, I have decided to add the references at the end of each chapter with a brief orientation as to their content. I hope that will offer a starting point for further, more in-depth, studies of issues of particular interest, at the same time not overburdening the text itself, and giving credit where credit is due, as, again, this book aims at an overview over what there is, to thereby enhance our ability to identify where to turn next, and leave the readers with the material to build an informed opinion in that regard, and about economic matters more in general.

Denver, CO
November 2016

Henning Schwardt

Contents

1

Trends and Changes in Economies

I

How can we effectively protect people from negative trends in economies? To which degree can we do that at all, for that matter? Are there fundamental differences between different markets or are they essentially the same? Can we forecast economic crises? If that is too difficult, can we at least pinpoint potential problems in sectors of economies, e.g., the financial sector, and form an idea about how these may affect economic activity? How do we deal with economic crises once they have manifested? How do we balance risk and potential in economic matters on the one hand, and security and stability on the other? How do we treat the relation between economic activity and other social activities? Do economic growth and development have effects on the way the economic system itself functions? Or are there fundamental regularities that we can identify independently of context?

The overarching theme to these questions is how can we utilize the economic sphere to improve the conditions of people's lives, and support individual emancipation. Providing answers to these questions, economic thought may then also be able to contribute to addressing the – as of yet still unresolved – fundamental problem for modern

H. Schwardt, *The Path to a Modern Economics*,
DOI 10.1007/978-3-319-52785-7_1

societies focusing on individual well-being and emancipation. Namely, how to organize societies in a way that prevents stagnation and the petrification of social structures. Ongoing processes of change, in order to allow individuals to participate to their potential, and permit societies to reap the rewards of individuals' potential contributions, are the foundation for individual emancipation. Where such processes would result in ongoing turbulence, however, they would be counterproductive. While competition, as a generic concept, is a starting point for fostering such processes, it is thus not the endpoint. We have to understand, embed, and support competition to benefit from its dynamics. In economic matters, influence factors that shape a competitive environment and its potential will have to be understood. How they are understood may depend on the analytical perspective we draw on.

In fact, while the overarching theme is shared by all perspectives on economic systems, there are many answers to more specific questions, including similar, complementary, and contradictory ones. Not many things in matters economic are uncontested. One point is, though: economies are complex. It is this complexity that lies at the heart of controversies over economic issues: the complexity of systems has to be reduced in and for analyses – and there are many ways to go about this task. The different perspectives that result lie behind the different and diverse answers we can find. Views on economies and economic issues differ, and at times radically, exactly because emphases in complexity reduction differ. There is no one proper way to approach economic complexity that we could a priori identify and define as correct. However, as we will see, there may well be good reasons to be more comfortable with some approaches than with others – not because they have proven more satisfying ideologically, but because they appear more fitting for the situation at hand.

What unites the distinct views is a concern with patterns of production, distribution, and consumption in societies, and with larger-scale effects that result from the activities behind these patterns. What potentially pit them against each other are differing interpretations and explanations of observations surrounding these issues, born from the different analytical frameworks that different approaches to complexity reduction result in.

II

Economists (or, originally, philosophers, lawyers, politicians, clergymen, and people from all walks of life with an interest in these matters) have noticeably stepped onto the scene as Western societies started to change and set out on the path to industrialization. Describing and understanding emerging developments and trends in increasingly relevant economic activities and their impact on societies became a pressing concern. And from the very beginning of the formation of modern economics, analyses have been contested. The eventual consolidation of individual analyses into coherent theoretical perspectives followed later. Over time, which approaches commanded more attention and respect has continued to change. For an idea's time to come, a confluence of social, technological, and political factors has been required. Given that a reduction of real-world complexity is a necessity for the formulation of an analytical framework, we may surmise that this will continue to be the case, and dominant perspectives on how to best organize an economic sphere will continue to change as well. Therefore, an understanding of the general approaches to economic analyses can only help us when dealing with different perspectives on economies and economic policies. At least, we will be better able to determine which societal interests may benefit particularly from specific positions on economic issues.

How the different perspectives that result from different approaches to complexity reduction shape suggestions for engaging economic issues will be the topic of this book. We will find differences in the focus of analyses as well as entirely different questions being asked. Permitting more complexity into an analytical framework does frequently not mean a more complicated structure to arrive at a fundamentally similar result to that of a basic analytical setup. It often means very different results, for our interpretation of economic issues, for matters of market regulation in different markets, monetary and fiscal policy, issues of trade, and economic development, or, labor market organization, to name just a few. These issues cannot easily be relegated to the sidelines as fringe matters of limited consequence. Rather, they lie at the heart of modern economic activity.

Fundamental issues in economic systems and the way to approach finding answers to them have long been debated. Where to direct attention, which relations between influence factors to integrate, and how systemic effects may influence outcomes are by no means always easily discernible. And as the perspective shapes the interpretation, different assessments of situations can be passionately embraced by different people. If you have chosen to believe that there are fundamental factors in economic systems that will counter the exercise of private power, an assessment of regulatory measures will be very different from a view that identifies a number of aspects that may enhance the ability to exercise private power through economic means. How much support the organization of competition requires, as the modern tool to keep individual ambition within parameters that a society concedes, can be assessed very differently depending on the emphases laid down in the analytical structure chosen to wrestle with the realities that are being confronted.

In other words, what economists do and propose can differ quite noticeably. Their theoretical frameworks are built on foundations that direct their attention to different aspects of the system under investigation and offer interpretations of the same issues that may well be at odds with each other.

In fact, different economic theories and different world views go hand in hand – and, more often than not, it may be their world view that attracts people to a certain theoretical framework, not the other way around. The close connection of economic issues to the political system and issues of power also draws in ideological components. No theoretical framework in economics is free of values. What is important, what is to be achieved through coordination in economic matters, which relations of influence to focus on, and which problems to place at the center of attention are all questions that need answering, and that more often than not, do not come with objectively correct answers. That is, at least not in a pure binary formulation. Rather, we find a necessity for a differentiation by degrees of importance, which can shift over time and depending on the overall environment that is being faced.

In a society, decisions concerning economic issues are as much a reflection of prevailing world views and values as they then further shape that society's views and values by influencing the organization of a significant part of life and people's perception. More broadly speaking, economic theory, social structure, political environment, technological capacity, and individual aspirations, amongst others, inform one another and shape one another in a continuous process. Whether these connections and ongoing changes have a noticeable impact on the fundamental functioning of markets and the economic sphere is contested among different perspectives on economies. Some approaches hold that the constraints imposed on economic activity, in terms of profit requirements, for instance, are so pronounced that the logic applied to economic activity can always be the same, binding the system itself through equilibrium outcomes and eventually permitting to work with one set of valid economic laws, in analyses and for devising regulations. Other approaches see more scope for individual actions, and more degrees of freedom for effects on the systemic level to emerge. Given the complexity of the system that we are dealing with, every perspective will miss something, some more, some a lot, some, possibly, less. However, the way that complexity is addressed is not therefore necessarily unimportant. The proscriptions and suggestions of theoretical analyses have to be translated into meaningful real-world actions, and, as we will see, the potential for a successful translation may differ. We will also see that all perspectives on economics and economies require a functioning political system to support economic activity. The temptation to relegate political responsibilities to other societal spheres, in this case the economic sphere, to overcome political shortcomings, has consistently proven to be a recipe for disaster.

Still, our understanding of modern societies, in which the economic sphere plays a substantial role, has improved with and through the formulation of economic theories, and the different perspectives on economic systems we may discern can serve to enrich our understanding further, as I hope you will agree after further perusal of this book. Nevertheless, the fact that the focus is on different aspects of the economic sphere, and different aspects of influence patterns within these, means that the gain from any single perspective we choose will be somewhat limited. They may all offer a contribution to a larger view, though. Knowing a number of different angles to look from can only help create a better picture.

1.1 Toward Modern Economic Systems – Changes in Mindsets

I

Over the past couple of centuries, in matters of social organization, the continuous move of relations from the overwhelmingly dominant sphere of custom and command to that of economic exchanges stands out. Communities based on some degree of reciprocity (however meager that may have turned out to be in the realities of people's lives) and in which people's focus lay on fulfilling their predefined role in their social group saw continuous relative losses in importance. Born the son of a blacksmith you were eventually no longer destined to become a blacksmith. Individual aspiration was redirected toward individual ambition and gain, with economic means as an eventually accepted proxy for success. This process played out gradually or violently, nudged or forced, and people's reaction to this redirection was one principal driver for continuous change to become a basic characteristic of the newly emerging structures and systems.

Market exchanges were allowed a growing reach in social relations, and transactions among individuals consequently multiplied. Market valuation criteria have entered into social relations and shaped outlook, assessment, and motivation patterns of people. This increased reliance on markets as problem-solving devices has influenced societal values through an impact on people's perception of problems, evaluation of issues, and emerging thought patterns. Subsuming activities under an economic rationale means that some motives increase their relative weight compared to others. This, again, shapes perceptions and perspectives of the people engaged in related activities. On the scale of the community, a 'one-dollar-one-vote' rule for decisions, as in economic matters, provides a different logic for integrating individuals' valuations of issues into decisions than is common for decisions in the political arena, for instance. With the increasing reliance on and acceptance of markets as coordination devices, this change in perspective has continued to spread through modern economies. The economic-centered approach to organizing societies' interactions has developed in tandem with world-views and value systems since. This change in people's attitudes may be the most important overall economic development during the period under consideration.

How to structure and organize individual coordination, and what can be achieved through different forms of coordination, for the individual agents themselves and with a view on the larger group they are part of, has been a main focus of economic research from its very beginning. What is a desirable outcome, or which problem seems the most pressing to pay attention to, has to be part of such assessments. Markets are by no means the only option for fostering coordination and solutions, here. Exchanges that supplement markets, complement markets, or bypass markets (or supersede, control, and suspend them, from another point of view) may offer more attractive options for realizing some objective or other, from the position of the individual agent and from the viewpoint of the community. How related aspects may be evaluated depends in part on the objectives formulated, on assumptions about individual motivation and decision-making, and on assumptions about systemic effects outside each individual's control that may influence overall results of individual actions and how these are acknowledged and perceived. The same activity may be perceived and assessed differently depending on the perspective adopted. Chapters 2 and 3 will address related issues in detail.

II

In the wake of the widened scope for market-based relations in societies, more turbulent socioeconomic environments started to emerge. The risks emanating from an integrated economic system continued, however, to be borne by the individual agents at first. Over time, measures, such as unemployment support, were taken to mitigate those risks, albeit to different degrees in different societies. An understanding of economic systems as entire unit of analyses was only slowly integrated into economists' analytical apparatus, however. Phenomena related to aggregate indicators, such as unemployment rate, inflation rate, trade balances, or other issues related to business cycles, provide the focal points for analyses here. The perspectives that have emerged from these developments in economic theory tend to inform the broad guidelines for societal economic management and structure.

All the more important, it seems, is it, then, to note that fundamentally different views on economies and the relations and effects we observe in them prevail. One of the core distinctions we can draw between different perspectives is in fact their interpretation of economic crises, typically evaluated with a reference to unemployment. Views are ranging across the entire spectrum, of crises as a constant feature in modern economies to crises as normal occasional outgrowths of individual action in a complex economic system and crises as phenomena that only result from external disturbances to an otherwise orderly system. We will address related issues in detail in Chapter 4. All the aspects discussed in Chapters 2, 3, and 4 will be taken up in Chapter 5, where frameworks for economic policies will be our topic.

III

Changes of the role of the economic sphere in societies went hand in hand with changes within the economic sphere. Ever since the late eighteenth century, not only the superficial realm of expanding volumes of production in existing product classes and designs has been touched by processes and dynamics in changing societies. The composition of economic activity saw the relative emphasis shift from production in the industrial sector to services and within those categories saw an increase of the importance of production goods relative to consumption goods, and of services related to production relative to personal, household, services. The organization of value-added chains saw an increasing concentration of economic activity, under the roof of one concern, corporation, trust, or other. Lately, this integration of production processes under one roof has begun to disperse into value-added chains formed as networks of independent links, with one dominant company coordinating the activities in such diverse aspects of activity as development, production, or marketing. Given the increasing concentration, or monopolization, of structures in final goods markets, we may still argue that the focus on some core business in terms of final products has been going hand in hand with an increased influence by fewer actors, as the dominant network members typically hold a strong influence over a wide range of aspects of their related companies' operations and activities. Over the last few decades, the expansion of financial sector-related activity has been especially noteworthy as well. In turn, the changing relative weight of finance has triggered changes in the emphases of the strategies pursued by productive companies, and has likewise further strengthened the trend toward increased control by fewer actors in production structures. We will come back to this.

In sum, the economic spheres of societies have continuously been redefined along various dimensions over the past two centuries, from impulses that result from economically motivated and economically relevant behavior, but equally importantly in an interplay with social relations, and the political sphere. The integration of newfound technological knowledge into the economic and broader social spheres of societies exacerbated these trends. Economic and other societal structures are necessarily intertwined and interdependent, and hence inseparable. For instance, labor is not separable from the person providing it, and that person is at home in more than one societal sphere at a time.

Whether we need to make amends for this fact in economic analyses is a continuous point of contention. A mutual influence of economic, social, cultural, political, and other areas of individual interaction is one thing. The logic and constraints that economic valuations impose on activities may, however, reach further, and thus constrain potential influences if these run counter to economic requirements in a sustained manner. Whether all economic activities can be approached with the same basic models in mind is contested. Again, Chapters 2 and 3 will offer overviews of related aspects.

Societal decisions regarding which activities to actually bring into the economic sphere have differed noticeably over time and across regions. The reach of the economic sphere is not the same in different societies, and it continues to change. The shift in the general mindset toward more market-based coordination is shared in modern economies, though. It is embodied in the increasing integration of nature and human life and activity into the economic sphere. The changes in the nineteenth-century British Corn Laws and the British Poor Laws may be taken as symbols for this shift. The expansion of the market sphere has started this 'great transformation' and it has continued to influence people's minds ever since.

Ownership and a set of positive rights of owners have first claim to recognition. For instance, the integration of nature into an economic arena means that monetary gain, even if only for the few, can trump nonmonetary losses, including for the many, as soon as the few can find a way to establish rights of ownership over nature. Examples for the conversion of nature into land (referring to all natural inputs into economic processes), as well as attempts to put some barriers in place to limit the reach of this process, may for instance be found in the enclosure movement, the establishment of nature preserves, or permissions or prohibitions of pollution. In other areas, intellectual property was invented, and software became proprietary after its open-source success led people to understand that it may be worthwhile to create conditions actually allowing to sell it. Natural remedies can be patented.

On the other hand, actions have also been taken to counter the increasing reach of economic valuations into social arenas. The degree to which human activity (or human beings, for that matter) has been exchangeable as labor has been constantly adapted, amongst others in regulations concerning child labor, female labor participation, work safety rules, or regulations of the length of workdays, and workweeks. Products, such as certain chemicals, but also natural products, such as hemp-based ones, amongst others, were removed from officially sanctioned markets in some countries, typically because noneconomic motives, be they health concerns, cultural prejudice, or other, gained or lost in importance in the assessment of situations.

Exchange relations in markets are not static, and neither are the arenas in which they take place. Nonetheless, there are patterns to them, and whether the changes within the market sphere actually affect the functioning of markets in general is contested. In fact, the majority of economists maintains that the underlying dynamic of market relations does not change. For them, all markets can potentially be understood in the same way independently of time and place, or object of transaction, and in a manner that allows to derive generally valid statements about markets. So can the economic system as a whole. Where factors interfere, a reference point that depicts the proper functioning and results can be formulated and serve as an orientation for potential corrective measures. Other economists disagree in various ways, and at times arrive at very different positions regarding the treatment, embedding, and utilization of markets for solving issues of coordination among economic agents. Less optimistic assessments of market structures and economic systems and their potential tend to be developed from perspectives that take the complexity of the real-world system into account more pronouncedly than the more optimistic colleagues do in their formulations.

As a result, we will employ a general categorization of economic perspectives to cover two larger groups. The first group, dominating current economic research, works with concepts assuming specific constraints at the relevant systemic level – whether whole economy or individual market – in the form of equilibria that bind individual decisions. Typically, in fact, one unique and stable global attractor is presumed to exist at any given moment. Other assumptions can be amended to some degree, as long as the resulting analytical structure is still characterized by such equilibria. The second group permits openness at the systemic level. Characteristics emerge from the interactions of individuals. As behaviors can change under different circumstances, so can the characteristics of parts of or the entire economic system. An understanding of potential dynamics from individual interactions, and hence an understanding of the system without imposing a certain shape from the start, is typically sought, here.

1.2 Toward Modern Economic Systems – Changes in Structures

I

Before the economic sphere started playing an increasingly significant role in the organization of human relations, trade was mostly limited to luxuries and spices. Production of manufactures was not at a level, and possible at a cost, at which widespread trade would have made much sense. Transport was expensive enough to act as an additional prohibitive factor. Once standardization had reached a point at which increased volumes of production became feasible, mechanization could advance, and the organization of work processes started to make this potential accessible, the creation of national markets to allow for volumes that would make trade in increasing numbers of goods worthwhile was the necessary next step. This was partly a question of changing trade rules. Additionally, however, the infrastructural developments of the second industrial revolution were necessary complements for further expanding economic activities. Transport infrastructure made resources as well as product markets more easily accessible; communication infrastructure furthered producers' access to markets and broadened the potential for the organization of processes of production and distribution. The advantages of large-scale production depend on the constant throughflow of production factors, on the one hand, as well as the ready distribution of products, on the other. Changes in the technological environment enabled the size-growth of companies seeking to enhance their control over their environment. The increased efforts required for establishing and maintaining these larger structures made control of their environment vital for companies, at the same time.

Seeking to support processes of technological upgrading in economic structures, governments set out to establish policies to develop manufacturing, later industrial, capacities in their territory. The promises of wider economic activity and gain had started to become an important influence for motivating agents, private as well as public. Economic gain had started to become an acceptable signal for social success. Economic activity – replacing force and inheritance or grants of land – was on the way to becoming a dominant means for directly increasing control over resources, and rules and laws were adapted to permit related purchases. The expanding economic sphere offered a new set of tools for exercising power, gradually replacing older ways for accomplishing this end. Economic potential and influence also became a notable factor in external relations.

At the same time, the increasing weight of economic activity and the continuous reorganization of societies meant an increasing weight of interests related to economic activity. Sooner or later, such interest groups found entries to the political arenas of their societies for an articulation of their interests, laying the foundation for further adaptations of the rules structuring the economic sphere in concordance with those interests, whether focused on individual aspiration, economic influence, or risk-reduction with a view on possible negative effects from systemic developments.

Capitalism shows its own dynamics of expansion, independently of the varieties in place in different countries, with influences ranging from the technical requirements and machinery used in large-scale production to the rules and laws in place to support and protect economic activity, and an acceptance of related values and mindframes. Private property and its use for for-profit productions are the markers of such a system. Formerly socially organized issues have been brought under the purview of a market mindset, and new products and eventually product categories are constantly introduced leading to a further increase of the relative weight of market exchanges in societies. Capitalist systems rely on the steady introduction of new gadgets, demand for which has to be created for them to be viable within an economic sphere – we will see a few perspectives that arrive at the view that in capitalist systems, invention is, in fact, the mother of necessity. A stable demand-side is as important as the availability of suitable production structures. In the interplay of developments of production technology, transport technology, and economic considerations, societies continue to change.

The formal rules, regulations, and laws applying to economic activity, which have been structured and restructured in the political sphere, have played a pivotal role for changes in societies and their market spheres. Pressure for such changes from increasingly influential interest groups may be seen as the flip-side to the technological developments and the options these have opened. As an example for the importance of formal rules, the eventual introduction of limited liability in operations made developments toward larger-scale production for profit a lot easier, as economic agents did no longer have to consider their entire possessions as collateral. The scope of operations could expand more easily following the underlying shift in attitude. This may, in fact, have been one of the major breakthroughs in social technology. (Limited liability had been refused as unacceptable in terms of doing business for the longest time, as it was felt that personal responsibility was diluted if business operations were carried out without full personal responsibility for their outcome.)

II

Companies grew larger and increased their reach in economic relations, in developments that closely resembled each other in the United States, the United Kingdom, the German states, and, a little later, Japan, amongst others. At first, this mainly meant higher volumes of production. Capital-intensive production processes (steel, chemical industry, large-scale textile production, etc.) lay behind this dynamic. Subsequently, more aspects of production, distribution, and marketing processes were increasingly brought under one roof, leading to a further growth in the size of companies, and eventually the establishment of corporations and conglomerates. The growing volumes of products and related requirements led to the establishment of management levels, specialized occupations overseeing companies for planning and organizing processes within those companies. Supporting size growth, in many production processes, increased production leads to a reduction in unit costs. For the higher levels of production, the continued availability and flow of inputs and products is crucial, requiring ever more refined planning within companies as well as general infrastructure to facilitate these flows. In fact, planning and control for reducing economic volatility have continuously grown in importance for economic activities. Overall, organizational factors and planning have become more and more important for maintaining economic activity.

Until the eighteenth century, ownership and management of assets tended to be in the same hand, unless larger agricultural estates were concerned. Economic endeavors themselves had largely been limited to trading ventures, in which the merchants involved put up their own capital. Production had typically been undertaken for subsistence and exchanges in barter, not for monetary profit. All this started to change then, with the first manufacturing sites, maybe even already with larger-scale putting-out operations, and has continued to change since. Day-to-day operation and ownership of assets were beginning to be separated. The new management class did typically not have ownership claims to the assets they managed. As the flip-side to this, the distance between owners and their assets grew, diminishing their control over these assets. Owners were increasingly relegated to passive positions, holding shares in larger ventures.

The separation of ownership and management of assets introduced possibilities for fundamental changes in investment behavior – you could trade your shares of asset ownership now – and laid the foundation for the development of the financial sector as we know it. As stockholders, owners' influence on the decisions in companies has continued to dwindle. It is not uncommonly minimal to nonexistent nowadays. Holders of stock gain and lose in the stock market and have settled in a role as passive recipients of payoffs who do not have to rely on particular effort or savvy for their returns, their 'unearned income.' Still, the general notion of shareholder value-focused operations has gained a firm foothold for swaying company strategies, and with enough stock in hand, investors can and do exert pressure on producers. As can, of course, the possibility of take-overs that emerges now.

The increased weight of the financial sector is the most recent broad structural change we can observe. The financial sector has started to enjoy an increased control over the cashflows emanating from the rest of the private sectors since the late 1970s, more or less, further expanding its presence in economic relations. Regulatory changes permitting an extension of the scope of financial sector activities lie behind this particular trend.

As a flip-side to this development, we can identify effects in terms of a refocused outlook in strategies of companies in the real sector of the economy. In broad terms, where the large conglomerates were focusing their efforts on maintaining their internal capabilities to finance long-term endeavors in research and development and productive investments up to the 1970s, modern companies tend to focus their operations on short-term financial indicators. For shaping these indicators, it is not uncommon to utilize profits for buybacks to influence their stock prices, for instance, instead of investing in their production potential. At least in part, this has originally been driven by defenses against financial institutions' brokering of (hostile) takeovers and other fee-generating activities. Once the pattern had started to develop, the focus on 'shareholder value' as a justification was not far behind ('the dumbest idea in the world', as it has come to be called by some of its originators), and the development of company strategies has followed the path laid out since, even though more pronouncedly in some countries than in others, to be sure. One noticeable aspect of companies' reorientations has been the willingness to more actively engage in financial sector endeavors, as well, in a bid to increase their profits, integrating (de facto) banking or insurance businesses under the roof of legal entities formerly focusing exclusively on production processes. The acquisition of profitable businesses or small companies with some innovative success has likewise become more popular to extend one's portfolio without incurring the risk related to R&D, or to improve profitability, even if only in the short term, without incurring efforts that seem too risky. The acquisition of patents is undertaken with similar objectives in mind. We can note that the volatility in economic activity has noticeably increased again since financial markets have been given more scope for influencing productive and service activities in economies.

In the real sectors of the economy, lately, the spread of routine production capacities has increased the scope to disassemble and reassemble value-added chains, on comparatively short notice, introducing an option for exercising control that differs from integration and growth. This can be assumed to have strengthened the position of the strongest network member. The network structure increasingly pursued in the organization of production processes may itself have helped fostering a process to allow changing the network components more freely. One reason, or at least facilitating factor emerging on the systemic level, may be that the interests of the different groups involved in economic activities in a territory are no longer as strongly aligned as they were more immediately after World War II, for instance. Relocating parts of the production chain is easier when the conditions in any one individual market, or economy, are of less consequence to any one company. Such a dynamic might be a good example for a possible decline in standards and conditions, brought about by agents seeking individual advantages, in the process jointly contributing to a deterioration of an overall situation.

1.3 Risk Reduction and the Role of the Public Sector

I

The inherent dynamics of change, the fluctuation of economic activity, and the possibility for negative effects that lie outside the immediate control of any individual agent, as, for instance, in a recession, have led people to try and protect themselves against the risks that have arisen with their integration into markets. Increasing one's degree of control of one's environment, especially for companies, and control of the impact of unforeseeable economic events, for all agents, have become possibilities in societies in which the main risks emanate from man-made social structures, and not so much the natural environment any longer. Shaping one's environment increasingly came into the reach of powerful agents and interest groups in societies.

For private agents, gaining some measure of control over their economic environment may allow to stabilize it and reduce the risk of adverse developments to contend with. Strategic behavior and the attempt to shape one's environment to one's advantage are major issues in economic relations. How agents are allowed and able to do this depends on political decisions (regulation of concentration of companies, unionization, relation to land and labor, etc.). How far there may be factors inherent to economic activity that counter this trend and prevent individual influence and power to solidify is a major point of contention in economics. How to deal with such occasions is also one.

In any case, companies have good reasons to try to establish a position of dominance. The desirability of control stretches across the entire value-added chain, from input sources to suppliers, and customers and the planning of sales, in the triplet of superseding, controlling, or suspending market operations in favor of other mechanisms of coordination. Companies can succeed in this endeavor, and have done so over nonnegligible time spans. Where they have succeeded, the search for causes is undertaken in various directions, depending partly on the complexity reduction system to which one subscribes. The professed belief in a competitive drive, and the ability to break up positions of power pursuing it, for instance, leads people to search for political interferences with the working of the competitive mechanism. Other perspectives might focus more on technological characteristics in production processes, and cost effects that go hand in hand with those, offering advantages over competitors and vis-à-vis potential competitors. Further scope for private actions to avoid competitive pressure is another possible option, which like the former ones can come in numerous shapes, forms, and colors. That a tendency exists to try and gain control over one's economic environment is a shared assessment; that rules formulated for regulating economic activity may be subverted and turned into measures of protection is as well. How to deal with related issues is contested. To which degree faith is to be put in an economic sphere or whether an extension of democratic controls in the political sector, instead of a more technocratic approach, for instance, may be more promising for promoting individual emancipation, depends on the position taken with regard to individuals and their objectives and abilities as well as characteristics of their economic environment, and that environment's place in society.

For individuals, the principal risks they face have shifted from those emanating from the natural environment to risks that are rooted in the socioeconomic environment. As subsistence vanished as a way of life and people were finding themselves integrated into a large-scale division of labor, developments within the newly constituted economic sphere have affected them, possibly pronouncedly. Systemic effects, that affect individual agents, as people or companies, can be countered as a community. Those systemic effects have resulted in enhanced levels of economic vulnerability of individuals. This vulnerability translates into different levels of economic insecurity, depending on how it is dealt with, for instance in the details of the social safety net structure. Dealing with economic vulnerability and the insecurity this has led to in modern economic systems is a principal area for public policies. Various measures have been put in place to cushion the effects of negative systemic developments, like the mentioned recessions. To this end, social, technological, and political means have been employed in continuous actions and reactions to systemic developments in attempts to change the risk exposure of individuals, or groups of individuals, over time.

For all the questions referred to so far, some trade-off between different objectives tends to be involved. How to decide between different objectives requires decisions that, in turn, need a foundation of values. A price mechanism may be suitable, but more stringent rules and policies may be required as well. How different objectives may be affected by different measures, and how the overall functioning of an economic sphere may respond to such measures, may be evaluated differently by the different perspectives that offer suggestions for addressing individual demands. The recommendations for addressing the threats of vulnerability and insecurity can differ noticeably depending on the perspective from which they have been developed.

While caution against overreaching policies is certainly merited, that does not mean research should voluntarily avoid results that point to a potential for advantageous measures. Flawed policies – addressing symptoms instead of treating causes, for instance – do not invalidate policy potential. Choosing not to try to tap into that potential because of side-effects, blowback, or problematic political developments that may follow is a decision that may be well-reasoned. But one that should be communicated freely and clearly.

II

The public sector has seen its shape adapt in response to newly emerging interest groups in and to demands from societies. The expansion of the market sphere necessitates an expanded role for public agents, actively or passively, collaborating with private agents or overseeing them. Stabilizing markets as well as the larger economic system that these markets form is a core task of economic policies. How such stabilization is best achieved, again, is debated. To which degree measures to stabilize activity might interfere with structural changes and upgrades is as well. As stated earlier, here, we find ourselves in a problem area that societies have not really found good solutions for, so far.

It is uncontested that government activity is a part of modern economies, just as government is more broadly speaking a constitutive part of modern societies. It provides protection and guarantees that are required for private economic activity, and contributes to and regulates the availability of complementary factors to economic activities, such as educated workforce and infrastructure. Public agents participate in economic activities, alone or jointly with private agents. Governments finance a substantial share of research and thus contribute to, or rather, provide, the technological foundation for many new products. They also tend to offer the most stable demand position that companies can service (through military spending, for instance). Public agents can intervene when markets are incomplete tools for coordinating activity, through regulatory measures. This can be resulting in a shift in the relative ability of private groups to pursue their respective more narrow objectives, but may also stifle private coordination at times. Still, government and private agents need one another for their activities. Policies also shape the distribution of risks and costs from various activities among groups that are more or less involved, or simply affected as bystanders. Typically, deregulation, or liberalization, in fact stands for a re-regulation that shifts costs or risks related to specific activities among societal groups (or to other societies). Not uncommonly, so-called deregulation allows scope for more powerful private agents to claim larger shares of returns, or divest themselves of parts of risks and costs, as changes in rules reduce the counterweights they may have faced before. It thus stands for an elevation of selected private interests over others; and in public perception, possibly rather frequently. However, of course, a shift in the focus of regulation can also open space for private activities that are deemed desirable by society at large. There is no neutral reference point for assessing these decisions. There is not a general antagonism between public and private agents, either. Perceiving relations between private and public agents as mainly antagonistic distorts more than it clarifies the view on relations of different constituents in modern economies.

Finally, societies have decided to make use of the potential that government offers and shield their members at least from some of the risks related to submitting some areas of life to markets and economic motivations. And utilizing the potential of the public sector to intervene in economic and social structures also includes at least some leveling of the playing field for individuals, or expanding on the promise of human development, through education and health care provision, amongst others. That a for-profit orientation in such activities would benefit societies as a whole cannot be maintained in the face of the observations that are available to us.

1.4 Analyzing Complex Economic Systems

I

The increasingly pronounced role of markets as one principal means for organizing and coordinating activity, with their own logic and specifics, in societies undergoing tremendous structural changes sees the parallel rise of the discipline of political economy, and eventually the shift to economics, as the more scientific sounding moniker. The economists' role has been to describe the system, to try to break it down to its roots, and lay bare the relations that ultimately form it and the outcomes produced in it. Based on the resulting understanding, factors interfering with the working of the economic sphere are to be identified, and suggestions made for possible changes to improve situations. Economists try to comprehend what can be achieved in, and through, economic actions and the economic sphere. An understanding of the relations in the economic system and the paths it may take can provide the foundation for offering warnings, focuses for potential improvements, options for arriving at a goal following a relatively less costly route, or an enhanced awareness of trade-offs between different objectives, amongst others.

However, while the changes that industrializing societies have undergone are issues we can observe, how they may be reflected in economic theory is another matter – how to cut through the complexity of the situations that present themselves to us is by no means clear. As the approach taken will typically lend itself to offering arguments more suitable for the interests of one or another group in societies, this is probably only to be expected.

For the reduction of complexity, we have to formulate an approach that combines two things: the choice of what we believe are critical components of the system under consideration for the question we are interested in, including their influence relations, and the choice of technique for the reduction of complexity to be able to handle any resulting analytical framework.

Simplifying situations to get a grip on them is not wrong, nor bad – we all do it, every day, and because we have to, to be able to act purposely.

We are accustomed to operating in social environments in which potential complexity has already been reduced to levels that appear manageable to us. Repetitiveness means stability of expectations, here, and social customs and habits bring stability to behavior and reduce the number of possible behaviors to expect in interactions, allowing us not to decide anew every time we come across a specific constellation. Still, in our environment, complexity persists and some measure of further complexity reduction is necessary in order to act purposely and consistently with a view on achieving specific goals. That necessity endows us with tools that can at times throw up obstacles as well, however: behavior patterns and customs are oriented on past occurrences and problem structures. In a changing environment, such patterns may have to change in order to allow for an effective utilization of whatever potential may be accessible. This is by no means a given, nor an automatic process. Over time, thus, groups' abilities to handle situations and enjoy the possible gains from their potential are not fixed. The relative ability to cope with the problems of the time fluctuates. An environment that is too stable has historically always stagnated, at least in relative terms.

II

Before complexity reduction and model construction even become the focus, another question needs to be answered, actually: how do you approach your analyses in general terms – building on general (first) principles or on observations? This is, fittingly, one of the first controversies on the way to our current economic theories, although discussed in philosophy before that already, between rationalists and empiricists. What it comes down to is that a black-or-white view is likely to obscure more things than it can shed light on. Pure reason without experience is said to lead to illusions, whereas experience without reason is purely subjective, which means that it cannot be systematized, communicated, assessed, and thereby serve to formulate a structured understanding of relations, causes and effects, and consequences. The drastic positions may help to clarify some issues. A workable way forward can typically only be found in their synthesis. This last point is, of course, an ongoing pattern. Scientific quarreling is not infrequently driven by the more extreme positions, if not a miscommunication due to the use of ill-defined terms, and eventually some way to integrate them may be proposed, or they stand off as opposing camps. As an example, in our context, we might consider whether individuals are autonomous agents, whether individual action is determined by their social structure, or whether, maybe, a combination of the two influences may be the most promising framework.

The first principles approach is deductive. You formulate basic axioms and derive your analysis by following the logical implications of these. Based on empirical observations, on the other hand, you try to identify patterns that eventually may allow for generalizations – patterns within the sets of patterns that apply to a larger set of situations. Eventually, the formulation of a framework for analyses may follow, by trying to insert reason into structuring those patterns. We will find both types of approaches represented in the models we draw on for the exposition later. In any case, regularities are to be found, in the system, or in behavior with reflections on the system, and built on for analyses. The improved understanding of complex systems and ways to approach them analytically, in part due to computational advances, have broadened the scope of what can be undertaken in terms of analytical structures over the last few decades as well, as system characteristics have come to be within easier reach. Critical components, conditions, relations, junctions, etc. have become more accessible. Whether regularities identified in such analytical structures have general validity, and how much they depend on circumstances such as environmental states, is contested.

Whichever way you choose to go forward for gaining a better grip on a situation, your analysis always has to be supplemented by a story in order to be able to communicate its results. Moving back and forth between model framework and the aspects of reality you deal with, you need a link between them. As your theoretical construct is a simplified version of its purported real counterpart, and as its relations and interactions are more reduced than those of said counterpart, that link has to be an artificial construct itself. The connections you decide to present are embedded in the story you tell. How the relationship between theoretical concepts and the conclusions presented based on them is conceived is not trivial. Not only do reduced analytical system and reality have to be connected, but the more convincing your story is, the more likely that you will be heard. From choice of vocabulary to touching a nerve with a relevant share of the people you address, many aspects outside the analyses proper can have an influence on the impact that is achieved.

No matter how it is derived and set up, an analytical system that falls in line with prevailing social structures, or conventional wisdom, for that matter, will have an easier time finding open ears. The classical economists' writings came at a time and place of social restructuring and ongoing changes in technological capacities. They offered a framework for addressing the developments that societies started to face at their time, and for alleviating worries that un-controlled transactions and trade might lead to chaos. Newly emerging societal interests found proponents of ideas that offered a foundation for supporting their interests, and promised order in societies even without the structure and stability of a monarchic overlord overseeing and regulating exchanges. Shifts in values to make this more widely socially acceptable increasingly took root. Patterns of changes can complement, strengthen, and reinforce one another in social developments. In fact, if they don't, the momentum for change is likely to be short-lived. Classical economic thought lent itself to supporting dynamics that accompanied and shaped the remaking of then-prevalent social structures. We were no longer born into a specific position and our life's role was no longer to fill it according to god's own will and law, but we held our own destiny in our own hands. Eventually this has been translated into thinking that if we only tried hard enough, we would make it; if we do not make it, well, we simply have not tried hard enough. This is easy enough to understand and implement, and it justifies whatever hierarchy may have established itself, offering some legitimacy to existing structures, and thus providing some stabilizing effect for societies on a philosophical level as well. Integrating systemic effects and a more complex setting into our tool set for analyzing economies, typically results in qualifications of such simplistic views.

III

Any structured and purposeful approach to economic matters needs an analytical framework on which to draw. This may of course be taking shape over time, drawing on a number of more specific analyses that share assumptions which can be developed into a coherent analytical framework. Later authors can draw on established structures on which to place their analyses, then. In any case, these foundations are where it does get controversial. We need to reduce the complexity of the system we want to analyze – so far, so good. How to do this?

Very basically, a system is complex if it is not that easy to describe it. Particularly forecasting future states of the system, at a given time, rather than necessarily just having a grasp of its components and their potential relations is hard. Even if you are able to grasp the system and offer a general description of it, you may not be able to produce forecasts, at least not beyond rather trivial ones ('it is going to rain again at some point in the future'). However, an understanding of such systems, even that there is a system that we may define somewhat accurately, and their general characteristics is already a great advance over a puzzled look of wonder about which deity may have been displeased with which behavior and retaliated in kind.

A general understanding of the system can, for instance, alert us to changes in its functioning at some critical point, or area. Once some critical value of one or more parameters has been reached, the character of system behavior can change in complex systems. Being aware of that possibility may mean a focus in regulating that particular system can be on keeping it inside a certain pattern of functioning, or outside another. Financial markets can serve as an example here, when viewed as complex systems, showing differences in their behavior and likely outcomes, depending on the risk exposure of agents in them, for instance. Their particular state at a given moment is then depending on the behavior of constituent individual components, underlining the fact that individual agents can have an impact on the functioning of the system they form, just as they are influenced by the state the particular system may find itself in.

IV

Possible sources of complexity are numerous different components (such as agents) with numerous relations between them and interactions in the system. The problem for analyses arises from the fact that all relations and interactions jointly shape the behavior of the system as a whole. One route for complexity reduction taken in some economic analyses is to restrict the scope for dynamics within the economic system. One key assumption for maintaining a manageable, or tractable, analytical environment involves a notion of negative feedbacks as the dominant dynamic in the system, thus maintaining order, or, at least, stability. Divergences from proper values lead to changes in activity which counter the diverging trend, and lead the system back toward its equilibrium state. On this foundation, we can also approximate estimates concerning the system around its equilibrium state.

But if we do not limit possibilities in the system from the outset, we can also see nonlinearity in complex systems: influence factors are not having the same impact on their environment over the range of their values. Examples of nonlinearities include threshold effects (think of a critical mass that is required before an impact is felt) or plateau effects (once a certain level is reached, there is no further impact from a specific influence factor). Other influences may have a positive impact first, reach a saturation level, and then not remain there but upon becoming stronger produce negative effects. For instance, output is not directly proportional to inputs in many production processes. It may grow quicker than input expansions would suggest in a linear relation, at first, but eventually slow down, and at some point, expanding input factors further may even produce overall negative results by reducing output, such as when more and more farmhands are added to cultivating a field of a given size. The expansion of one input factor may result in increasing costs without generating more output in other cases, such as industrial production, with its fixed number of workers for operating certain machines, where an additional body will not be able to contribute anything, really, and in the worst case will just be in the way. More complicated dynamics between influence factors are also possible, of course, and can include influence patterns like a circular and cumulative causation, and positive feedback effects. Removing such effects from the grasp of an analytical framework may prove problematic once a translation into approaches for handling an economic sphere is undertaken. Certain characteristics of the system can vanish entirely in the operations that have to be carried out for the approximation. Whether that matters at all, and how much, is, again, a point of contention we will identify in more detail in the following chapters.

When we integrate more aspects of our complex reality into our models, we usually accept a trade-off in the form of a reduction of our ability to make clear-cut statements. What the proponents of the various approaches following this route maintain is that the understanding of the system is more important than the ability to offer a simple binary statement, or an easy explication, or description, rather, after the fact, in favor of a more in-depth understanding of the system itself. Such understanding, in this perspective, offers an improved ability to identify potentially damaging dynamics, and thus a better chance to prevent crises from unfolding.

A final aspect to bear in mind is that the reduction of complexity also entails to decide what is entirely left out of an analysis. The complexity reduction referred to in the preceding paragraphs deals with the complexity within a system. An economic sphere is a part of societal relations, however, if you want, a sub-system of society. Even if understandable as a sub-system, it remains connected to the rest of social relations. As a consequence, there may always be relations between factors that have been left out of an analytical framework, but which can have a noticeable impact on economic activity, just as economic activity may have an impact on them. How such factors are assessed and taken into account in analyses may have a noticeable impact on results, or on the evaluation of effects that have been identified as possible, or likely. Once we translate our analyses into policy considerations, such effects will have to be considered. As variously pointed out, the open economic system, in fact, can extend its reach only by drawing on other societal, and natural, subsystems to facilitate that expansion. This, and the related influence on such other subsystems, cannot be grasped if we limit our considerations to economic matters alone.

How differing perspectives on economic issues may come about is probably easy to fathom by now. That there is no a priori claim to an enhanced scientific validity by some over the rest may likewise be convincing. At the danger of oversimplifying things, influences for currently dominant perspectives are therefore probably more easily found in social structures – *cui bono* has remained a powerful guidepost for assessing proposals – and in the ideological mood of a moment, than an inherent superiority in grasping economic phenomena.

V

The foregoing cautions notwithstanding the translation of assumptions and models into mathematical constructs can cast light on complex systems for analytical purposes, and for some issues to an otherwise unachievable degree. Mathematical formulations thus offer some principal advantages over purely verbal approaches. They may make it more easily possible to see whether assumptions are logically compatible, for instance; not that the results would necessarily be heeded, as some perspectives in economics arguing for the extension of mathematical foundations, at the same time have a long history of ignoring inconsistencies in their analytical frameworks. More importantly, mathematical formulations offer possibilities for reaching levels of analysis that a purely verbal approach cannot hope to reach. An example would in fact be the understanding of properties of complex systems. They can be more clearly identified and communicated and it may well be that they, in fact, only become accessible through the framing of relations in mathematical language.

With few exceptions, the competing approaches to economic analyses have sooner or later been translated into a mathematical vocabulary. For those schools for which this has proven impossible, the general mathematization of economics has meant that they were relegated to the fringes of economic thought. A heavy reliance on mathematics may not be unproblematic, however, all advantages it can offer notwithstanding. The clarity of structure that mathematics allows may make people too confident in their analysis. Especially, they may show themselves to be willing to overlook the fact that substantial complexity reductions were required before a mathematical model could be formulated, so that the suitability of an approach, in general or to specific questions, may turn out to be more limited than they would like to think. Also, even if we have a clear mathematical framework, we still require the correspondence of its components to tangible concepts, and a translation of a mathematical result into a statement about an economy, including its implications if we want to attain any degree of relevancy. This always entails some degrees of freedom for the researcher, or policy-maker relying on these representations.

Most importantly, however, and this particularly merits bearing in mind, some aspects of our environments are not translatable into mathematical vocabulary – uncertainty, for instance, in its true sense (not as risk) means that there are 'unknown unknowns' in the future. These are distinct from 'known unknowns' – things you know may play a part, and that might be accessible as risk. Of course, they are also different from the 'known knowns.' The verbal approaches to economic issues tend to integrate uncertainty proper, whereas mathematical formulations have to assume that uncertainty could be approximated as risk. However, behavior under risk, as we will see, can differ significantly from behavior under uncertainty, and misinterpretations, blind spots, and distorted focuses may easily result if we decline to distinguish risk and uncertainty, no matter what vocabulary we choose to assign. This does not prevent economists from re-defining commonly used terms for their purposes. As such changes in meaning are not necessarily explained, the impression that certain statements create is even further removed from any tangible mathematical representation on which it appears to be based. We will take this up in more detail later, especially in Chapters 2 and 5, and will see that examples include terms such as competition, dynamics, uncertainty, trust, or rationality. *Honi soit qui mal y pense.*

Actually, to deal with those unknown unknowns and the possibility of unknowable future events with adverse consequences is a main motivator of individual behavior. Aspects of behavior may be rational under uncertainty that would not be if everybody involved knew everything of relevance, as actions promising the establishment and maintenance of control and a reduction of the effects of future events can take different shapes, or be different entirely if uncertainty and not only risk, much less certainty, has to be contended with. Behavior in an environment in which uncertainty is a relevant factor can thus differ noticeably from behavior in environments where it is not. Also, as this behavior is directed to future circumstances, it can have an impact on the development of the system agents are moving in. Losing sight of the fact that only risk is translatable into the language of most economics models may mean that behavior patterns observed in the real world are misunderstood or misjudged. If we integrate uncertainty into an analytical framework, this much we can say here, the role and function of markets can change noticeably, and may, for instance, depend on what is actually traded in the market under consideration, as individual behavior may be different where different goods are concerned. A perspective viewing economic activity as an ongoing process, beyond the reach of equilibrium-based analyses, may press itself upon the analyst more forcefully.

VI

Over the following chapters, we will discuss how complexity reduction is undertaken when formulating different perspectives on economies and economics, which problem areas come into focus under which perspectives, and which measures for limiting negative developments for individuals and their societies have been proposed. We will start by venturing into the realm of individual agents and the environment they move in, in Chapter 2. We will then take a more specific look at particular types of environments, namely markets, for transactions involving particular goods, or types of goods, in Chapter 3. From there, we will take a further step, in order to see how the interplay of markets and their results from the perspective of an entire economy has been approached, in Chapter 4. Having identified factors that may interfere with reaching desirable outcomes over the preceding chapters, we will address possible remedies to such disturbances in Chapter 5, discussing frameworks for economic policies that result from the different analytical perspectives. The final Chapter 6 will offer a brief overview and some general points to derive from the more specific ones discussed until then.

References

For the full list of references, see the bibliography at the end of the text.

Arthur, W Brian (2014) Complexity and the Economy. Oxford University Press, Oxford et al.

This book offers a collection of papers by one of the first economists to explore in a formalized manner the implications that an approach to economies as complex systems have.

Ayres, Clarence E (1944) The Theory of Economic Progress: A Study of the Fundamentals of Economic Development and Cultural Change. Chapel Hill, University of North Carolina Press

The author analyzes processes of change in economies and the influence that the formal and especially also informal rules and norms in a society have on the shape of the process.

Beinhocker, Eric (2006) The Origins of Wealth: Evolution, Complexity, and the Radical Remaking of Economics. Harvard Business School Press, Boston

The author integrates a large number of concepts and approaches to evolutionary and complexity economics to provide the foundation for rethinking what we thought we knew about economics.

Bell, Daniel (1976) The Cultural Contradictions of Capitalism. Basic Books, Inc., New York

The author argues that in capitalist societies, the cultural developments that have gone hand in hand with it will eventually lead the system to break down.

Berle Adolf A., and Gardiner Means (1932) The Modern Corporation and Private Property. The Macmillan Company, New York

The authors analyze the structure of corporations and the impact that the separation of legal ownership and control of a company has had.

Chandler, Alfred (1977) The Visible Hand: The Managerial Revolution in American Business. The Belknap Press of Harvard University Press, Cambridge and London

The author analyzes the changes in the structure of economic activity, with a focus on the nineteenth century.

Chang, Ha-Joon (2007) Bad Samaritans: The Myth of Free Trade and Secret History of Capitalism. Bloomsbury Press, New York

The author shows that successful economic development processes have always relied on government interventions and support.

de Soto, Hernando (2000) The Mystery of Capital: Why Capitalism Triumphs in the West and Fails Everywhere Else. Basic Books New York

The author analyzes the importance of legal property rights for capitalist economic systems and their expansion.

Dobb, Maurice (1973) Theories of Value and Distribution since Adam Smith. Cambridge University Press, London

The author presents a history of economic thought, stressing the importance of ideology for its development.

Eichengreen, Barry (2003) Capital Flows and Crises. The MIT Press, Cambridge and London

The author addresses the issue of capital flows, and their potential for positive as well as negative effects on economies, from a number of vantage points.

Eichengreen, Barry (2007) The European Economy Since 1945: Co-ordinated Capitalism and Beyond. Princeton University Press, Princeton et al.

The author discusses the particular cultural and institutional background that has fostered economic development in postwar Europe.

Friedman, Benjamin (2005) The Moral Consequences of Economic Growth. Alfred A. Knopf, New York

The author analyzes how changes in the standard of living can affect openness, democratic structures, and political stability.

Galbraith, John K (1958) The Affluent Society. Houghton Mifflin Co., Boston

The authors argue that in rich modern societies, the notion of scarcity is no longer the principle problem of economic activity to address, and analyze the consequences that abundance has for economic activity.

Galbraith, John K (1967) The New Industrial State. Houghton Mifflin Co., Boston

The author analyzes the influence of large corporations in the economic sphere, and in society more in general.

Hall, Peter A, and David Soskice (eds.) (2001) Varieties of Capitalism: The Institutional Foundations of Comparative Advantage. Oxford University Press, Oxford

This edited volume offers a framework for understanding the differences in the specific forms the capitalist systems have taken, and a number of case studies to show these in more detail.

Heilbroner, Robert (1953) The Worldly Philosophers: The Lives, Times, and Ideas of the Great Economic Thinkers. Simon and Schuster, New York

The author presents and analyzes economic thought and ideas, embedded in the times and circumstances of those who articulated them.

Hirschman, Albert O. (1981) Essays in Trespassing: Economics to Politics and Beyond. Cambridge University Press, Cambridge et al.

This collection of essays brings together a number of the author's writings, many of them concerned with the relation between economic development and institutional environment.

Kapp, Karl W. (2011) The Foundations of Institutional Economics (eds. Sebastian Berger and Rolf Steppacher). Routledge, London and New York

The author analyzes the role of institutions in economic systems.

Keen, Steve (2001) Debunking Economics, The Naked Emperor of the Social Sciences. Zed Books, London

The author presents a detailed discussion of short-comings and inconsistencies of standard economic theory.

Lazonick, William (2009) Sustainable Prosperity in the New Economy? Business Organization and High-Tech Employment in the United States. W.E. Upjohn Institute for Employment Research, Kalamazoo

The author analyzes the impact of the changes in the structure of economic activity over the last few decades.

Maddison, Angus (2007) The Contours of the World Economy 1 – 2030 AD: Essays in Macroeconomic History. Oxford University Press, Oxford et al.

The author analyzes long-run trends and dynamics in economic activity, to identify principal influence factors behind them.

Milberg, William, and Deborah Winkler (2013) Outsourcing Economics: Global Value Chains in Capitalist Development. Cambridge University Press, Cambridge et al.

The authors analyze changes in the organization and structure of production processes, and the impact this has had on modern economies.

Mirowski, Philip (1989) More Heat than Light – Economics as Social Physics, Physics as Nature's Economics. Cambridge University Press, Cambridge et al.

The author discusses the influence of physics in the development of neoclassical economic theory.

Mokyr, Joel (2002) Gifts of Athena: Historical Origins of the Knowledge Economy. Princeton University Press, Princeton

The author analyzes how complementing technological developments and institutional structures have shaped economic development processes.

Myrdal, Gunnar (1953) The Political Element in the Development of Economic Theory. Routledge and Kegan Paul, London

The author analyzes the ways that ideological components enter economic analyses.

Nell, Edward (1998) The General Theory of Transformational Growth: Keynes After Sraffa. Cambridge University Press, Cambridge et al.

The author analyzes how ongoing innovations in markets change the functioning of the economic system.

North, Douglass, and Robert P. Thomas (1973) The Rise of the Western World: A New Economic History. Cambridge University Press, New York

The authors analyze the role of property rights in the process of economic development in Europe.

Olson, Mancur (1982) The Rise and Decline of Nations: Economic Growth, Stagflation, and Social Rigidities. Yale University Press, New Haven

The author analyzes how the increasing impact of special interests can hinder economic activity.

Penrose, Edith T. (1959) The Theory of the Growth of the Firm. Basil Blackwell, Oxford

The author analyzes internal structures and the performance of firms.

Perkins, John (2004) Confessions of an Economic Hitman. Berret-Koehler Publishers, San Francisco

The author describes how development policies and organizations are used to extract wealth from less developed countries.

Pickett, Kate, and Richard G Wilkinson (2009) The Spirit Level: Why Greater Equality Makes Societies Stronger. Allen Lane, London

The authors analyze numerous studies on the impact of economic inequality on societies.

Polanyi, Karl (1944) The Great Transformation: The Political and Economic Origins of Our Time. Farrar and Rinehart, New York

The author analyzes the interplay of increasing economic turbulence and political developments.

Schmookler, Andrew B (1993) The Illusion of Choice: How the Market Economy Shapes our Destiny. State University of New York Press, Albany

The author illustrates how a market-based approach to relations cannot provide good solutions in a number of areas of life, and how it affects our behavior where relations are organized using markets.

Schumpeter, Joseph A (1954) History of Economic Analysis. Oxford University Press, New York

The author provides overview, interpretation, and analyses of a few millennia of economic thought.

Sen, Amartya K (1999) Development as Freedom. Oxford University Press, New York

The author develops a broader concept of freedom than can be captured by increased average per capita income.

2

Individual, Economic Environment, and Mutual Relation

The individual agent and her relation to her environment have always been a key interest for economists, to draw on for explanations of the environment we perceive, and the results we create and experience. Different potential constraints or interfering factors that may counter the materialization of desired effects have been pinpointed, different approaches for dealing with them identified.

We need to combine the discussion of individual and environment because conceiving of an individual agent without a conception of her relation to the environment she moves in cannot result in a meaningful analytical framework. An individual perceives her environment and she moves in her environment. We define her in relation to the environment, need to have an idea of how far she can grasp this environment, or where characteristics of that environment itself may shape what an individual can do. There may be an influence of the environment that constrains or, on the other hand, enables individual activities. In short, the description of the individual by itself is void. Only in the embedding into the system do we gain insights.

Different ways for approaching an analysis at this level have been pursued, with regard to the conception of our model-individual, as well

H. Schwardt, *The Path to a Modern Economics*,
DOI 10.1007/978-3-319-52785-7_2

as in regard to the environment she moves in. We can broadly categorize them in two groups, those that assume equilibria in the economic system around which analyses can be undertaken, and those that assume ongoing processes shaped by individual interactions at the heart of their frameworks. We will call the first group top-down perspectives and the second one bottom-up. This chapter will explore the main perspectives developed in each of these groups.

We will label the currently dominating approach to economic research the reference framework, and its core reference point the benchmark model. This is not to embrace the perspective embodied there, nor its research direction. It merely reflects the fact that a substantial share of economic research, and policy suggestions derived from it, are drawing on this perspective in some way. It is a top-down perspective, in which one unique and stable equilibrium exists in every market, and for every economy, that reflects a resource allocation in an economy in which everyone participates in the best way possible for them.

One core assumption in this perspective is that this benchmark is generally applicable to economic issues. Even where market interactions result in different outcomes, a benchmark estimate can be made and serve to quantify the impact of distortions. This will prove to be crucial to analyses even where the specific analytical framework is more involved because it offers a reference point against which to evaluate alternative scenarios. Over the past decades, the basic approach to economic issues embedded in this perspective has shaped our perception and general thinking about economic issues, and increasingly societal issues at large. The fostering of a focus on specific economic criteria in the organization of societal relations has been supported utilizing this view, as we will see.

The brunt of the burden for bringing this benchmark solution about is borne by the economic environment. In short, the structure of the economic system is assumed to guarantee the existence of a solution that should be aspired to, and can serve as a reference for cases, where it cannot be reached in an outright fashion because other factors interfere. This structure has also, more recently, permitted a certain relaxation of assumptions regarding individual agents and aspects of their, for instance, technological environment, as compared to the benchmark model. Especially this aspect, on the other hand, serves to stress how crucial the equilibrium assumption really is for the entire analytical framework. Criticisms leveled against specific aspects and assumptions of this analytical framework therefore usually do not have much of an impact. We will see, however, that giving up the equilibrium framework can lead to drastic changes in perspectives.

Following a more detailed look at the frameworks for equilibrium-based, top-down perspectives on economic analyses, we will address the main components of bottom-up models. We must note, again, that once the equilibrium framework has been established, aspects of these bottom-up approaches can be woven into equilibrium analyses to some degree. However, the bottom-up perspectives open the framework to permit aspects that may lead to an analytical framework that is complex in and of itself. In particular, the economic environment emerges from individual actions as the sum of individual actions shapes their environment as agents act. Different sectors, markets, and whole economies may function differently as a consequence. In shaping the process, agents can distort outcomes to their advantage, or change the relevant environment in unforeseeable ways, for instance. Typically, societal values have to be addressed explicitly in the process of deciding between different potential paths.

As a general rule, in these frameworks, a reference solution cannot be defined. The understanding to be obtained by such analytical frameworks typically aims at gaining an understanding of potential pitfalls in ongoing economic processes. Typically, such perspectives come at the cost of obtaining less clear-cut results for a specific question at a moment in time.

In terms of the view of economic systems they lead to, these approaches can point into a markedly different direction for understanding economic issues than that given by the reference framework. The more complex analytical structure entails space for effects and developments that the uncomplex benchmark cannot address, nor the top-down perspectives in general, for that matter, and that these frequently exclude by assumption. For the fans of Occam's razor, therefore, a reminder may be in order that it asks for as little as is needed for an explanation of the relevant observations, not as little as possible to offer any kind of story that is purported to explain a particular outcome (after the fact). Alternative analytical frameworks may therefore very well be worth their effort, as they stress aspects of economic systems that remain hidden from the viewpoint the reference framework offers. Put differently, more involved analytical frameworks do not simply result in similar perspectives, derived in a more complicated setting. And while different does of course by no means generally imply better, these frameworks can point to aspects of economic realities that are more intricate and more intricate to handle than what the scope of equilibrium formulations can accommodate. Faced with a complex situation, this should not be discarded lightly.

2.1 Equilibrium or Process, and the Value of Goods

I

The reference point for a substantial share of considerations in economics, as the so-called perfect competition outcome, is derived in a very basic setting in which complexity reduction has pretty much gone as far as possible. This benchmark outcome is alleged to hold as a neutral reference point against which all other outcomes can be measured. It represents an optimal resource allocation pattern in an economy. Results of analyses of different situations are compared to the outcome estimate provided by the reference point scenario, losses and problems are assessed on the basis of differences between these outcomes, and policy measures are suggested with a view on bringing results closer in line with those in the perfectly competitive market outcome.

At least as importantly, comparisons of different model outcomes are assumed to allow to identify generally valid influence patterns in economies. The standard approach in economics following this strategy for research and analyses is to proceed with model structures that offer clear-cut, deterministic, solutions. Basic assumptions are formulated, and results are deduced from these. The first principles approach referred to in Chapter 1 has established a firm claim to superiority in many economists' minds. An economic sphere, separated from the rest of society, in which clearly identifiable rules and transmission channels for influences derive from the basic postulates, results.

The research strategy attempts to assess how specific changes in selected parameters impact the model outcomes. You determine the reference outcome and introduce tariffs to see how the result in that specific exchange arena may be affected by them, to choose a simple example. In this way, effects are to be understood in isolation, in order to identify the tendency with which they can be expected to impact the economic sphere in general. The results obtained are assumed to represent fundamental relations, laws even, that can be transferred to more general, and complex, settings. For more complicated analyses, the different factors and influences that have been identified in model exercises are combined. Overall outcomes in an economic sphere depend on their relative influence. Even if the general approach is followed, it may be clear that this opens possibilities for dissent, as the actual influence of different factors can hardly be assessed, much less actually measured, so that different stories relating to events, but especially to potential developments to expect, are very much possible.

The crucial factor to the entire analytical system is an assumption about the system itself; namely, that for a given situation it was characterized by the existence of one unique global attractor, the equilibrium toward which activity was drawn. Comparing different equilibrium outcomes allows to identify the influence that a change in an influence factor has on the analytical system, by extension presumably on an economic system. The comparison of equilibria leads to the possibility of statements about the relations of factors in economic systems.

However, even within the same theoretical framework, evaluations of the applicability of the basic analytical structure differ. Some economists are willing to take the very basic models rather literally. Most are not, but treat model formulations as heuristics that mainly serve to discipline thinking. However, it is fair to say that the majority are willing to take comparative analyses of static situations as adequate for an identification of single effects, and the foundation for approaching policy issues from there. The comparative static nature of analyses, as the comparison of two points, does not preclude these two points being start and endpoint of a process, where models include the description of the way from A to

B. Such settings are not dynamic in the sense that systems dynamics researchers use the term, however.

Other economists take a more reluctant stance on this kind of research strategy. Even if the isolation of specific effects and transmission channels for influences under specific conditions were possible that does not necessarily have to mean, that these effects would work the same way in a different economic or social environment, or when emerging in concert with other effects. So far, no reason has been presented to justify an a priori exclusion of the possibility that the economic environment, representing a host of factors, has an influence on how a single factor actually impacts economic matters, especially when it is assumed that such influence was persistent over time. In the same vein, it is not an a priori given that joining different isolated effects into one analysis may be done easily or nonarbitrarily when turning to analyses. Addressing the different perspectives in detail later will clarify these notions.

This being said, the criticisms also run deeper and integrate the notion that in complex systems that are continuously changing, static analyses abstracting from the complexity of the environment will prove to be inadequate. Removing the complexity of the system itself, allows a high degree of flexibility in model formulations, concerning what is included, as well as how. From a more critical perspectives, this resembles arbitrariness more than flexibility. Suitable models still have to be selected to address specific situations, and interpret observations. This may be seen to mean that analyses in top-down frameworks happen outside the actual analytical system, which is in fact a communicational tool only, not a tool that offers particular insights into economic systems. The following sections and chapters will address these aspects in more detail.

For a brief example at this point, and to illustrate at least some of the issues raised, we may draw on some perspectives on the labor market: It is sometimes analyzed independently from the rest of the economic sphere, in the basic logic assumed in the benchmark view. Then, price increases induce demand reductions, so that higher wages mean less labor being demanded by companies. Minimum wages that have an impact then lead to the exclusion of people willing to work. A second perspective involves the notion that employers may be able to dictate the terms of employment, in variations of so-called monopsony market structures, or if they dominate the product market they service. Then, the market outcome may be improved by changing the rules structuring exchanges in labor markets. A minimum wage, for instance, may increase employment, because in this scenario the calculations for employers change in comparison to the benchmark structure. Without minimum wage, or other provisions, hiring additional workers is only possible by increasing the wage rate, in this perspective. When a minimum wage is given, however, every worker costs the same until everybody willing to work for that wage rate is employed. Only then does demanding additional workers increases the wages that have to be offered. Therefore, there may be a range in which a minimum wage will increase employment because of the effects it has on the profit calculus of potential employers. How a market structure is interpreted will influence how labor market measures are assessed.

Alternatively, demand for labor can also be seen as derived from transactions, from the demand for goods and services, and therefore connected to and dependent on the state of the rest of the economy. In an extension, it may even depend on the expectations about the development of demand. This view stresses the fact that wages are not only costs for companies, but simultaneously represent cost for companies and purchasing power for workers. Supply of labor and demand for labor are not independent of each other. Then, a simple price–demand relation cannot be derived, as the overall conditions in an economy have an impact on the labor market and, for instance, higher wages may lead to an increased demand for goods and services and thus an increase in demand for labor in order to produce for that increased demand. For minimum wages that will mean that their impact on employment will depend on the economic environment. It is entirely possible that an increase of the minimum wage has a positive effect on economic activity at first, and on employment with this, as the demand for goods in an economy increases. That does not mean that this statement would be globally valid, of course, as we may assume this effect to turn negative after wages have been crossing a certain threshold, as hiring people will become more expensive than is worthwhile.

II

The formulation of top-down perspectives was motivated by the desire to turn political economy into something to be considered a real science. The economists working in this direction took the physics textbooks of the middle to late nineteenth century and reinterpreted the equations they found to serve as a foundation for approaching economic issues. These are formalisms describing equilibria of forces in mechanics and thermodynamics. In translation, economic model structures have been set up under an assumed equilibrium state in economic structures. The reference point, the equilibrium, represents an optimal outcome in this environment, under suitably defined criteria for optimality.

The equilibrium foundation adopted from those physics models also allowed to connect to earlier economic writings, which worked with the assumption of so-called natural prices of things and a tendency for real-world prices to converge to these in economic environments in which producers compete with each other. An equilibrium and a tendency of the system to move toward it provide the foundation for analyses there as well. However, a major distinction between earlier and later authors is due to different conceptions of the value of goods. Prices of goods in markets are assumed to reflect the values of these goods, with relative prices (the ratio of the prices for different goods) showing the relative value of one good in terms of another. Originally, it was assumed that value was based on cost of production, which in the final reading meant labor. The more labor required to produce something, the more valuable it was seen to be. Later, the concept of value was reinterpreted and the idea was introduced that value originates in an inherent utility of things. If it is useful, it is valuable. Still, the assumption of an inherent value of a good is shared, either deriving it from the labor required to produce a good, or the utility the good has for the people using it.

In our reference framework, thus, external to transactions, value derives from the usefulness of goods. That usefulness is given. It may change over time, and can even change within a particular structure to drive jumps from equilibrium to equilibrium, but that variation does not impact the fundamental understanding and, top-down, structure of analyses. The desire for useful goods motivates activities in market economies. The scarcity of commodities and their potential uses lead to exchanges, in order to tap into the profit-generating potential of goods and services. In other words, production and exchange are driven by consumers' demands for useful goods. Prices, in their relations as relative prices, reflect the value of goods.

Where value is the result of labor utilized in production, on the other hand, the value of something depends on how much labor is used in its production. Prices are not signals of value unless all prices have converged to the natural prices that reflect labor requirements in production. Prices do influence whether production can continue, though. If a product can command a price that is sufficient to reimburse the inputs utilized in its production, including capital, then a company can stay in business. If a price a good can command does not adequately reflect its value in terms of labor, companies do not turn (sufficient) profits and will have to leave the economic sphere.

We can also distinguish different kinds of value, depending on the purpose of a good. The principal categories that result are use value and exchange value. The denomination of these different kinds of value describes their foundation. As we will see in Chapter 4, this matters because motivations may differ depending on which kind of value an agent focuses on. Workers are usually assumed to decide based on use value. They trade a commodity, their labor power, and use the proceeds to acquire goods that have a higher use value for them, than their labor power does. People who invest, or capitalists, more narrowly, decide based on the exchange value of goods, or their expectations concerning the development of that exchange value. When they buy commodities, they do so expecting that a transformed good or commodity can be sold at a profit.

Taking a different approach, the value of goods may be created in transactions, at least partly. Examples may include frameworks that take into account that individuals as social beings seek status and position, or prestige more generally. In our modern societies, status is commonly conferred to those signaling control over resources, not infrequently through their consumption spending. Which consumption goods are seen as particularly worthwhile to that end can be influenced by producers. Black pearls, for instance, did not become an item for conspicuous consumption until their prices were drastically increased and their marketing focused on creating a strong impression of exclusiveness. In this case, the signal value of goods means that value may actually be created in the exchange itself, and not be preexistent prior to that act of exchange.

Value may also be shaped by the conditions in the economic environment. An example is goods that are more or less valuable depending on the number of other people using them. For a positive connection, think of communication devices that become more valuable, the more people you can actually reach with them because they own a compatible device. The value of a good changes over time, here, and depending on others' actions, with a positive feedback with more acquisitions. For a negative impact, think of consumption items meant to set the user apart from others, where the value to the individual is reduced with the number of users. Such sources of value also introduce the possibility for ongoing shifts in consumption behavior, based on the drive to set oneself apart, for instance.

Another, possibly even more relevant example, concerns the fact that while the technological value, as measured in productivity, or production potential, depending, of machinery, does not change, there monetary value does. That is, future income flows will change, depending on the decisions of economic agents, as these decisions influence the level of demand in an economy. If many companies invest, demand is higher, and employment increases, leading to more demand. If few companies invest, the opposite is true. Others' decisions have an impact on the viability of your own course of action, and, in terms of value, at least the monetary value of your assets. We will come back to this point repeatedly, and from different angles.

2.2 An Approach to a World of Scarcity

I

The story to embed the basic benchmark model is built around the, by now somewhat infamous, homo oeconomicus. This creature is characterized by some remarkable features. It knows everything it needs to know, can make instantaneous decisions processing literally infinite amounts of information – and optimal decisions at that – and is not influenced by its environment. It knows what it wants, independently of others, and pursues the best way to get there. Of interest in the economic sphere is consumption, the more, the better. Some modifications, in newer models, so to say, have been introduced to see how far the equilibrium structure can carry analyses. The general outline holds, however. But we take these modifications to signal that it is the equilibrium character of the system that matters most of all for the analytical frameworks.

The only way homo oeconomicus communicates with the rest of society is through price signals for production factors and for consumption goods. Resulting market prices are parameters for consumption decisions for every individual. Given the constraint of their budget, agents execute their personal optimal consumption decision. An agent is simultaneously worker in a production site and owner of that production site. In fact, it also is an entire household. All we ask for capturing it for analyses is how much utility each unit of a good affords to this agent in consumption.

On the production side, companies receive the same price signals. They produce as much as they can without incurring a loss. They know the price for which they can sell their product and adjust production so that the revenue for the last unit produced equals that unit's cost. As an individual is described by her utility from consumption, a company is described by the cost it incurs in production. All companies producing one specific type of good operate with the same cost structure. They are identical for the purpose of the benchmark view.

Even though everybody strives toward the realization of profits, the actual existence of economic profits signals that markets are not running smoothly. Such profits are a sign of companies being able to influence market outcomes, and keep prices above production costs. While desired by everybody, and motivating economic activity, from a systemic perspective, economic profits are a signal for distortions in the workings of the economic system. (Economic profits are profits that are earned beyond the normal, market, rate of return on investments.) In fact, while we may motivate behavior by a desire to realize profits, the analytical structure is one that rests on use value alone. All income is spent, so that we have to assume that the ability to acquire goods is the ultimate motivator behind actions. We see a barter economy in which the sole purpose of money is to ease transactions.

These assumptions are made to permit a specific approach to economic occurrences. The idea and motivation is not to provide an adequate picture of specific situations. It is to provide an understanding of basic effects that factors and their changes have on economic activities. These effects are drawn on for more generalized analyses, then, combining individual effects that have been identified in different models for assessing a specific situation.

II

The larger problem to address behind the reference framework is that of scarcity. Humans presumably have unlimited material wants. The means for satisfying these are, however, limited. The best way for allocating scarce resources and consumption rights then presumably becomes a core question for societies. The basic model referred to here describes a scenario in which an allocation would occur that is defined as economically optimal – and it comes about by every individual pursuing her narrowly defined self-interest without regard for her surroundings. The story that embeds the models tells us that competitive markets guarantee this result; perfectly competitive markets, actually, to be precise. The perfect market requires specific characteristics of goods, production technologies, agents, as well as the economic environment and system itself.

To make sure that the optimal outcome is in fact realized, transactions are only allowed at the equilibrium price. That means that everybody with an interest in a specific market signals their intents to the central planner (how much are they willing to buy and sell for which price), and this central entity then calculates the price at which amount demanded and amount offered will be equal. At this point, transactions are allowed – 'perfect competition' thusly at work produces desirable allocation patterns. Everybody who wishes to partake in the transactions in a specific market can and will, all those who do not partake either feel the price is too high for them to acquire a product, or see that their costs are too high to be able to produce without incurring losses. Everybody gets to decide what they want to dedicate their funds to. Nobody is left out of a market against their will. If all partial markets are in equilibrium, general equilibrium has been achieved. In order to serve as a reference point that allows to determine presumed economic laws, this outcome of overall market activities has to be unique and stable in a given situation. In the case of multiple equilibria, for instance, there is no market mechanism that could be drawn on for selecting one equilibrium over another. The clear identification of effects that the comparison of two unique equilibria is set up to allow would be impossible.

III

The economic system itself plays an important part in facilitating results within this analytical perspective. The basic setting for market analyses is facilitated by assumptions of a potential demand that increases the lower the price of the good in question, and a potential offer that increases the higher the price, the economic 'laws of supply and demand'. There is one price vector where supply and demand of and for all resources, intermediate products, goods, and services, etc., are equal, leading to the optimal price-quantity combination in all markets. This represents the unique equilibrium for economic activities. This basic setting forms the foundation for the analysis of every kind of market, at least by offering the reference against which to determine distortions in other settings. It is given by assumption, not because of observation or any other kind of determination. A rule of thumb of increased sales following price reductions no doubt works in a number of sectors, at least for a certain price range and time period. However, this is not the same as constructing a unique equilibrium on the basis of given values, individual wants, and their ability to pursue these. Furthermore, we will see later that there are many, and important situations, in which we may expect different behavior, if we allow for a little more scope for individual action and a less constraining economic system.

Guaranteeing that these required equilibrium conditions hold for a system is not easy to accomplish in formal terms. In fact, the choice of mathematics as the language to work with, here, has allowed to stress just how difficult it turns out to be. It is actually practically impossible to construct such continuously upward and downward sloping curves from individual components simultaneously in all markets. Pretty much any shape for the respective aggregate functions can result even if every individual's demand function is showing increased demand for decreased prices. The reason is that initial changes in, say, demand lead to changes in demand, thus change in input demand and therefore changes in income patterns, affecting the demand schedules in a given market differently at different prices. That the one form needed for a unique equilibrium solution may result from the aggregation of all individual demands is unlikely, to say the least.

So, that there was one unique and stable equilibrium has to be introduced as an a priori assumption, the model structure then tailored to permit its existence. Even agents that are endowed with the peculiar skill-set and preferences of a homo oeconomicus produce effects through their interaction that emerge at the systemic level and prevent a unique outcome, unless these effects are curtailed by additional assumptions. You need a world of identical individuals to achieve the complexity reduction required for the desired equilibria to result from their interactions. These identical individuals have to not only all want the same things in the same proportion, but have to want them in the same proportion no matter what their income level. Whether you have one hundred, one thousand, or one million currency units at your disposal, you always spend them in the same proportion on the same things. If not set up this way, model interactions would threaten to produce results that are not amenable to coaxing economic laws out of the comparison of unique equilibrium outcomes under different parameter settings. We can begin to feel that these laws are not only man-made, but may well be only made on and confined to paper.

IV

As a result, the reference model is, basically, uncomplex. Concerns for analyses thrown up by the complexity of the subject of analyses are addressed by removing their potential impact by assumption. All potential for influences beyond those that do not interfere with the desired analytical results is excluded before the analysis is actually started. On that foundation, ad hoc extensions are integrated into models for identifying and understanding specific mechanisms and impulses. This makes the reference framework a very flexible setting in the eyes of those working with it. For more complex analyses, the results of a number of models are then drawn together, depending on what is assumed to be important. That there is not necessarily agreement on what, in fact, are important influences in a situation in question, may not come as a surprise. Even following the same general research strategy, people can quarrel without problems; in this case about which of different models may be best applicable to a situation.

The clear-cut results in the individual models mean that for deciding their application and applicability, factors entirely outside their scope of explanatory ability bear the brunt of the analytical work. Which model or models are the appropriate ones for a given situation have to be determined somehow. This 'somehow' lies outside the scope of the models themselves.

Viewed from other perspectives, thus, a certain arbitrariness in the formulations and application of the benchmark framework appears to be a more prominent feature. The uncomplex analytical environment leaves many degrees of freedom for the choice of a specific model as well as the translation of the model structures into stories about the effects of certain changes in complex economic environments. And as no real-world environment can ever conform to the reference model assumptions, the choice of where to put the emphases in an analysis and in a story lies with the story-teller. If you deem a situation you observe satisfactory, you might put your emphases on the aspects that conform to what you consider an appropriate, or desirable, environment. In the case of adverse outcomes, you might do the opposite.

2.3 Suboptimal Outcomes Within the Benchmark Framework

I

In relation to the perfect market outcome and the benchmark it offers, higher prices and lower quantities in an equilibrium in an alternative scenario signify a worse outcome than would be possible under proper conditions. In case of such disturbances in markets, some consumers will not make the purchase they would in the undisturbed environment. Price or quantity distortions thus mean that some agents are worse off than they would otherwise be because they do not participate, and others are worse off, because they overpay.

A number of fields are identified thereby in which individual activity is expected to lead to suboptimal results. We can group these into two large areas. One branch shows that agents who can exert an influence on others in their economic activities distort results, to the disadvantage of those with no, or at least lesser, influence. The second branch focuses on characteristics of activities themselves that lead to suboptimal results. Within that second branch, we can distinguish three different basic situations leading to problems for the allocation of resources through markets. The first focuses on issues of differences in information availability for different agents who interact. The second focuses on effects that activities have on other agents, which are unaccounted for and therefore not reflected in market prices. Such an effect will lead to the over- or under-provision of goods as related activities do not take all of the effects they have into account because price signals are flawed. The third, finally, focuses on characteristics of goods that make it unattractive for private agents to supply them, even though the group can benefit from them.

II

In the first branch, suboptimal outcomes result when companies can exert an influence on markets. Producer influence is assumed to be exercised either by reducing the amount on offer and thus manipulating the price per unit upwards, or directly setting a price above the socially optimal one. If the number of producers is limited, there may be scope for such a scenario. Monopolies (one company servicing a defined demand segment) or oligopolies (few companies servicing a defined demand segment) constitute such situations. Market structures of monopoly or oligopoly allow the realization of economic profits for producers; or workers, for that matter, if they can organize effectively against employers who find themselves as one among a large number.

The more producers there are the less pronounced the influence of each on market outcomes is assumed to be. In the limit, then, no influence by an individual producer can presumably be exercised at all. The perfectly competitive market is approached. In that limit case, the reference point, no single participant in a market can, by assumption, change the situation in the relevant exchange arena to their advantage. In the monopoly and oligopoly model markets, consumers are robbed of some possible benefits of that reference situation, as pointed out. Regulation of markets showing such structures is typically suggested with the reference point in mind – set a maximum price that mirrors some estimate of a competitive price, or mandate respective output quantities. For monopolies, such regulation may further prove practical, for instance, because breaking up large companies may lead to undesired side effects such as increased spending in production structures, or delivery structures. It is just not very reasonable to have a number of overland electricity networks side by side, for instance, competing for business. For oligopolies, additional attention may then be paid to the behavior of companies, in order to ensure that there is no coordination between them, aiming at jointly changing conditions to the disadvantage of customers. There may also be ways to try and get producers in such structures to behave as if they were competing properly. However, it may also be estimated that regulations will introduce further distortions that are even more costly than the original damage they set out to alleviate.

There is no scope for strategic behavior in this analytical setting. The power of dominant producers in markets is still rather limited, therefore. Their power is constituted by their ability to move the price-quantity combination observed in the market in their favor. The overall set of possible price-quantity combinations is, however, defined by consumer preferences, which are out of reach of anyone in the economic world, on the one hand, and the generally known production technology, which is in reach for everyone in the economic world, on the other. So even the cases of 'market power' are limited by the individuals' given preferences, placing the assumption of the autonomous consumer at the heart of the model formulations even when their counterparts in exchanges are assumed to have power for manipulating these exchanges to their advantage on the market level. Why companies would dedicate funds to measures to establish strong brand signals, strengthen their grip on market niches, or go other ways about customer attraction has to remain a puzzle from this perspective. Integrating such measures into an analysis under this perspective will always run the risk of contradicting the assumptions made about individuals for the unique equilibrium setup.

III

Three general settings in which suboptimal results are the outcomes of market activity and market characteristics have attracted rather detailed research interest as well. These three general settings provide the second branch for systematic divergences from optimality conditions in markets in the reference framework.

At the heart of these fields of analyses lie what are called external effects and information asymmetries, or incomplete information for some agents, with so-called public goods accounting for the third group. External effects result when an individual is affected by the action of other individuals outside of market transactions. These can be either positive (e.g., education increases the technological capacity in a group and therefore others' earning potential, producing a benefit that is not accounted for and not reimbursed) or negative (e.g., pollution affects another's business negatively, producing a cost that is unaccounted for and not covered).

So, externalities mean that costs or benefits are caused by economic activities but are not paid for. In consequence, resources are misallocated. Something is either overproduced – if costs in its production are not accounted for – or underproduced – if benefits from its production are not paid for. The reference point then allows to produce estimates regarding optimal levels of activity for markets where externalities play a role. Any impact that may be felt in the noneconomic parts of society lies outside the scope of this perspective. Cultural, social, political, ecological, and other spheres are not integrated into analyses as there is no monetary price to put on them; even though a price would come about if they were integrated into market relations, which is not uncommonly seen as a potential solution to aspects that have been identified as problematic in noneconomic spheres of societies.

Information asymmetries refer to situations in which some partners to an exchange have more information about the product in question than others involved and can use that information to their advantage. It is not infrequently covering fraud of some kind, albeit under a more lenient vocabulary. Information asymmetries can arise in different circumstances and contexts. Principally, the advantage may lie with the seller or with the buyer of a product. Markets where these asymmetries have a noticeable impact may collapse, or not even constitute themselves in the first place. At the very least, a number of additional costs can be expected to arise, for a protection against contingencies, monitoring, reassurances, and other objectives.

As an example for an advantage for the seller, think of used cars, or other products that the consumer cannot fully experience or gage immediately (such as a new house, or a financial advisor's suggestions). Consumers may be wary to enter such markets without additional measures or assurances in place. Such adverse selection may lead to markets not even constituting themselves; at least, noticeably reduced transaction volumes are to be expected. On the side of customer advantages, the most prominent examples are probably found in insurance markets. The sellers of insurance policies cannot be certain what the risks of an individual agent are, or how the existence of an insurance policy may affect their behavior. An insurance premium would be covering the average risk in the group insured, which may turn out to be so high that low-risk people would overpay, and hence stay out of the market. This would drive the premium up to cover the new higher-risk pool, driving more potential buyers out. The more private information about specificities of their risk exposure individuals have, the more of an advantage they potentially have over insurance companies. Additionally, moral hazard plays a part here, as, because of the insurance cover, people might show riskier behavior than before, and thus change the foundation for risk calculations for companies. This can lead to severe problems in private insurance markets. Particularly for health insurances, we can note that no theoretical economics perspectives suggests that markets would work even remotely well, if coverage is in fact the objective pursued. The public good (see below) character of public health, and the fact that market power is a noticeable factor to contend with from insurance companies further exacerbate problems for market-based approaches to health coverage.

Mandatory participation combined with competitive market environments to keep prices for customers reasonable may be seen as a way out here. This critically relies on competition on the side of the providers of insurance, however, assuming that a competitive mechanism existed that would force insurance providers to see the purchasers of policies as customers that they needed and wanted to retain through proper service. To raise the chance for that to happen, the profit motive on the supply-side and a shareholder-value orientation of structures has to somehow be kept in check. Every payout is a cost to the provider, which gives an incentive to reduce these. The worst-case scenario for insurance markets would therefore entail a mandatory participation, in an environment where price and service competition is unlikely to materialize so that agents are forced into a role of customers to profit-seeking companies. Regulatory approaches to such situations are not unlikely to prove rather involved and costly, and it is probable that a cheaper option would be to offer insurance through a nonprofit provider who can set a benchmark price. Private companies, if charging higher prices, would have to offer an actual advantage in the services paid for if they were to maintain a presence in such an environment. In a sector like health care, where input costs have to be considered as well, additional regulation of medication prices, for instance, may prove necessary for keeping overall costs at a reasonable level given the high market concentration of producers in the pharmaceutical sector.

Even where a competitive benchmark solution is assumed, a privately organized market for health insurances is regularly used as one of the prime examples of a market that brings all ingredients to make it fail entirely, and if not, come with pronounced cost distortions and underprovision. Markets in which private agents are left to themselves cannot be adequate solution mechanisms in areas such as health care provision. This does not even address ethical considerations of a decision to make a person's health a marketable good and leave health provided on an ability-to-pay base in a private market.

Public goods, finally, are goods from which everybody profits, but where it is difficult, or at least highly impractical, to charge individuals for their use of the goods (national defense is one typically used example, on a smaller scale a lighthouse, for instance, can qualify). Once they have been made available, it is practically impossible for producers to amortize their investments and thus to make it worthwhile for private producers to engage in production activity. Therefore, private producers who have to rely on users paying for the rights of usage usually have no incentive to offer public goods. Even though people will benefit from their existence, their nature means that a profit-centered environment will not be able to guarantee their supply. Public goods provision is a main task recognized for the public agent here.

2.4 The Economic System Forcing Beneficial Results for Agents

The view on markets' potential as solution mechanisms for societies as embodied in the reference perspective is not necessarily unique. Another perspective that proposes unimpeded markets as the single best tool for addressing social problems assumes individuals to be limited in their capacities, and market interactions to proceed as ongoing processes instead of equilibrium-based static states. However, the economic system still constrains individuals' scope for action, and provides the outline for decisions that are ignored at the agents' own peril.

The market itself collects and aggregates information. Values of goods are given for every individual at a point in time. The desirable outcome is defined as reflecting such valuation to the best possible degree when judged on the social level. This cannot be assessed or measured from the outside, however.

By pursuing their own objectives purposely and clearly in market interactions, individuals provide information that is reflected in market prices, in turn signaling the values of goods relative to other goods. Markets that operate without interference offer all the information individuals need for making their personal best decisions, oriented on the prices they face. Every interference, on the other hand, means a distortion to this outcome and leaves some members of society denied their best course of action and is therefore to be avoided. In a variation of the top-down perspectives centering on equilibria, here, we assume that economic systems develop along the best possible path if functioning properly. While basic relations, conditions, and identities that economic agents have to heed provide structure and limitations, economic laws are outside the scope, and interest, of analyses, here. A number of the identities, conditions, and constraints formulated for deriving results and informing interpretations is shared with the reference perspective, however. This applies especially where analyses of entire economies, in macroeconomic settings, are concerned.

Wariness of unwarranted influences is certainly a valid point. However, the faith put in markets as systems for collecting and aggregating information to reflect underlying valuations in the best possible way cannot be upheld without qualification when confronted with general analyses of complex systems. Outcomes in such systems are by no means necessarily particularly good, even when decisions or actions are taken independently of each other. Such independence, however, is a strong assumption for economic settings; without it, feedback cycles become possible and likely, even, in some markets. For example, as the agents in such a system become too homogeneous – say, motivated by the same conclusions based on the same worldview they were taught, or group-think – there is a good chance that an unstable system results in which damaging developments are likely to recur. More generally, and for real-world agents, information problems, and rules of thumb formulated that may center on an imitation of presumably advantageous behavior patterns, and thus the dependence of one decision on others, may exacerbate such problems, and thus lead to an increased volatility of activities.

As an additional point, the perspective stresses that some kind of mechanism giving structure at a higher level than the individual components is required for the economic system to function. This structure is reflected in the postulated market environment. Then to simply assume that the higher level mechanism will produce advantageous outcomes, if only allowed to work properly appears to be a limitedly useful solution.

Support for market interactions and the participation in these interactions is necessary, and the constitution of a framework for markets to function is required. The theoretical framework itself only allows general statements concerning such supporting frameworks. Hence, we find a system in which some influence is acknowledged to be necessary. It cannot be clearly determined or delimited, though, leaving it to the researcher to formulate an opinion as to whether measures are still required for a functioning market sphere, or represent unwarranted influence taking and distortion. The recognition that market activity provides information is a valuable contribution, to be sure. The attempt to exclusively build on it for a fully-fledged foundation for economic policies cannot convince, however, given that the assumptions about the economic system set limits to its functioning that our knowledge of complex systems does not justify. While the same areas of potential problems – market failures – identified for the benchmark case, Section 2.3, are acknowledged, they are assumed to be of minor relevance; or still better than any attempt to alleviate their effects through policies could hope to be.

Furthermore, the evaluation of situations and the driving force for changes rests on a monetary foundation. Economic issues trump all else, and, thereby, the economic sphere can be interpreted as a source of dynamics of societal change. Economically disadvantageous issues are assumed to be resolved, as competition supposedly drives them out of the economic sphere, and by extension out of societies. That behaviors mirroring discrimination, for instance, draw on other aspects of humans, and are carried by groups and societies, however, alerts us to the fact that things are more involved, and that 'one-dollar-one-vote' cannot a priori be expected to serve as enough of a motivator and influence to overcome their reflections in societies. Regarding discrimination, for instance, we see a pattern that is carried by a larger group, and that is reflected in that group's behavior. A theoretical advantage for producers from ignoring prejudices may never materialize if their customers continue to discriminate, then, if they are willing to do so even at a monetary disadvantage. Hence, economic competition may be tasked with carrying more than it can reasonably be expected to stem. In environments in which markets emerge from individual interactions, these may just as well strengthen existing structures, and maybe even be more likely over time to do so, than to weaken them.

2.5 What if Agents Directly Influence Each Others' Results

I

A first step toward increasing the complexity of the analytical framework can be to allow that the actions of people have an impact on others' results, at the same time that they are affected by these others. We had referred to external effects already, where someone's action has consequences for others, changing results for other people in a positive or in a negative way. Originally, what economists had in mind when referring to external effects were effects that result from actions where the people experiencing the consequences do not have much of a choice but to accept them. Furthermore, and possibly even more importantly, the effects in that case are unilateral as the affected agents do not have an influence on the person who causes the effects in the matter of concern.

For analytical purposes, it is therefore convenient to treat external effects distinctly in situations in which influences are mutual. In this case, it is not uncommon that the best possible behavior is contingent upon others' actions. Agents can no longer necessarily execute an unambiguously advantageous behavior. Such situations may still exist, but there is no a priori reason to suspect that they may be the norm. Still, for the description of outcomes of interactions, mutually compatible expectations and behaviors are assumed, so that we remain in an equilibrium environment. However, multiple equilibria typically exist, and some are better for the agents than others.

Two aspects matter. The first concerns itself with the stability of outcomes, that is to say, whether behaviors are compatible in the sense that no one can achieve a better result as long as no one else changes their behavior. The second aspect asks whether the environment may permit better results than the one settled on, that have not been reached by the interacting agents.

Problem structures that agents may face are variable. Individually good decisions by no means necessarily result in even only particularly good outcomes for the group as a whole, or even the individual concerned, for that matter. If we leave the model environment, problems can get rather intricate when mutual influences are involved, as situations have to be mutually understood and considerations about others' behavior have to be formed.

When assessing actual economic situations, for such individual interactions, thus, other coordination mechanisms than prices matter; here, the social environment comes into play. When agents know that their results depend on what others do and they know that their action has an impact on others, their decision situation changes relative to situations where the direct mutual influence is not given. Agents then have to form expectations about others' possible actions, and, potentially, about others' future reactions if they interact frequently so that current actions may be sanctioned in the future. These intricacies can only limitedly be reflected in the analytical setup, which therefore focuses on providing descriptions of problem-structures.

II

A number of basic decision structures can be thought of in situations where agents interact in interdependent problem structures. These cover a range from situations in which single unambiguously advantageous behaviors exist, to those where a behavior pattern is individually preferable if analyzed by itself but produces overall negative results on the communal as well as individual levels if enough agents adopt it, the dilemma problems. For the latter, depending on the issues at stake, we can carry some or some more people exploiting a communal structure, but eventually it will collapse, for instance.

In between those two cases lie a number of situations where the individually best decision in a moment depends on what others are doing, so-called coordination problems. In those, a range of scenarios differing in details, such as the distribution of the overall result achieved, can be represented. Coordination is better than noncoordination, but different outcomes may be favored by different people. Finally, there are situations in which one agent gains while the other loses, or any combination of them where more people are concerned.

The dilemma structure has proven rather popular analytically. The individually best decisions result in a socially suboptimal outcome, in which each agent is also individually worse off than they could be. If everybody behaves pro-socially, substantial gains can be reaped. However, if everybody else behaves pro-socially, whoever diverges to a different pattern may gain even more. But the more agents switch course to a less inclusive course of action, the stronger their impact and the worse the overall outcome produced. This tension between individual and social level has, in fact, been a recurrent theme in economic thought, ever since modern economics started with the writings of Adam Smith.

In the face of the individualistic incentive to pursue a socially damaging course of action, different groups and societies have been able to devise a number of ways, socially informal as well as politically formal, to deal with such situations, and create some cohesion and communal outlook. Still, how well individual groups have fared has differed noticeably within and across cultural borders. As a general rule, in smaller groups, pro-social behavior is more common than in larger, more anonymous ones. Social control mechanisms tend to have a firmer grip in the former. However, there are then mechanisms to transfer what has been learned at a small level to interactions in larger groups. Still, the larger ones offer more scope for overly individualistic behaviors, and thus at least open the door to undermining the more pro-social patterns shown by others over time.

The exploitation of commonly accessible resources, such as forests, fisheries, grazing grounds, or on a larger scale, environmental issues such as clean air and actions with an eventual effect on the larger climate, is a prime area of examples for dilemma situations with economic relevance. Another example is the provision of public goods. As the question of the provision of public goods here relates to interacting agents, it does center on whether freely interacting agents may be expected to utilize their private resources for the production of public goods, even if they could just as well wait and hope for others to undertake the effort instead.

Where economic activity draws on social structures as inputs, there may be an impact on individual possibilities in other areas of life. If the impact is a negative one, but the economic sphere functions more smoothly, or at least, temporarily more profitably for some, then a dilemma-type situation might be discernible. An example may be a race to the bottom-kind of dynamic in companies, where longer work-hours by some induce others to follow suit until informal standards concerning expected overtime have been established that leave everyone worse off (assuming people have had the time to develop enough personal competence to enjoy leisure). Nothing indicates that overworked and tired people would be more productive than those who are not, but social standards require attendance. Eventually, the people working may well be worse off, while the company may not gain much, if anything, either. Labor standards more generally fall into the same category if we look at the results for companies that are pushing for lower standards, because of short-term cost considerations, for instance. Here, we might draw on the fact that when standards decline, people's productivity does not increase, while eventually we may note negative effects on the demand side, especially if stagnant or even declining wages are part of the process. Here, we may also note that our perception of the situation faced will influence our description, which in turn may feed back into behavior. Changes in the time horizon considered, for instance, can alter the problem structure we assume.

III

We can utilize a scenario of investment decisions by companies in different constellations for an exemplary overview of some basic coordination and dilemma structures. Depending on what other companies do, your best option for a course of action may differ, already in the simplest case between making an investment and not making an investment (that is, without further decisions where exactly to invest or how to split an overall amount between different locations, how to finance if external sources are required, etc.). The case of two agents is a baseline to illustrate the basic problems that may be faced. All of these situations may be considered as offering the foundation for describing different problem-structures as well, depending on the details involved.

As a starting point, we may look at a situation where two companies face an investment decision where, if they both invest, a positive outcome for them may result. Say, jointly they are strong enough to push some new product that individually they would not have been able to market. If one hesitates in related efforts, however, the other one will be better off abstaining as well. Taking up investments in a recession may provide another example, where joint investment efforts may be helping an economy out of a slump, and amortize therefore, but isolated individual efforts would fail. Aspects of industrialization in countries with more agricultural production structures may be captured by the same line of thinking, as enough venturing entrepreneurs may provide each other with customers for their products, either directly, or through increased purchasing power of their employees. Note that – and we will take this up in Chapter 4 – the production capacity of investments does not depend on others so much, the extent of the potential market, however, does. It is the income flows that are triggered which shape outcomes for companies.

It does get more complicated if the companies involved can expect to profit differently. Say, one company has expertise in variation A of a standard, the other in a variation B of that standard. As it is, both companies will realize losses due to a lack of demand. However, market volumes are expected to increase noticeably if they both offer the same variation, as wider use and potential for interoperability will attract more customers, but also, as their joint efforts can create a wider reach for marketing efforts. Both have to converge on the same version in order to realize the higher profits, meaning one has to move toward the other company. Who blinks first and adopts the other's version will be comparatively worse off regarding that particular variation, as new knowledge has to be acquired, and the competitor has an advantage in experience. However, it is conceivable that the situation overall means that such outcome will still be preferable to not coordinating at all even for the one realizing weaker profits. If neither one is able to create a sufficient market alone, neither can realize profits. If they agree on one variation of their standard, and the market grows as expected, they do realize profits, even if to different degrees.

Finally, and beyond the coordination issues raised, we may also end up identifying a dilemma scenario, where it would be enough for one of them to invest, and the other to enjoy the positive results this may generate without investing herself. Again, assume that for the creation of sufficient demand for their products, some initial effort is necessary, including various marketing measures. If no one invests in an initial effort, then there will be possible gains that are not realized. However, if the efforts of one agent are enough to expand the potential market, or even constitute it in the first place, for that matter, then either one has a reason to wait in order to forgo that expenditure and only reap the rewards.

IV

Note that in none of these situations can a price signal alone produce a socially desirable outcome. The proper price of alternatives, if there was one, would change depending on others' behaviors. It would change reflecting monetary variables, as income flows are created and changed with individual's decisions. A perspective focusing solely on price-based coordination as the solution mechanism for agents in economic settings may misinterpret or fail to grasp related problems. Additionally, the market mechanism coordinating agents, as pointed out earlier, relies on a large number of such agents for its existence. In cases of few agents pursuing joint objectives, or common objectives, different mechanisms, in the social and political spheres, for instance, or a determination of negotiating strength, have to be drawn on. The interest of companies does by no means have to coincide with that of the larger group. However, some kind of coordination has to be permitted. Overall, the negotiating position, strength, and tactics employed by the agents involved will play a critical role in determining outcomes under multiple options; such additional options for shaping which way a situation is to turn are not technically part of the analytical framework, however.

V

In the broader set of problem structures that agents may be facing, with a set of tools that allows some tentative first approaches to situations in which different interests may be involved that have to interact to produce an outcome, we get a more variable view of interactions and possible outcomes. We can also more easily broaden the scope of analyses.

Additional perspectives on situations may open up as well. As an example, we might think about owners, or capital, and workers, or labor, who have to come to an agreement regarding the distribution of the value created in production. For some questions, an understanding of situations may be suitable that involves an interpretation of a struggle for the distribution of income as a main force shaping economic structures. Typically, the view embodied is one of antagonism between labor and capital. Whatever is afforded to one group, or class, is not available to the other. Patterns of distribution respond to the distribution of power that affects the negotiating positions when it comes to wages and reimbursements for owners of capital.

The approach to this kind of struggle contains two aspects, namely, an assessment of a current situation, in the distribution pattern, and an assessment to changes of those patterns, in the zero-sum view – what is taken from one is given to the other. The distribution pattern can take a number of forms, of course, as long as every group involved in the production processes gets access to enough of the production value to sustain themselves over time.

As a third point, we may decide to integrate time into our analysis in order to reflect that agents may continuously encounter one another – in labor relations not unlikely, for sure. The zero-sum perspective on changes is then not the only view that can be adopted. Even though there is no arguing with it at any given moment, there is still the option that a situation does not have to deteriorate into a struggle. Once the understanding of interdependence has matured, groups may be willing to compromise in an understanding of mutual needs and necessities, and thereby enlarge future gains more easily than would be possible in a situation of antagonism and struggle. This is not so much collusion, but simply a willingness to hold back in pushing for short-term advantages in order to realize a medium term improvement. The immediate changes to a situation matter less for its evaluation than the longer running processes that get started through the interaction patterns of the groups involved. Such potential for showing an enlightened self-interest is not limited to economic issues, of course. An interesting side effect of both of these alternative perspectives on the same basic situation is that, insofar as the interpretation of the situation influences and informs behavior, by assuming a specific interpretation the behavior that follows contributes to creating an environment confirming the assumptions made before.

The economically very successful first decades in the wake of World War II show patterns that indicate a broader consensus among different societal interest groups in a number of industrialized economies.

Participation of each group in economic gains brought a number of advantages, from stable demand for large corporations, coupled with employment stability, to political stability, and continued technological advancement. Interests were rather well aligned.

This is interesting insofar as the shifts in the structure of current production activities may mean that such an approach to economic relations may not be easily replicable. Interest groups' relations may have changed in the course of the changes in the organization of production processes over the last decades. The spreading localities of production sites, organized within networks of company relations, can be seen to mean, simplified, that capital is in one place and labor in another. A number of concerns that seem to have been playing a role in the relations between capital and labor in the postwar years may not be perceived as too relevant any longer. The purchasing power of labor in its locality is of lesser concern to capital. The same is true for more general overlapping social and political interests and stability. This may also be seen as a reinforcement of the need to acknowledge that the economic sphere is created by the rules and norms set up to structure it, and not a natural given, with natural law-like relations.

2.6 What if Agents Can Influence Others' Economic Environment

I

For describing problem structures as the perspective described in Section 2.5 does, agents accept the decision situation that they face. What we think of where strategic behavior is concerned, however, is frequently directed at attempts to change the problem structure actually confronted. Once individuals have formed an assessment of their specific situations, scope for strategic behavior may open up. There may be ways for changing the decision structure that oneself, or other agents involved, face. Companies, for instance, can try to make a situation less attractive to (potential) competitors, either by influencing supply-side conditions in their reach or demand-side conditions in the market segment of interest. If done successfully, this would reduce the space of options that are suitable for the respective counterparts.

Competitive behavior of this kind does not have much in common with the perfect competition of the reference framework. Rather, it focuses on forcing changes in situations and problem structures in an attempt to increase control over one's environment. Imagine a monopolist who knows that she is vulnerable to other companies' market entry. Once that entry has occurred, there may be no viable way of protecting the profits the company is used to. But, there may be ways for her to try to prevent others from entering the market in the first place. These would center on making the entry decision less attractive relative to decisions to focus attention and activity elsewhere. What may appear like over-investment in production capacity, or excessive spending on marketing measures, among other things, may make a lot of sense when seen as attempts to gain, establish, or maintain a certain control over a specific market segment or niche by making it less attractive to others. Actions taken to that end may include preemptive price cuts, investments in enhanced production capacities for lowering costs per unit, or marketing campaigns for strengthening brand image and market segment control, for instance. Profits might drop below prior levels, but still be above what they would fall to if other companies started to service the market segment under consideration.

Other options include strategic partnerships, with potential competitors, as well as with suppliers, distributors, or retailers, depending on the specifics of the situation involved. They might also include the tying together of previously disconnected areas of activity in which interests of oneself and potential competitors are affected, or which may help to weave a tighter network of products into which to tie customers. Of course, ties to political actors that may afford some protection are rather attractive options as well.

Before actually establishing a monopoly position, competition for a certain demand segment may play out in a way so that the first investor may gain an advantage over latecomers, because of later brand recognition, quality advantages because of a longer learning period to implement improvements, or compatibility issues where standards are concerned that dominate once they have been established and attracted a critical mass of followers. A first mover may be able to force other companies onto a path of action that is advantageous for the first one, including the others' abstention from a market entry. However, in other instances, companies may be better off waiting to see what competitors do before they move themselves and then act in a more settled, and hopefully more predictable, environment.

Of course, price competition in and around demand segments may happen, too. However, no company really has an interest in price competition. The only reasons to engage in it anyway include trade-offs between short-term and longer-term considerations. This may focus on the capturing of market shares at competitors' expense in the short term in hopes of a more secure position in the longer run, for instance through a push in production to exploit characteristics of technology that often allow lower unit costs at higher production volumes. Other reasons may be born of a certain desperation for short-term revenue generation for there to be a longer term at all. Still, price competition is not usually the preferred method of choice for engaging in interactions with others. Once they have established their positions companies tend to have ways to avoid cutting into each others' profit margins (too badly).

In different areas of economic activity, or economically relevant activity, shaping one's strategy environment can have a more positive connotation, for instance, in setting the structure for participating in a network of companies that collaborate in research and development matters. Here, collaboration and cooperation are to be enhanced, not market entry hindered. In such an environment, structures that support long-term collaboration may be able to make more novelties accessible as efforts in research and development can be bundled and results shared, thereby potentially also cutting down waste. The influence on the strategy environment would focus on making long-term relations profitable enough to overcompensate the foregoing of short-term gains from breaking relations. Of course, viewed from a different angle, such collaboration may elicit a different interpretation.

II

As seen previously, one way to approach economic issues in which the focus of analyses lies on the individual is to assume that all resources and goods have a clearly understood value. Knowing what they want and how much it is worth to them because of its usefulness for them, agents participate only in those exchanges in which they can realize an objective gain in use value. This framework offers a foundation for the positive assessment of market economies' ability to deliver a plethora of consumption goods. With given values, outside influences that may lead to positive feedback loops between agents and their decisions can be avoided.

However, companies may be able to exert a direct influence on consumers; observation suggests that they can, to say the least. Agents among themselves may have an influence on each other; observation suggests that they do. Both aspects may steer consumption choices in random directions. For new products and product classes, customers have to be educated and trained in order for a market to actually emerge. In fact, for modern economies, the nomer 'invention is the mother of necessity' has repeatedly been applied. In social environments, individuals compete for recognition, and consumption choices may be employed as a tool for that end. There is scope for influence-taking there. New products come before the demand for them. Customers have to be created by and in the system for the whole process to be viable in the first place.

Allowing for the possibility that desires may be created and stimulated, and the consumption focus thus steered, the positive assessment of a market system is no longer unequivocally possible. Instead of being good at finding ways to satisfy existing consumer demands, the system relies on the ability to create such demands. These demands are themselves part of the system and the ability to shape them is an integral aspect of allowing the expansion of economic activity, and the continuation of the system as it is currently set up. The parts of the system are such that it keeps itself running. A simplified positive assessment of this system based on its ability to satisfy consumption urges runs into a circular notion.

The fact that people get bored with what they have got can open space for new products, as well. Teaching consumers to seek satisfaction through consumption then can be a worthwhile strategy for maintaining potential demand that can be tapped into for new products or services. Either way, for a continuous satisfaction from consumption, continuous stimuli are required, and typically, that also involves changes in the sources of these stimuli. The view of a market system to address people's wants and needs in the best possible way gives way to an image of a donkey chasing a carrot; for some aspects, at least.

III

If preferences can be shaped, then market power becomes a different thing as well. Market power does no longer only refer to picking the point at which price and quantity sold permit the largest profits, where companies, instead of the social planner of perfect competition, get to pick a combination from the set of accessible ones. Shaping preferences and creating demand for products mean companies can influence their environments to their advantage, just as they may make a situation less attractive for potential competitors. They are not confined to some influence in defined spaces, in terms of moving a result one way or another, but can be creating spaces over which they can exercise some control.

Market power becomes much more concerned with capturing demand segments, in that case. Such market power relies on the attraction of demand to the products offered and on reducing the impact that other companies can have on one's own position. Connected to the establishment of brands, for instance, we may also note that habits in consumption behavior do play a role so that a choice once made can more easily be reinforced in, eventually habitual, repetition. Competition is more adequately understood as competition for markets and market segments, not within markets where the danger of price competition might become more pronounced, then. Once a demand segment has been captured, companies cannot be oblivious to potential competitors within that segment, of course. Possible means for avoiding competitors, or discouraging them, beyond those already referred to earlier, also include the ability to create advantageous production structures, in cost and quality, and the tying of products into networks of established standards, which limits the space for potential competitors to enter. Of course, influence from outside the economic sphere can also be sought.

When aspects such as the ones referred to in this section play a part, we see that the economic environment itself is shaped by individual actions. Back and forth of strategic action and reaction can shape and change this environment in an ongoing process. We have thus taken a first step toward analytical perspectives in which the sum of individual actions leads to the emergence of a particular environment. These are analytical perspectives that ask what environments may look like, once individuals can influence them, no longer only how individuals' actions may impact the outcome in given environments. Hence, we start to see bottom-up perspectives on economic issues, and as a result economic environments in which functioning and outcomes depend on what exactly individual agents can and do.

2.7 What if There is a Mutual Influence Between Individuals and Environment

I

Finally, regarding the relation between individual and environment, we may look at situations in which individuals influence their environment, at the same time that they react to influences from that environment. Notions of circular and cumulative causation can frequently help describe dynamics under such conditions. Factors that shape economic outcomes may be found in the economic, technological, or social environment, among others. We will discuss a couple of examples drawn from these areas.

An interesting starting point in this context lies in the establishment of standards. Standards refer to commonly used or applied measures, objects, norms, or protocols, depending on context and situation. Where technological standards are concerned, they eventually converge onto a product variant offered, whether the product is material or immaterial, and are therefore connected to some producers' originally marketed offer. In areas in which the characteristics of products are particularly prone to the emergence of standards, typically related to interoperability in a wide sense, either between different producers during production processes (e.g., in a value-added chain), between different consumers when using products (e.g., communication software), or in the actual act of using the product itself that requires additional supportive structures (e.g., the internal combustion engine), one of two general routes is then open for private producers. Either they try to set the standard or they wait until a standard has emerged from competing varieties, and only then start their activity in a specific market or segment. Perceptions of others' actions, expectations regarding other producers and potential consumers, and estimates regarding the properties of the standard to emerge, as well as technological factors in production, such as economies of scale, compatibilities to other potential alternatives, and own capabilities and specialization all will influence decisions, and assessments of situations will therefore likely differ.

The general patterns of the adoption of a standard by the customers follow similar concerns. The product class that will eventually converge onto a certain standard offers some feature that may appear desirable upon availability. Hence, the product may be purchased before the standard has been established. This, however, runs the risk of later having to undergo the same spending again, if the version one has opted for is not compatible with an eventual standard (e.g., producing software for the wrong operating system, buying Beta vs. VHS player). It may therefore also seem advantageous to wait and see which of competing alternatives may become dominant and only then make a commitment to it. To some degree, consumer decisions shape the market that becomes established. Later consumers take that market environment into consideration as they make their purchasing decision.

But someone has to go first. Not only hesitant producers, a hesitant demand-side may then actually lead to a nonconstitution of a market for which potential demand may well be high. This is partly due to the fact that the emerging environment is important for customers. If you have committed to a losing alternative, your investment, or just spending, will be lost. Too many hesitant potential customers may then mean that a good may never make it to general market penetration, even though the potential for it existed. If enough people decide to make a purchase, on the other hand, a standardized solution to a specific problem may be established.

In the process toward such a lock-in on a standard, coincidences may play a role, short-term assumed advantages may easily dominate considerations over long-term advantages (say, in terms of environmental considerations, or for labor standards); marketing strategies that are superior while the product itself may not be can have a marked influence on the outcome, as may numerous other factors. All of them can open situations up to the possibility of allowing inferior variants to become dominating. Again, once a critical mass of adopters has been reached, it may simply be advantageous to follow them for reasons of compatibility, not any inherent characteristic of the variant or standard in question. Each one of them, reacting to the influences around them, contributes a small impulse to the direction of the overall process, shaping their path as they go. No one can determine the eventual outcome by themselves. Production cost advantages that come with volume and eventual research advantages from continuous tweakings of a standardized product may make it difficult, eventually, to recognize or realize alternatives, however.

Market interactions can then easily lead to disadvantageous outcomes, even if everyone does what they think is best for them. Once inferior outcomes have materialized, the customer base they have attracted may well be too large for alternatives to stand a chance and out-compete the dominant one in any relevant time-frame. The environment matters for the choices of the individual agent, and for the sensibility of such choices. What consumers prefer may differ noticeably in different environments. The usefulness of products depends on the environment created in the process of choosing them, at times. There is nothing in the process to guarantee a long-term satisfying or particularly good outcome to this process. There is nothing in this process, either, that would automatically produce the same outcome as a kind of simultaneous vote would. The system is not moved from state A to state B in one leap. It moves, and decisions along the way shape that way. The time-component itself plays a part, and an abstraction from time, here, means that critical factors vanish, and potential outcomes and problems with it.

As the usefulness of the standard depends on the state of the environment, there is also no inherent and fixed value to each individual standard or variation thereof. Value depends partly on user numbers, among others, introducing additional components that change depending on the environment that has emerged, and that may also change over time. This cannot be reflected in current prices, either, as it cannot be known at the outset, so that the information available to agents by observing prices in exchange arenas for products of interest here is of limited usefulness.

II

A primary entry for the actual creation of wants is the fact that humans as social beings are embedded in a social environment. We live in groups, and place and status in those groups are important for most if not all individuals in one way or another. Fashion, fads, trends emerge from this environment, in an interplay of human individuality and human sociality as group signaling and emulation of higher ranking status groups and individuals. Peer groups and aspiration levels shape individual reference points and focuses. Status signals are defined within the framework in which agents have been socialized and in which they are moving. Human individuality is expressed and communicated through consumption choices in our modern economies, as is group affiliation.

In modern economies, consumption plays an important role for status and status signals as well. Therefore, consumption goods can carry at least two characteristics that influence their appeal to individuals, one is their usefulness in a given environment, and the second, their appropriateness as a status signal. Such status signals are not limited to luxury goods or brands, but have made it all the way to the most basic consumer goods, with store brands, for instance, toward the bottom of the pile, and fancier brands toward the top, even though the usefulness of products themselves may differ by degrees, if at all. The two aspects of usefulness and status signal will generally both be present in a particular good, albeit to differing degrees. A useful good can always be produced in varieties catering to different consumption potentials. For instance, building on the social nature of individuals, mobile technologies offering constant access to the peer group apparently tie into very basic desires and wants of humans as social beings. On the other hand, the more the standard for contact is tied to new devices, the more necessary it becomes to keep consumer spending levels up for meeting the requirements of technological givens. And, of course, the devices themselves may become increasingly attractive for signaling consumption ability on a general level.

III

This aspect of human behavior may lead to changes in our perspective on activities mediated through market transactions. In societies as rich as the Western ones, for instance, capacities to solely address basic needs have long been left behind in relative importance in economic activity. Poverty is for the most part not an absolute concept any longer, but a relative one, where poverty signals deprivation from capacities for a participation in regular societal activities. Part of economic activity may nowadays be more appropriately described as a device for the creation and signaling of status within the respective peer group. This has consequences for an interpretation of the observations in exchange arenas by the individuals as well, for instance, in terms of the information that economic activity and its indicators, such as changes in prices, may be seen to offer individuals.

For instance, if fashion rules in some areas, a price mechanism may play a minor role in the determination of demand. It is entirely feasible that demand even increases with rising prices. This may be seen as another instant in which the value of an object or service acquired is actually created in a transaction. If specific goods are particularly attractive among higher-status groups, a trickle down to lower status groups, in attempts at emulating more successful group members, is not uncommon. Increased user bases, however, will threaten to devalue signals again, so that once consumption goods are accepted as signals for social status, by whichever group in society, a continuous flow of goods may be expected in a higher turnover to the latest model available, or latest category included in status-conscious shopping lists. Whether these will then fade again, or eventually transform into perceived necessities, is probably difficult to assess at the outset of a process. A differentiation between groups and the signaling of status will require a constant change in the details of the signals sent, to the latest product line, trend, or gadget.

Certainly, a defined usefulness of goods can no longer be assumed, as the fashion component shifts and changes. Just as the value of some goods may depend on how many others use it in terms of interoperability and connectedness, so may the value of a good here depend on the right people perceiving the signal that is intended, and a limit to acceptable numbers of those actually employing a specific object for sending it. Consumption goods being an acceptable status signal in Western societies, in combination with a trickle down of specific status signals, increased purchasing power, and scale economies in production, have resulted in a constantly increasing material requirement for participating in society over the last decades. Participating in transactions takes on an air of keeping up, more than one of actually improving one's well-being.

Also, status is a zero-sum game, as we cannot all accede the status ladder at the same time. That market interactions would generally result in advantageous results cannot be upheld as a statement in an environment in which status competition is pursued through activity in the economic sphere, therefore.

While individuals have been motivated by group-oriented and status-oriented considerations (whether consciously or habitually) for as long as we can trace back in time, and therefore the offer of signals meets a, possibly latent, demand, the way the economic sphere is utilized for such signaling is relatively new. The concept of relative deprivation is likewise a recent novelty, as material progress to the point where absolute poverty does not have to be a concern in a number of countries is a recent advance as well, shifting the focus to aspects of deprivation related to societal participation that were less pressing as long as material deprivation dominated.

IV

Status, more often than not, to generalize, is connected to the control of resources, directly, or in some indirect way. The specific shape of signals observable will depend on values as well as technological capacity in groups. Signals showing control over resources can thus differ widely, across space and across time. Examples may include time dedicated to learning about some obscure fringe aspects of music, or wine; the resources to employ unproductive staff, and have them learn specific manners that take time to master; defining those plants as desirable that require attention and care, arranging them in some pattern, and weeding out the rest; a sports car; hunting; physical prowess; mobile phone; vacation spot; and so on. Note that a system in which these aspects play a role for human decisions and behavior depicts a possibility of a continuous dynamic of change built in as an integral part of the system. The direction for such changes is not determined at a given point in time.

Demonstrating resource control is what we may call status-driven behavior. Such demonstrations are not typically focusing on a prudent use of resources. Waste – from a productive standpoint – is in fact a much more promising way toward signaling and maintaining status. We may already note here that under this perspective, the 'one-dollar-one-vote' rule that guides allocation in economic matters does not leave a lot of reason to suspect a particularly useful resource allocation pattern to emerge. While the individual may benefit, the group will not. In fact, if interactions are predominantly mediated and coordinated by prices, we may expect overall disadvantageous developments to occur at times, and more frequently over time, under this perspective on economic activity. This would be exacerbated by the fact that the drive toward status likewise means a reorientation of activities, from productive and instrumental for solving problems that are faced on the group-level, toward unproductive and ceremonial, motivated by hierarchical considerations within the group. Such a shift in motivation coincides with a shift in values, as the focus of activities is drawn from taking group-considerations into account to increasingly individualistic perspectives, in the sense of an anarchic individualism that has no regard for others, not the rugged individualism of focuses on self-sufficiency wherever possible. As a flip-side, scarcity is much less of an issue to be concerned about in rich societies. We may also find this reflected in the fact that unemployment is very common, to say the least, meaning the principal production factor is in fact typically not used to its full availability, much less demanded beyond that and that crises manifest in overproduction, not a lack of available goods (which is a topic to pick up in more detail in Chapter 4).

2.8 What if There are Relevant Aspects that Cannot be Known in Advance

I

How the field of information is integrated into economic analyses differs among the two broad groups of top-down and bottom-up perspectives on economies. Two different fields are generally treated under the heading of information problems. In the first case, the information is in the system somewhere, and the task is to make sure an information advantage is not exploited by agents (see section 2.3). In the second case, information does not exist yet. Possible future events either are entirely unknown or may be known but cannot be assessed in terms of their likely occurrence. An unknowable future may be the result of changes and developments of which agents are simply unaware. Unknowable events also arise from the fact that in a complex system, consequences of actions can be unpredictable for individual agents, as the future is created in the processes they shape jointly. One action is not necessarily always linked to the same outcome, as others' actions matter as well. And of course, learning that is, for instance, translated into technological change cannot be forecast, and cannot really be factored into assessments of future potential by an individual.

The possibility of unknowable events is typically taken into account by human agents in individual and collective action. Included are a number of issues referring to the already mentioned protection against potentially disadvantageous future events, especially those emerging from systemic effects that the individual cannot do anything about, as well as the need for stabilizing measures in order to enable interactions among people in a structured and purposeful manner. Approaches to dealing with economic activity, then, when ignoring such issues of uncertainty, related motivations, and resulting behavior patterns, may be missing or misinterpreting relevant aspects of economic life and behavior.

II

Uncertainty and real time go hand in hand in economic matters. In processes, over time, conditions and environments change and new structures emerge. There is no predefined path for this process to follow. Hence, where it turns cannot be known in advance. Technological findings, norms and rules regarding their application, economic conditions shaping their viability, together with social and cultural factors influencing their acceptability in a given society, all combine to shape the foundation and specificities of economic activity. This economic activity provides the foundation for further processes of change and thus the future foundation and shape of activity. Current conditions may have a formidable influence on future conditions; developments in the systems under consideration from this perspective can be described as path-dependent: original conditions have an influence on the paths that are open for changes to follow. Which form they take is not knowable to the agents. As a side effect, the agents can only choose one step along the path, and thus shape the future direction a little. They cannot choose future states of the system, as those result from the combination of all steps taken over time. Even if everyone does what is objectively best for them in a given environment, they cannot be sure that the overall outcome reflects the best possible state given the potential in the system at an earlier point in time.

The systematic and directed protection against specific events, or rather their consequences, may not be possible, and prove too limiting for the system and society overall. Again, the general issue of a balance between stability, and the tendency toward stagnation that goes with it, and the space for changes, with the potential for deep-reaching disruptions that it brings, will have to be an ongoing topic and concern for societies. What is possible is to try to limit the exposure to adverse influences and to the impact adverse developments can have in more generalized protection or insurance settings. An income stabilization scheme may be an example for such a set of measures. Where system characteristics are better understood, keeping system developments outside of potentially more threatening areas may also be possible.

Trying to create a stable environment is a general objective pursued in economic matters, whether by the individual, possibly by means of collective action, or companies. In order to protect oneself from the consequences of unknown events and unforeseeable developments, increasing the control over one's immediate environment is one route that has historically been pursued for increasing the stability of the environment faced. Branching out to different areas to reduce dependence in any single one is another general route pursued. While the disadvantageous development will still materialize at some point, a more stable setup may increase the chances of making it through the situation. That companies are planning structures within our market economies is one reflection of issues related to real time and uncertainty, then, as control and planning go hand in hand, even though uncertainty is not the only reason to organize production processes in companies, for sure.

For an individual, protection against adverse future developments may be sought through collective actions of some kind. Whether they are community-based, government-granted, or made available through markets in the form of insurance policies, for instance, such options have increasingly been made available to individuals over the last decades. The concrete trigger of an adverse development does not have to be known, here, as for instance a reduction in income may have been due to financial market developments affecting economic activity, a general loss in demand because of slacking real world investment, adverse exchange rate developments, or the closure of the production site of the principal employer in a region. Its impact can in any case be lessened by a mutual cover granted among the individuals or through some organizational structure put in place.

In a different area, a noticeable issue in the formulation of contracts and the framework to embed economic activity in an environment under uncertainty will be related to the distribution of costs that adverse future developments may produce. Regulating economic activity is to no small measure concerned with the distribution of costs related to it, including the prevention of income-generating activities if these threaten noticeable harm on others.

III

Uncertainty may also be a de facto state, as there may simply be too much data for agents to assess, process, and then filter for relevant information. That is to say, even if a future were calculable at a given point in time because everything relevant could be known, this would still be impossible because human capacities are too limited to do so. (And regarding such calculations, it is always worth repeating that sensitivity to initial conditions can matter a great deal in complex systems, requiring incredibly precise data sets if accurate results where to be obtained. Also, already the physical limitations of calculators and computers – you cannot carry all decimals in iterations after a certain point, for instance – set limits, and can result in very different outcomes in calculations depending on the precise limitations and rules for dealing with them in place.)

Aspects of the environment may take on a role and importance for agents when they are faced with uncertainty that differs from that under circumstances in which uncertainty does not play a noticeable role. To some degree, the environment offers support through the structure that comes into being in the interaction of agents. Also, parts of the environment itself can become signals and have to be assessed differently in light of missing other information, as contrasted with a state in which everything relevant is known. For instance, expectations about others and about future developments can be based on the reflection of others' activities in economic indicators. Changes in such indicators can be viewed as important sources of information and can therefore increase their weight for individuals' consideration about reasonable courses of action. Prices and their changes are one example for this as possible indicators about others' expectation, for instance. When we turn to the functioning of markets, this can be a key aspect for addressing and interpreting observations in market activity, as well as the formulation of a framework of rules to embed activity in those markets. In short, where prices serve as indicators for others' expectations, decisions are not taken independently of one another any longer, and price movements may be expected to respond to positive feedbacks at times. In that case, a continuous motion driven by moods and expectations will be a normal part of market developments, not the reversal to a true price driven by negative feedback. We will return to these aspects in more detail in Chapter 3.

Finally, and to be addressed in detail in the following sections, human interaction itself is subject to a substantial potential uncertainty. Social structures help to limit the conceivable, normal, decision space for agents and make interactions possible thereby. Simplifying decision situations in order for structured and directed activity to be a viable option is a prerequisite to human activity. Heuristics provide the foundation for decision-making and action. Habits of behavior provide the foundation of human interactions. These are embedded in the institutional framework and guided by the social rules and norms that constitute this framework. From these rules and eventual norms emerges stability in the actions and interactions of agents. The applicability and usefulness of the resulting regular behavior patterns can be expected to differ depending on the environment. Just as different environments may bring out different emphases in behavior.

2.9 Structure Through Rules and Norms

I

Humans move purposely, in interactions with others and in pursuing objectives in complex environments over time. At the same time, humans have limited capacities for data processing and information uptake, while the space of potential behavior without constraint is large, and possible interactions and results may be multitudes larger. The space that humans draw on when considering behaviors has to be limited in order to become manageable. For human interactions, stabilization is achieved by social conventions, rules, and norms. Such stabilization is a necessary component of complex systems in general. Structure has to exist to allow their continuation in discernible form. The concept of emergence plays a key role for related issues. The interaction of individual components can lead to structure, without it being apparent by analyses of the individual components by themselves. Just as you cannot determine the state of an element by examining an atom, or molecule, so you cannot discern social structure, or spatial structure for that matter, by analyzing an individual agent. In the interaction of individual components, something more than can be grasped by focusing on them alone emerges. That still means that the structure would not exist without the individuals. However, in complex systems, the whole can be more than the sum of its parts, and a focus on the parts alone may therefore miss aspects of the system under consideration.

The complex of social rules and norms forms the institutional framework, or the institutions, that members of a group adopt or are socialized in and therefore have learned at some point in their lives. Included in those institutions are the values that guide the agents in their social interactions. In certain situations, certain behaviors are expected, and a value-system develops that supports, or even tries to enforce, certain actions. Deviations from expected and sanctioned behavior patterns come at the risk of incurring social sanctions, possibly encoded in formal law. Rules of behavior are also part of a larger system. This system itself, in turn, gains stability through an ideological framework that embeds the institutional framework and provides some coherence to the interpretation of the overall set of rules, as well as a justification for them.

The institutional framework reduces the complexity of situations and makes actions and reactions more predictable, thereby enabling human interactions. Complexity reduction by means of institutions works for the agents themselves as well as for their assessment of interactions. On the one hand, we see that rules, norms, and conventions guide behavior. The other way around, social expectations limit what may be considered acceptable courses of action by agents. The space of possible actions to explore is limited. Over time, typical action and response patterns develop, and come to be expected. In certain situations, you behave in certain ways without having to expand a lot of energy on assessing all possible courses of action. Thus, eventually, agents habitually show certain behavior patterns. The institutional structure is not automatically given in its totality at some point in time, nor is it the result of directed rational decisions regarding structure. It emerges from individual interactions, further responds to initial changes in behavior following learning and shifts in value, and developments in problem-solving abilities in technology. It stabilizes the interaction of individual components. None of this means that individuals would not be able to show different behavior patterns, possibly depending on their willingness to accept social repercussions from the group.

On the other hand, the ability to form expectations about others' behavior is enhanced at the same time through the same mechanism.

You have a reasonable idea of what to expect from others in certain situations, and grow used to certain patterns. This does not have to mean a single unique behavior will come forth, but at least should refer to a limited set of actions to expect. Also, in familiar environments, expectations are no longer necessarily the outcome of conscious efforts, but may be formed habitually as well, and drawn on subconsciously. As the institutional framework shapes the behavior of all members of a group, typical responses are alike, at least for comparable members in a group (status and hierarchy may play a role in what is considered appropriate in certain situations), and patterns stabilize on which the relevant agents can rely.

The suitability of different behavioral options is shaped in the process through which such structures have come into being. Once habituation has taken hold, whether additional options may exist that could lead to improved outcomes is more often than not, not even considered any longer. Humans do not normally question the relations of daily life, and how these are presented to them. Things are as they are. That makes them a lot easier to deal with. This is, on the other hand, another factor contributing to situations where stability can lead to stagnation.

II

We may interpret institutions in this framework as solutions by groups to problems they have faced over time. They do not have to have been actively sought, but may very well just represent patterns that have developed over time and have led to results that the group members could live with, possibly literally, in the face of more or less specific external and internal challenges for the group. Put differently, they have emerged from processes of interactions and problem-solving patterns, over time, and not been constituted in a concerted effort at one single point in time. More than one approach is likely to be able to offer a satisfactory outcome in any situation, and processes building on such outcomes can take a multitude of different forms. However, once a certain institutional framework has consolidated, further changes are more difficult to introduce as the existing rules and norms restrict possible novelties that are compatible with the system in place. To transfer rules from one environment to the other, and expect them to work in the same way, will not unlikely result in disappointment.

Furthermore, there is no reason to suspect that behavior oriented on satisfying results in the past would be particularly well suited to new technological environments, or otherwise changed conditions. Still, the social environment matters for what constitutes successful behavior within a group so that the behavior patterns themselves may be expected to be complementing and stabilizing each other. Patterns of complementing behaviors and responses have developed over time and are not easily abandoned, much less unilaterally. A number of effects combine that result in a relative stability of an institutional framework that is oriented on past conditions and problems, and integrates values past.

Integrated in the successfulness of behaviors is also a notion of social acceptability so that besides the direct outcome, a social component is brought to bear onto the individual who may consider changing settled ways. This will introduce a further conservative impulse – failing in the conventional way cannot be held against an agent, succeeding in a new way can always be attributed to luck.

Stability is further enhanced by an overall umbrella that typically provides a justification for behavior as an ideological frame. Whether it be god's will that you are where you are, or the incorruptible laws of the market that put you there, playing by the rules is your only way of advancing, or at least, not falling behind within an ideological and value-frame guiding group behavior and justifying social structures. The ideological justification, religious, political, or else, that contributes to the stability of the overall framework and embeds the behavior patterns regularly shown, constrains the space for possible adaptations of behavior. Values reflecting this outlook develop that agents adopt and internalize which likewise stabilize behavior patterns as alternative behavior patterns will no longer only be considered wrong, but actually feel wrong. Still, behavior is not determined, of course, and agents retain the capacity to change behaviors, just as their basic ability to experiment and learn is always available. How far they are allowed space for maintaining and developing this potential, and then exploring it, depends on the institutional framework itself.

III

Institutional change can happen along two dimensions, here. The institutional framework itself can change, in a process of an adoption of new rules, resulting in new social environments, and possible further adoptions. Learning and technological change can continuously open options for changes in institutions that may offer more effective possibilities for addressing problems in the social sphere. One group of effects providing momentum for change is assumed to be the integration of new technological possibilities with their accompanying behavior patterns for effective utilization, and impacts on social relations and hierarchies that may follow from these. Openness to change is an ongoing challenge for groups to master.

Change can also refer to the values behind behaviors, in the aforementioned shift from instrumental to ceremonial motivations. Ceremonial motivations refer to attempts at maintaining or increasing status in one's group. A basic assumption regarding dynamics of change along the instrumental-ceremonial dimension over time states that ceremonial motivations gain in relative importance in stable environments. Structures that may have stabilized because they did provide acceptable results for the agents involved are increasingly maintained because they serve specific interests. The values that motivate behavior may shift over time, from problem-solving to being oriented on hierarchical and status considerations. Preventing such stagnation and the resulting peterification of structures, and attempting to maintain openness to change go hand in hand.

IV

The value system shapes how recognition is given, and in which direction a ceremonialization of structures takes a society will depend on the values in place. A warrior tribe will set different standards from an agricultural village, or a consumer society, and depending on the experiences of different consumer societies' forebearers, they may set different emphases in their patterns as well. An institutional framework and the culture it is embedded in matter for behavior and matter for the future paths that are open.

In a value system that acknowledges economic success as one way to social recognition, the economic sphere, and the symbols connected to it – consumption, in our case – will play a core role for the agents involved. In the economic sphere, allocation patterns can be expected to be affected by shifts in motivations. Activity is oriented on showing the ability to excel within given structures for the sake of positioning oneself. Economic success is not an end in and of itself, but a means to an end. The value sets that have developed in modern economies over the last decades put consumption front and center of social signals; consuming services, like traveling, is part of the package. In this dynamic, consumption spending can be expected to continue to grow, as in a relational approach to consumption signals, there is never an end in sight. The aspiration level of the agents, on the different rungs of the income ladder, increases in reaction to perceived increases in the reference group drawn on for comparison. A relative aspect of success, outdoing others' success in a zero-sum setting, can be expected to be an influence on dynamics, then, that differ from relations in which absolute success is the only yardstick for the desirability of measures and changes, as is the case in the reference framework. Market-based interactions can cause a lot of stress and struggle; they do not unequivocally enhance the well-being of people, because the motivations for participating in them and the environment that we acknowledge are more diverse than a basic benchmark framework captures.

Companies and business activities are tools in such social status struggles. Business activity is aiming at the generation of profits, at least partly in order to permit social status-related activities. The inherent conflict between immediate profit and long-term ability to function and generate future profits has already been referred to. Focusing on profit, business decisions also mean that available capacities in a company are not necessarily fully employed, but rather may be partially laid idle in order to save costs. We can go a step further, still, recognizing that business considerations introduce a criterion into production processes that is removed from an immediate problem-solving. More appropriate solutions to social problems may in that case not be pursued if they will have a negative impact on profits, even if possibly only in a short-run consideration. Recall that we have moved to a perspective in which market mechanisms that automatically correct outcomes toward a socially more desirable direction have no place. Companies have influence over demand and over the way they structure supply, as well as resource utilization patterns. Time horizons between different interests may differ, future developments are not necessarily known, etc., and the price mechanism to send signals for correcting mis-developments can, at the very least, not be relied upon.

Beyond this first degree of separation between solutions to problems and the implementation of actual measures undertaken from a business perspective, further levels have increasingly come into play. Shareholders introduce additional interests that are further removed from the actual production process, and more oriented on the revenue stream it allows to tap into. Financial brokers push this to an even further diminishing interest in the actual activity that is taking place in production. Considerations are further and further removed from any actual, usually longer-term, activity that offers effective solutions to societal problems, and more and more oriented on financial indicators, which by their nature entail a short-term outlook, to evaluate suitable endeavors. An ability to arbitrarily include or exclude specific aspects of economic activity, such as environmental costs, social costs, or other negative effects of economic activities, in the economic sphere can be used to further increase monetary profits, but do reduce the serviceability of activities. Economic activities are by no means necessarily socially desirable or supportive of socially desirable outcomes in such an environment.

V

No matter how market structures are set up there is always an influence on the market participants. There is no neutral reference point and influence-free decision-making. Formal structures reflect decisions on cost- and risk-distribution. A liberalization of structures, as the withdrawal of more active regulation by public agents then may likely mean that the scope for private agents for exercising influence becomes more pronounced. A shift of negotiating strength to producers is a likely consequence, for the cost and risk distribution between producer and consumer, as well as the relation between producers as employers and their employees. This does not have to be bad, but should be acknowledged, in order to allow more informed choices about structures embedding economic activity.

Choices for policies and regulation are not typically reflecting a binary choice of either public or private agent setting the tone in interactions. They reflect a spectrum of relative influences by different interest groups involved, and concerning the distribution of potential benefits and costs from activities.

VI

We can also focus on rules and norms, as more narrowly defined institutions, from a starting point in the reference framework. In that case, economic problems are framed by the thought of an ideal equilibrium outcome. Market failures and a time dimension in interactions may be integrated into the analytical framework, however. Rules for structuring the economic sphere, and overcoming market failures, then serve to improve economic outcomes. Where time is concerned, a protection of agents against the impact of future decisions by transaction partners is seen as particularly important. Say, you make a payment now, and the goods agreed on are never delivered. Upgrades in production structures may lead to problems if your partners decide they would like to revisit the terms of contracts after you made investments that tie you more closely into their network. Contracts, their structure and enforcement, become relevant components of agents' relations.

How to approach problems that have been identified, here, is informed by a use of the economic laws identified in the reference view. For instance, imposing a tax on certain behaviors with a view on changing decisions to counter misallocations of resources can be a viable step where external effects have been identified. The changes in price structures signify an internalization of these external effects, as now social costs are reflected in private cost structures. All areas of economic activity can be drawn on for examples of developments that we may capture as external effects and that therefore may be gainfully addressed through the rules in place that structure this activity.

But even within companies, as planning structures that shape economic activity, these issues matter. Different companies have gone different routes for addressing potential problems they face, and the governance structures that have resulted are not the same in different companies. As networks of rules, they are stable and may work well for given companies. We cannot necessarily expect specific rules to be transplantable from one network to another and work in the same way there, however, as they are set up and function in connection with other such rules. Across borders and in different cultural contexts, potential hazards of simply copying someone else's approach are more pronounced, still.

Japanese companies, for instance, have given a lot of autonomy to the workers on their factory floors, allowing them to interrupt production processes as soon as they perceive something not going as it should. This usually allows to adjust whichever part of the production process may be affected rather quickly. In the United States, workers do not typically have such a degree of autonomy, and need to get supervisors and managers involved to address problems. The whole process is much more time-consuming. The level of trust between the different groups in the latter companies is not particularly pronounced, we may surmise, and rules to structure relations that draw on trust may not work particularly well.

2.10 Limitations of the Individual and Limitations from the Environment

I

For the larger environment humans move in, complexity reduction is typically achieved by heuristics and rules of thumb. Such rules of thumb may refer to systemic effects that are expected in particular situations, they may also refer to the adoption of behavior patterns, in which case copying agents who are successful in the given institutional framework provides a good first approach, though not the only one. So-called biases in behavior play a role as well that are the outcome of human evolution and direct attention to specific aspects of situations or problem structures that humans face. There are dozens and dozens of these biases listed. The term biases may have to be taken with a grain of salt, depending on the perspective adopted, as it may refer to deviations of behavior from the proper economically rational actions of the benchmark agent, thus accepting the validity of that framework. Human behavior that is conceptualized integrating human evolution and the state of the environment, and the further impact on that environment, then, may provide a more promising route for a fuller understanding of the goings on around us, at least for addressing some of the issues faced.

Regarding heuristics, the term bounded rationality refers to the effectiveness of short cuts for decisions, as heuristics that orient humans in decision-situations they may face while taking the limitations of human capacities into account. Given limited information and limited capacities for processing information, such approaches to decision-making can themselves be viewed as rational, again, the argument goes.

In areas in which decisions are more likely to be influenced by experience and institutions, as another set of guidelines and some kind of social heuristics, if you like, the same effects are observable. The additional layer that behavior patterns have emerged over time with a view on addressing social problem structures is being added here, though. People have learned these patterns, reflecting rules and norms providing social coherence to the group, and expand on them by experiencing and learning more. They are more prone to focus on regularly experienced issues. Transferring resulting social behavior patterns to new situations by analogy will work better at some times than at others. There is no reason to suspect that in a changed environment, heuristics and rules of thumb oriented on satisfying results in the past would be of particular use. Also, the objective behind behavior patterns has to be carefully assessed. For instance, men tend to show riskier behavior when women are around. Trying to attract attention and recognition would be the motive, most likely. Reproductive opportunities and success for men and women are not equally and evenly distributed, with a concurrent influence on behavior patterns in different situations. Without this aspect in mind, behavior may simply seem reckless and stupid, on the other hand; not that it may not be both at the same time, but it is so for a reason, if you like.

II

Heuristics are interesting for us as they influence economically motivated and economically relevant behavior in a number of ways that would not be considered economically rational under the perspective establishing the reference framework. The general idea is that, for human agents, optimality is not sought in decisions, at least not reasonably so. A result deemed satisfactory should usually be considered to be enough. Under limited information processing capacities, short cuts for coming to a decision without an attempt to take all potentially available information into account can be very sensible. Heuristics and rules of thumb describe such short cuts. Such decision-rules help to limit the amount of information actually taken into account in a decision, thus allowing a foundation that stands a better chance of being manageable by individual agents. Bounded rationality thus refers to a concept where a rational decision is taken based on purposely limited information. As an example, think of setting parameters for looking for a new apartment. You may limit the search to specific parts of town, limit the number of bedrooms or bathrooms, or search with an idea about an acceptable distance to specific features of cities (not more than a 15 minute drive from your kids' school, or your own, or at a certain distance from the railroad tracks, and not under the principal entry corridor for the local airport, etc.). That may mean that you miss the perfect place because it does not seem to confer to your parameters, but overall you can be reasonably sure that if something good, from your point of view, is available, that you will find it faster than without restrictions to your search. Similar scenarios may be thought of, for instance, when deciding among a number of models of a certain type of goods, as a physical product or a service, or when making decisions about your pension plans. Not uncommonly, we need to simplify a situation in order to be able to come to a decision at all.

Other kinds of heuristics can also be found. These do not refer to limiting the information utilized as the foundation for a decision, but go hand in hand with external impulses, and thus integrate the notion that humans learn from one another. Especially in a somewhat unfamiliar environment, for instance, limiting the amount of information for decisions may not suffice for coming to a satisfactory course of action.

More promising here are ways that permit to draw on others' experiences. Copying others who seem to move successfully in a territory we are unfamiliar with falls into this category. As this copies behavior that was good enough for others, it may promise to reach a satisfying outcome, at least with a higher likelihood than guessing into the blue might offer. Incidentally, however, this may be one way how behavior patterns that prove disadvantageous at the group level may gain a foothold. Copying others' behavior may also be expected to be one factor behind effects that prove destabilizing on the systemic level, as countervailing trends and impulses have a harder time to arrest self-reinforcing trends that may emerge. Similar results may be the outcome of transferring familiar behavior patterns to new environments where they may work, but not nearly as well as behaviors that are more attuned to the situation at hand. This can, for instance, also be an issue where technology transfers between different economies are concerned.

A satisfactory result is referred to as the aspiration level of agents. Solutions that are workable tend to be accepted. Once the related outcome has been realized, a revision of behaviors is no longer a priority. Whether improvements may be possible, how they might look like, or even only in which direction to start experimenting to find them, cannot necessarily be known. In fact, in a complex environment it is basically impossible, at the very least at the outset, to determine whether a result is just relatively good compared to close variations, or whether it is globally very good. Large areas of an environment are simply not accessible to the agents who would have to experiment with vast numbers of variations in order to determine the global quality of their approaches, individually and as a group, and under different environmental parameters. Given the limited capacities of agents, we are in any case in no position to constantly revise our behavior.

The aspiration level is, however, not static and no reflection of fixed internal valuations. Humans' aspirations are influenced by their environment. An aspiration level is hence a reflection of social relations and at least in part depends on observations among the peer-group of individuals, and therefore it can change over time. Human nature, and human sociality, means a potential for change is an ongoing factor in at least some spheres in societies that have taught themselves to seek satisfaction through consumption.

III

Aspects that have evolved over time steer agents' attention and guide valuations. In the application of these types of heuristics, human decision-making shows systematic biases relative to economically rational behavior, not just random deviations in the assessment of situations and decisions. These biases mean that we systemically make mistakes in our decisions, when assessed from perspectives focusing on economic rationality. While random deviations may be expected to even out over larger numbers and thus not influence the economic sphere noticeably, systematic biases may lead to effects in the economic sphere that would not result if agents were to act rationally.

Biases and heuristics, and the reasons for them, also may lead to openings for other agents to take influence and direct attention where it may appear desirable for their purposes. Successfully directing the attention of prospective customers can permit more targeted approaches to revenue increases for companies. As such influences are drawing on human behavior patterns, they cannot be avoided. That competition for profit would keep companies' ability to take advantage too pronouncedly in check, seems unlikely, as the more profitable route would appear to be to try to utilize these such aspects to their advantage.

A large number of effects that reflect the direction of human attention and jointly shape human behavior have been categorized over the last decades. The list is too extensive to be taken up in detail here, so we will limit ourselves to a few selected examples that may be particularly useful for illustrating problems that agents may face in their decision making in economic matters, and effects that may arise form others' influences shaping individuals' decisions thereby.

A first contact with a numerical value provides an anchor for later estimates. Price stability and a feeling of a proper price can have their foundation here, without needing to invoke a true value of a good.

The availability heuristic describes an effect that captures agents focusing more on things that are immediately available to them when making a decision. This way, for instance, certain moods or frames of mind can be stimulated by reminding people of specific aspects of their sociality. Decisions in the same situation vary with the mood that has been created, then.

Aspects that are not relevant to a decision situation, such as clearly inferior offers, can change the decision outcome. As irrelevant options, they should not matter. However, if these offer a clearly comparable alternative to one of the other options, agents are steered in the direction of the more attractive of the comparable offers. Being able to make a choice between an obviously better and worse option makes it easier to decide and, thus, allows to move us in a certain direction through the provision of an objectively irrelevant option. (Think of magazine offers were print only costs the same as the online and print access, and somewhat more than online only.)

Furthermore, human beings value things they actually own higher than they valued them before acquiring ownership. That value was an intrinsic characteristic of things material and immaterial is not borne out by human behavior.

A sensitivity of human beings to the way that factual information is presented, where choices systematically differ as a consequence of the presentation structure, is likewise interesting in our context here. Courses of action taken differ even when facing the same situation, depending on how the situation is presented and perceived.

We are not wired to intuitively grasp statistical concepts and numerical relations very well. Decisions result that are not even particularly good for the individuals, but may, for instance, be systematically overoptimistic, neglecting basic statistical properties of the decision situation, or an underestimation of risk. Additionally, a loss tends to evoke stronger emotions than an equal gain, something that is systematically underestimated when it comes to the evaluation of actually materializing effects.

In complex environments, that we selectively perceive and interpret, decision heuristics thus make immanent sense for agents. Evolved patterns, or biases, and learned social heuristics take part of this role. These steer attention in specific ways. They also allow an opening for directing activity and interests. What those aspects of human decision-making show, among others, is the importance of environmental conditions and context, be they natural, technological, social, or other, for specific decisions. There is no neutral reference point, in consequence, that we could rely on in analyses. Without knowledge about context, we will miss important aspects of motivations, and thus may misinterpret behavior and patterns we observe.

IV

A final issue to address for us here concerns the abstraction from the spatial structure of interactions. If the likelihood of interactions with different agents differs, interaction results for agents in neighborhoods can differ from the results that an average of the entire group would show. As a neighborhood, we understand groups of agents with relatively high interaction likelihoods. The term may also refer to networks of agents, therefore. Neighborhood in that case does not necessarily entail geographical proximity so much as it refers to agents with whom connections exist, and some relations are entered into. A modern production network that is spread over numerous countries may serve as an example for such a case.

Once such spatial and network structures are taken into account in analyses, results are found that are not within reach of analyses that abstract from the specificities of such structure in agents' environment. This is a reflection of the fact that every interaction pattern between individual agents, or even more generally, components of systems, is embedded in a structure that exists as a higher level of organization. Different behavior patterns may prove successful, then, depending on the neighborhood, for instance. The institutional framework referred to earlier is another example for such structure-giving higher level, as is a policy environment in a more concrete case.

Using network structures to capture economic realities draws on the relations between agents, which may, for instance, be conceptualized as information flows, or flows of goods and services, and incomes and payments. The connections between agents can then be analyzed to find structure and order among them, and then discover what specific structures and relations may mean for economic activities and outcomes. With connections, and ongoing rearrangements of connections, we have tools at hand to capture economic processes, and find out more about the impact of structures on these processes. An equilibrium state, and thus outcome-based viewpoint, cannot help to identify issues that come into view when processes and ongoing change are considered. Networks to trace relations that explicitly assume limited connections of, thus flows relating to, each agent can offer a foundation for process-based analyses, on the other hand. Different agents are differently important for the system at a given time. The rules that influence structures and stability matter, because of how they may impact developments and flows. As a side note, an approach that is focused on the flows of information, funds, and goods, among others, can no longer treat supply-side and demand-side separately in a meaningful way but will have to consider them as being connected.

2.11 Structure to Enable Economic Activity, and Top-Down Versus Bottom-Up Approaches to Formulating an Analytical Framework

I

In this chapter, we have focused on how the individual and her environment are integrated into analytical frameworks in economics. The organization of individual activities is the key issue for the economic performance of groups and societies. The interplay of different agents, as competing companies, collaborating companies, companies and suppliers, companies and customers, customers competing for status, but also researchers, and so on, requires for them to be able to interact in a structured and purposive manner. Individual abilities and environment jointly shape how individuals compete and can coordinate, and what they can achieve, for themselves and as groups. A participation in those structures is pretty much a necessity for people, given the organization of production and distribution of goods in place.

The picture that respectively emerges from the conceptions of individual and environment depends on the ability of individuals to grasp their environment and the options that are open for them for acting in it. These options, in turn, are partly determined by the environment itself. Only the interaction between environment and its characteristics and individuals and their abilities lets an analytical framework emerge that allows interpreting behavior and identifying potential problems of individual agents pursuing their economic undertakings. This observation mirrors the fact that in complex systems, some kind of structure is required for the interaction of the individual components of the system. Conceptions of how the structure of an economic environment comes about and comes to exert influence on individual action and ability shape the different perspectives we have seen concerning individuals as economic agents.

Depending on how we approach the decision-making environment for individuals and the ability and capacities we endow them with for making decisions, our view on the economic sphere changes, as do our interpretations of outcomes. The same behavior may take on a different significance in various interpretative frameworks. In consequence, problem perceptions may be different as may the answers given to specific questions. This is not only true for the analyses we offer but can also refer to the perception and subsequent behavior of the agents themselves. The perspective and the behavior shown according to an evaluation of a situation and related expectations can impact the way the situation develops, including the possibility of contributing to a situation so as to generate a self-fulfilling prophecy.

II

Individual interactions in a complex system cannot be expected to show discernible patterns or regularities over time without a structure to embed them. In complex systems, there is no stability and no scope for structured and planned behavior without a (self-)regulation of the system. For an ability of agents to act purposely and in a structured manner, the system itself needs structure. As an adaptive system, economies show such structure, emergent from the interactions of their component parts - individuals create order through their interactions. This structure limits the options for individual behavior, but also, and at the same time, enables individual behavior, by reducing the complexity of the situations the individual agents, as human actors or companies, for instance, face.

All approaches to economic analyses assume structures that enable individuals to maneuver in their environment. This ranges from approaches that rely on system characteristics as their main focus to those in which individuals employ various strategies for reducing uncertainty and exercising control that lead to the emergence of structures in social processes, with one area for coordinating activities being markets. Shape, scope, and results of coordination efforts can vary noticeably. Whether there is a structure that might permit the undistorted reflection of given values in market prices, including the existence of such values, is then an assumption to introduce into the analytical framework.

When the complexity of the economic system is more explicitly acknowledged, the emergence of such stabilizing structure plays a key role in related processes. As structures for human interactions emerge from their relations and learning over time, there is no reason to suspect them to be particularly good at solving each individual problem they address. They just need to continue to be good enough to possibly be maintained. Even where individual agents discern possibilities for improvements, they will have to foster changes in an existing stable structure that has come to be stabilized by adaptations of ideology and social mores to further its existence and the support of interests that have developed in reference to the narrative and structures of earlier times.

III

Interests within societies are not homogeneous, and the fact that setting up exchange arenas requires structure may mean that heterogeneity of interests finds a reflection in respective structures. The rules given for providing structure thus may always represent a compromise between different interests and interest groups. This does not only refer to short-term economic interests but may include such issues as reservations regarding the transition of activities from the social arena to the economic, for instance. Not everybody involved may put increased economic output above all other possible societal objectives, for instance.

It may also be seen as likely that continuous attempts to find ways around regulations would be sought, leading to an ongoing process of evasion and reformulation. A fixed set of rules will not be adequate, here.

Additionally, groups whose interests are affected by the structures in place at a given moment in time may not necessarily find a representation that permits to make sure that these are taken into account. Discrimination, for instance, based on race, religion, or sexuality, may persist even though it leads to potential competitive disadvantages and various other losses of potential. If nondiscriminating companies face social repercussions from their customers, who are after all the carriers of the discriminatory mind-set, then they may vanish from the economic sphere before any potential economic advantage they could enjoy because of more humane behavior may manifest. The people in companies may not be interested in any changes, when they are the same carriers of prejudice. Affected groups, on the other hand, are by definition of discrimination not infrequently barred from equal participation in the political arena, where formal rules are actually decided that may provide an inroad toward offering more support to them.

While private competition may very well still offer the least bad option for remedying societal concerns in a number of occasions, it cannot be expected to do so without a supportive embedding structure. Interactions reflect social structures and values and may easily strengthen and reinforce them. Countering narrower interests requires supportive economic, political, and social environments. As we will take up later, especially in Chapter 5, in more detail, there is no reason to assume that a misfunctioning political sector could be constrained and corrected by individual agents striving for profit. They may just as well – and maybe are rather likely to – abuse such a situation to further any advantage they have.

IV

It is entirely feasible that processes at the individual level and effects connected to the overall framework do not favor the same traits, behaviors, or structures. A biological example can refer to evolutionary pressure on the individual level favoring behavioral traits that reduce the successfulness of groups who find themselves in competition with each other. At the systemic level, then, evolutionary pressure for prosocial behavior can exist. When groups are facing competitive situations, there can be selection for the pro-social traits, as the level of competition favors those. A transition to economically relevant matters would entail a dilemma-type problem-structure in which individualistic behavior is curtailed by institutional provisions. How well those issues are addressed by groups, as a result of cultural evolution, then can become a key point for the successful sustenance of groups, depending on the competitive situation they find themselves in with regard to other groups, or even environmental pressure that groups face, which may result in the vanishing of groups composed of too individually minded members, for instance. This we will take up in more detail later as well.

V

In broad terms, we have characterized the previously mentioned perspectives on individuals and their economic environment as top-down or bottom-up. On the one hand, we have perspectives that assume certain characteristics of a (properly working) economic system, in which individuals try to realize the best economic outcome possible, constrained by the system and the regularities that are a part of the system and its functioning. For the developing narratives, the individuals are then endowed with whatever characteristics or abilities they need to have, in order to close a story. There is some flexibility as to what can be permissible while maintaining an equilibrium structure.

On the other hand, we have seen perspectives that are developed based on conceptions of humans and their interactions, asking what kind of system might emerge from these interactions. In this case, we see an endogenously moving and potentially changing system and try to understand how the individual actions and interactions within the system may shape its path and the outcomes individuals face. Probably not surprisingly, considerations regarding the economic sphere differ among these broadly based perspectives. While it is agreed that participation in the economic sphere is required in modern economies, how to structure that participation in support of an ongoing individual emancipation is assessed differently, in consequence.

When the system itself is assumed to come with a fixed structure, in terms of regularities or laws that are regular parts of the system, we need to figure out how to use the existing economic laws and regularities in support of the economic outcomes we desire. From assumptions about the shape of the system derive statements about the mechanics in the system. These are taken to have a general validity, being able to point to effects that they generally induce, therefore. We have to consider how to remove, overcome, or contain obstacles that prevent the system from working to its full potential. From assumptions about the system we also define how individuals can move within a system. Their behavior affirms the system that they cannot but accept. Some distortions to further one's own advantage may be possible, depending, however, within the structure that the system's general functioning establishes.

When we assume a bottom-up perspective, we consider how to stabilize the system along its path, trying to assess how to best reach mid-term and longer term objectives. The resulting views are ones of nonequilibrium processes, not a disequilibrium to be corrected. Over time objectives turn into the tools and foundation for reaching further objectives, acknowledging a path-dependent dynamic playing out over time. Opposed to the regularities in the functioning of the system that may be undermined within certain parameters to distort results for personal advantage, we find emerging social and political structures. The economic environment results from individual, cumulative, efforts, and actions. Depending on context, the impact of actions may change. A process results that is shaped from these actions, showing the emergence of social structures and institutions, from learning and reassessments by individuals, and communications and actions that may follow. There will still be regularities. These, however, are the reflection of man-made structures and depend on social values and technological conditions, and resulting habits and relations, not on ethereal systemic characteristics.

Starting out with the individual, there are no single directions of influences, but rather circular ones, from individual behavior that shapes the emerging system, and those structures then influencing individual behaviors that is oriented on the larger guidelines that the emergent structures provide. Behavior can affirm existing structures but can also lead to changes, in the detailed, as well as, cumulatively, the larger aspects of the economic sphere's shape and functioning. Adapted and changed behaviors happen in reaction to observations, reassessments, and learning. They are part of the system, as they are part of human nature. Therefore, we find a potential for systems that are constantly in motion, as behavior depends on circumstances; as uncertainty about the future makes attempts to secure or control the environment attractive; as, relatedly, strategic behavior focuses on expanding the own or limiting others' options; as economic objectives may not be all that matters, but may rather constitute only one of a number of means to other ends; as individual emphases and focuses change; as the perspectives rest on human agents who are curious and can learn; and so on. All of these aspects are regular parts of a normally functioning economic sphere and process, not the reflection of attempts to undermine a solid system; even though they may be directed toward undermining, or strengthening, depending, current structures, of course.

Still, basing the analyses on an understanding of the human behavior involved, allows to gain an idea of general trends and developments. Recurrent phenomena can be identified, and systematized. General motivations and the direction of actions can be described and understood, and an understanding of the potential dynamics within the system may be formed. Where such dynamics are not constrained from the outset by the system itself, by assumption, change becomes a part of the system we see emerge for analytical purposes. An understanding for potentially damaging dynamics becomes a possibility, thereby.

VI

Some cautions and observations are shared by all approaches, typically relating to the use and potential for an abuse of power. Cautioned against at the outset, this is then not something that any one perspective can claim as an explanatory success under its belt. What can be offered regarding their detection, containment, or prevention depends on the focus pursued, from short-term and static to longer term and with a view on the processes and functioning in and of the system, from a top-down definition of the system or its bottom-up emergence. So, that areas of concern are shared, is one thing. We may take that as an indicator that certain problem areas are more easily discernible.

In sum, we get not only different types of models but different views on economies under different perspectives on individuals and markets. Additional aspects in analytical frameworks, and particularly the top-down and bottom-up distinctions, do not only make results more complicated to derive or interpret, analyses more tricky, that is, while arriving at principally the same conclusions as simpler analytical structures. On the contrary, the view on the economic sphere changes when more complex analytical structures are employed. A single solution mechanism for problems of coordination or the determination among trade-offs, such as prices, is no longer adequate when the system itself does not force individual ambition onto a path serving the public interest. A single control mechanism, such as competition, is no longer adequate for containing abuses of power, even though, properly conceived and embedded, it will be a major component of structures set up to that end. A broader set of coordinating tools will be required for improving the economic and technological foundation and performance of groups and for making the economic sphere serviceable to the society it emerges from.

References

For the full list of references, see the bibliography at the end of the text.

Adelman, Irma, Cynthia Taft Morris (1988) Comparative Patterns of Economic Development 1850–1914. The Johns Hopkins Press, Baltimore.

The authors examine development processes to find underlying causes for the diverging experiences of different economies.

Akerlof, George A., and Robert Shiller (2015) Phishing for Phools: The Economics of Manipulation and Deception. Princeton University Press, Princeton et al.

The authors explore the consequences of the insight that market interactions do not necessarily lead to improvements for everyone involved in transactions, because our decision-making allows consumers to be deceived and manipulated by producers and sellers of goods.

Ariely, Dan (2008) Predictably Irrational: The Hidden Forces that Shape our Decisions. Harper Collins, Scranton.

The author shows that irrational behavior of humans shows discernible patterns that can be utilized by others to sway our decisions, and that should be taken into account when formulating policies.

Arrow, Kenneth (1974) The Limits of Organization. W. W. Norton & Co, New York and London.

The author addresses different ways to organize economic activity, including markets, governments, the internal planning of firms, and communal approaches.

Arthur, W Brian (2014) Complexity and the Economy. Oxford University Press, Oxford et al.

This book offers a collection of papers by one of the first economists to explore in a formalized manner the implications that an approach to economies as complex systems have.

Beinhocker, Eric (2006) The Origins of Wealth: Evolution, Complexity, and the Radical Remaking of Economics. Harvard Business School Press, Boston.

The author integrates a large number of concepts and approaches to evolutionary and complexity economics to provide the foundation for rethinking what we thought we knew about economics.

Bell, Daniel (1976) The Cultural Contradictions of Capitalism. Basic Books, Inc., New York

The author argues that in capitalist societies, the cultural developments that have gone hand in hand with it will eventually lead the system to break down.

Bowles, Samuel (2006) Microeconomics: Behavior, Institutions, and Evolution. Princeton University Press, Princeton et al.

The author analyzes how the interplay of individual preferences and economic environment shape the economic sphere and its ongoing change.

Dobb, Maurice (1973) Theories of Value and Distribution since Adam Smith. Cambridge University Press, London.

The author presents a history of economic thought, stressing the importance of ideology for its development.

Elsner, Wolfram, Torsten Heinrich, and Henning Schwardt (2014) Microeconomics of Complex Economies – Evolutionary, Institutional, Neoclassical, and Complexity Perspectives. Elsevier /Academic Press, Oxford et al.

The authors present a number of different perspectives on microeconomic issues.

Friedman, Milton (1962) Capitalism and Freedom. University of Chicago Press, Chicago.

The author argues that uninterfered economic activity is a necessary building block for political freedom.

Galbraith, John K (1958) The Affluent Society. Houghton Mifflin Co., Boston.

The authors argue that in rich modern societies, the notion of scarcity is no longer the principle problem of economic activity to address, and analyze the consequences that abundance has for economic activity.

Galbraith, John K (1967) The New Industrial State. Houghton Mifflin Co., Boston.

The author analyzes the influence of large corporations in the economic sphere, and in society more in general.

Gintis, Herbert (2009) The Bounds of Reason: Game Theory and the Unification of the Social Sciences. Princeton University Press, Princeton et al.

The author discusses how game theory has to be integrated with broader aspects of social theory to provide a meaningful tool for analyses.

Hayek, Friedrich von (1944) The Road to Serfdom. Routledge Press, London

The author presents his views on the political dangers of public sector planning in the economic sphere.

Hazlitt, Henry (1946) Economics in One Lesson: The Shortest and Surest Way to Understand Basic Economics. Harper Brothers, New York.

The author argues that, no matter how well-intended, economic policies that try to improve a situation for a selected group in economies will eventually make the situation worse for everyone.

Hodgson, Geoffrey (2015) Conceptualizing Capitalism: Institutions, Evolution, Future. The University of Chicago Press, Chicago.

The author analyzes the importance of the legal framework for the development of capitalist economic structures.

Hodgson, Geoffrey (2012) From Pleasure Machines to Moral Communities: An Evolutionary Economics Without Homo Economicus. The University of Chicago Press, Chicago.

The author analyzes how a nuanced understanding of human beings as self-interested and moral individuals enhances our capacity to analyze pressing issues in economic environments and economic policies.

Kahneman, Daniel (2011) Thinking, Fast and Slow. Farrar, Strauss, and Giroux, New York.

The author discusses how our minds actually work, and the impact this has on our decision-making.

Kahneman, Daniel, Paul Slovic and Amos Tversky (eds.) (1982) Judgment under Uncertainty: Heuristics and Biases. Cambridge University Press, Cambridge et al.

The authors present a collection of papers that examine biases in people's behavior, and the heuristics in decision-making that lead to them.

Kapp, Karl W. (2011) The Foundations of Institutional Economics (eds. Sebastian Berger and Rolf Steppacher). Routledge, London and New York.

The author analyzes the role of institutions in economic systems.

Keen, Steve (2001) Debunking Economics, The Naked Emperor of the Social Sciences. Zed Books, London.

The author presents a detailed discussion of short-comings and flaws of standard economic theory.

Marshall, Alfred (1890) Principles of Economics. Macmillan and Co., London

The author presents, systematizes, and expands the state of economic analyses at the time.

Ormerod, Paul (2005) Why Most Things Fail – Evolution, Extinction, and Economics. Pantheon Books, New York.

The author analyzes why failure is common in complex systems, and what economics and economic policy can learn from this fact.

Potts, Jason (2000) The New Evolutionary Microeconomics – Complexity, Competence and Adaptive Behavior. Edward Elgar, Cheltenham.

The author develops an approach to microeconomic analyses that draws on various economic schools of thought and combines them with the analytical tools of complexity science.

Schelling, Thomas C (1978) Micromotives and Macrobehavior. W. W. Norton and Co., New York.

The author shows how decisions by individuals can have large cumulative effects that were unintended by any one of them.

Schmookler, Andrew B (1993) The Illusion of Choice: How the Market Economy Shapes our Destiny. State University of New York Press, Albany.

The author illustrates how a market-based approach to relations cannot provide good solutions in a number of areas of life, and how it affects our behavior where relations are organized using markets.

Scitovsky, Tibor (1976) The Joyless Economy – The Psychology of Human Satisfaction. Oxford University Press, Oxford et al.

The author applies current psychological knowledge to analyses of consumer behavior.

Sen, Amartya (1970) Collective Choice and Social Welfare. Holden-Day, San Francisco.

The author studies group decision-making and what conflicts may arise, drawing on economic theory and a number of disciplines beyond that where required.

Simon, Herbert A (1957) Models of Man – Social and Rational. Wiley and Sons, New York

The collection of essays presents analyses of the rational and nonrational aspects of human decision-making and behavior.

Sweezy, Paul M (1942) The Theory of Capitalist Development – Principles of Marxian Political Economy. Oxford University Press, Oxford et al.

The author examines Marxist theory, and analyzes how far it can help to understanding the dynamics of capitalist systems.

Veblen, Thorstein B (1899) The Theory of the Leisure Class: An Economic Study of Institutions. Macmillan, London and New York.

The author analyzes the impact of social and economic structures on individual behavior, and resulting dynamics of change in socioeconomic environments.

Veblen, Thorstein B (1904) The Theory of Business Enterprise. Charles Scribner's Sons, New York.

The author analyzes the role of companies in modern economies.

3

The Function and the Functioning of Markets

Different approaches to complexity reduction result in different views on the individual and the environment in which she moves. Characteristics of this environment, in turn, influence what individuals can achieve, and how. Of particular interest within the economic environment are markets as the arenas for exchanges that are most prominently connected to economic activity. Markets take a preeminent position in economies and economics, and are, in fact, the arenas for what is usually considered first when thinking about economic activities. Even though planning is at least as important in modern economies, the reference is always a market environment – does a company plan instead of using the market, does it control, bypass, or supersede the market, is more likely to come to mind as a question, than do they use the market instead of planning (their nature as planning structures themselves notwithstanding). The options for strategic action we have referred to above in Chapters 1 and 2 are likewise introduced with a view on limiting the exposure to market volatility, making the market exchange the starting point, and a reaction to the effects that these exchanges can produce the consequence.

Different views on specific markets and market-based activities result depending on the emphasis in and the scope of complexity reduction

H. Schwardt, *The Path to a Modern Economics*,
DOI 10.1007/978-3-319-52785-7_3

pursued with regard to individual market participants as well as the market arenas themselves. In the top-down perspectives, all markets are assumed to function in the same way, in the sense that there are specific regularities in the system that apply to all of them. The information that prices hold bring about certain behavior patterns which can be identified in every market. In the bottom-up perspectives, we can indeed identify characteristics of specific markets that differ from others, as market functioning emerges from the behavior of individual agents, which can differ for goods with different characteristics. In turn, the views on the role that markets can play in societies diverge, to larger or lesser degree, as do the roles assigned to them in the tool-set of policy relevant measures. In this chapter, we will consider different perspectives on markets in general, as well as specific markets that are of particular interest, including labor market and financial sector.

3.1 Markets and Individual Agents and Societies

I

Businesses and individuals enter markets with objectives in mind. Businesses seek profits. These are required for a continuation of their activity, at the same time that these businesses are sources of profit for different agents with a claim to the revenue stream business activity generates. While profit as a driving force behind business decisions is generally recognized, integrating the notion of profits into an analytical framework is less straightforward than would appear at first glance, among others because of potentially conflicting behaviors from the different interests involved in a business. On the other market side, individuals enter market exchanges as these are their path to accessing the necessities and amenities of life in modern economies. The potential for revenue and profits that comes from the potential demand of individuals should motivate producers to offer goods that people want to buy.

Producers, even if we view businesses as individual agents at times, are not homogeneous entities. Owners, shareholders, managers, and financial market actors, but also workers have an interest in revenue and profits.

A short-term perspective on profits focuses on their generation, and a longer run perspective focuses on attempts to permit their sustained generation, usually subject to acceptable short-term results. Such different time horizons can lead to different emphases in decisions regarding business strategies. In fact, with the increased willingness of companies to use financial markets and to interpret changes in share prices as a signal for a company's potential, financial market actors have come to take a more influential role in shaping patterns and strategies in the economic sphere, directly or indirectly, in a development that has been particularly noticeable over the last couple of decades.

As businesses account in monetary terms, monetary costs and profits may be shaped by shifting parts of business operations to their environment. This can involve the natural environment, for unaccounted waste disposal or pollution, for instance, but also wider social infrastructures, such as through publicly provided education and training. A socialization of costs can also be reflected in the specific relation, designed to be shorter or longer term, for instance, with employees. Rules that permit to shift costs to the social and natural environments are in the interest of individual businesses, but not their larger environment.

While broadly speaking still capturing the function of economic activity by producers, profit generation as a generic term for business objectives may then at least be falling short of capturing motivations and actions that do have an impact on the economic sphere. An increase in short-term profits is not necessarily commensurable with long-term profits, or the long-term continuation of a business, for that matter. It may as easily undermine the longer term potential of a business. Thus, what purpose profits serve may matter.

For individuals, market activity offers access to goods that play a part in different facets of life, from current livelihood to future income generation, or insurance against adverse future developments and risks. A shift of activity from the areas of custom and command to the market sphere means that individuals may have a higher degree of freedom when deciding whether they want to participate in a specific market, or not. An avoidance of the market sphere, however, is practically impossible for members of modern societies. As one consequence, that means that for the labor market, the function is very different from all others, as it is the participation in labor markets that enables the participation in modern societies by granting access to money for most people. As subsistence activity has largely vanished in modern economies with their very complicated division of labor, a participation in the economic sphere is basically a must for individual members of societies. The labor market therefore plays a unique role in the organization of modern life. A one-size-fits-all approach to markets may still be able to capture the fundamental characteristics of labor markets as well, but at the very least, the fact that a participation in the labor market is required for individuals to make a living brings it to a special place in public perception. The fact that a withdrawal from the labor market is practically impossible, for the most part, may, however, mean that labor markets differ from other markets, as the possibility for sending signals by abstaining from participation does not exist, here, for starters. For financial markets, it is their orientation on future outcomes that we cannot know completely, that may make them different from other markets.

II

On the social level, the function of markets involves a number of issues that may well be incompatible to some degree. There will be trade-offs to consider, between different objectives stated for the entire society in question, and between different groups within that society, currently or over time. How related decisions are to be made is assessed differently under different perspectives.

Markets and market activities are to serve to improve the way that resources are allocated according to societies' demands. They are supposed to enhance effectiveness in production processes by producers competing for the profit potential that servicing specific demand segments makes accessible. They are supposed to foster technological change as a reaction to competition for and in specific markets and market segments, and following the detection of something that is believed to be marketable, thereby creating new markets. Finally, the information that market activity generates serves to orient the participants in a market. Relying on one of the hallmarks of modern societies, competition between individuals, transactions in markets are to foster individual energy and ingenuity to drive improvements in all these areas. Whether we may assume such changes, and outcomes of market activities in general, to be generally desirable and positive, or not necessarily so, is contested. The role consumption spending plays in modern societies may mean that we continuously chase after consumption options, to the detriment of developing other areas of life.

In other examples, profit-based incentives themselves may also undermine the social functionality of market arenas. Unless market competition suffices to force companies into behavior that is the best possible from a neutral societal perspective, there is the option that companies objectives and social objectives diverge, without an immediate negative impact on said companies. For instance, a pharmaceutical company's research funds are not very likely to go to learning more about prevention, as their continuation as a company relies on being able to sell a cure to a disease, or, even better, on making it chronic. A media company sells eyeballs to its advertising customers. What the public might desire from a media outlet, or gets used to, and what a public service would require, may not coincide. The reporting on the 2016 US primary campaigns may serve as an example. Now, that there exists theoretical room for improvement does not mean that this can be put into practice. This will be taken up in more detail in Chapter 5.

As a final point, without that necessarily being a function of markets at the societal level, or at least having been perceived as such at the outset, the increased utilization of markets has enabled the increase in prosperity we have witnessed in some societies over the last couple of centuries. Division of labor and specialization have provided the foundation for enhanced productivity, themselves being based on the technological changes that have allowed standardization and mass production. This, in turn, has allowed to continuously extend the organization of the social provisioning process through the economic sphere. Reach, influence, and impact of a market mindset, with a concurrent impact on the valuation of things, have thus continued to expand over the last decades, slowly starting a couple centuries ago, really.

III

Given the key role of markets in modern economies, their functioning has been one of the principal objects of economic analyses from the start. How the structures for stabilizing market environments are interpreted specifically and filled with content and meaning in detail depends on the perspective taken in the formulation of the theoretical framework drawn on. How markets can be utilized in support of more concrete objectives, and how they have to be structured to avoid them undermining societies' objectives is contested, then, between the different perspectives that approaches to complexity reduction open up. The focus in this chapter will lie more on the functioning of markets and the role they may therefore be able to play supporting societal objectives. Policies to support markets to function advantageously for societies will be discussed in more detail in Chapter 5.

We can distinguish two top-down perspectives, actually, that assume that market transactions lead to outcomes that cannot be improved if functioning normally and properly. The burden to be borne by the market environment focuses on structuring a static resource allocation in the one case, and the signaling of profitable opportunities to introduce novelties, and undermining existing positions of influence, in the other. In either scenario, if they choose to ignore the information emerging from the market environment, agents will be forced to abandon their activities, as there is no freedom to pursue them against societies' collective wishes reflected in prices. Furthermore, as long as market forces are permitted to work, behavior that might damage profits is expected to vanish because it is assumed to lead to a disadvantage in the market sphere, by narrowing the spread between revenue and costs below its best possible value.

Even though they approach the economic sphere and its problems very differently, the two perspectives both assume a view on markets as social technologies that prohibit the exercise of individual power if they work the way they are supposed to and do not face interferences from the private or public sector, usually in conjunction with one another. Where characteristics of goods or production technologies may lead to market failures, while the underlying functioning of the market is not affected, outcomes may be suboptimal. Whether private competition or public regulation is the preferable way for dealing with resulting issues depends on the stance of the researcher in question, such as the assessment of potential distortions that measures introduce relative to the situation that is supposed to be improved. Coming down on the side of private competition as the long-run better option to pursue is not an uncommon stance.

Presenting analyses and their results, the reference or ideal-type market is typically termed a free market. How specifically such a market looks like is unclear though. Exchanges are understood to have to rely on functioning legal frameworks and other social structures. Ownership rights have to be granted. Free therefore cannot mean without a structure constituting a market but has to refer to the result, namely, the best possible reflection of the values of goods in market prices. Analyses focus on finding distortions relative to these outcomes. Where such distortions lie and how much of an impact they have is by no means uncontested even among economists following the same general route in their analyses, however. There are some degrees of freedom in translation of analytical perspectives into applications and policy suggestions. In fact, how to translate findings of assumed distortions into measures to overcome them cannot be answered in detail from within these analytical frameworks. Additional assumptions and political preferences come into play at that point.

Note that the view of the economic sphere itself is rather different for the two views focusing on markets as most suitable problem-solving devices. Where the properly functioning market will be in an equilibrium state that does not permit economic profits to be realized in the one view, focusing on static resource allocation, profits are part and parcel of an ever-changing economic sphere in the other view, and necessary signals for agents for identifying promising pursuits. Agents striving for profit are what drives changes in societies, and given the assumptions, the constant improvements these changes embody and that characterize a capitalist economic system. The static system is set up to derive regularities and laws for the economic sphere, and the changing system is set up to try and understand development dynamics in capitalist societies. In the changing world, the economic laws of the static world cannot be derived, as the reference point provided by the presumed equilibrium state cannot be defined. Even though thus incompatible because of their foundations, in the public discourse, arguments are frequently freely drawn from both perspectives when support for a specific notion is sought that relies on human ingenuity and markets as the best social technology for guiding individuals through their complex environments.

Under the bottom-up formulations, neither individuals nor markets are necessarily endowed with the abilities or characteristics to automatically produce desirable outcomes if behaving or functioning normally. Markets are one of a number of coordination devices for agents. In that case, one in which economic valuations are the yardstick for assessing exchanges. Market activity serves individual interests, and to which degree and in which direction that interest can be pursued depends on the rules and norms in place. Rules and norms are always required for allowing market exchanges to be undertaken. To some degree these rules and norms can be set up to align individual interests and societal interests, but that is by no means always the case.

Agents' capacities and markets' aggregating capabilities point more explicitly to the importance of the embedding of market activity. How to structure interaction arenas matters; not that it wouldn't in the top-down frameworks, but there is rather little that can be said about such embeddedness from within those analytical perspectives.

An environment without a supporting structure of rules and norms to restrict individual actions is generally seen as more likely to result in positions in which power can be exercised and abused, than the other way around. Relations of influence and power are a part of the market concept, as the market is a social construct like any other arena for human relations, and there are no natural mechanisms that would dilute them or render them inconsequential. The functioning that is assigned to markets based on economic laws of supply and demand or as an automatic property emerging from large groups of agents interacting in markets is not taken for granted, nor given by assumption. Socially particularly desirable outcomes are by no means to be expected from market outcomes.

Against this background, then, the participation in markets as motivated by economic considerations is not necessarily separated from the rest of social activities. It is entirely possible that economically motivated actions may lead to results that are undesirable from economic perspectives, or other possible ones, be they socially, environmentally, politically, or culturally inclined, among others, in markets that are working normally. These issues play a role in the evaluation of the suitability of markets as social-solution devices, though. Focusing on only some effects of a cause can distort the picture that emerges rather noticeably. Again, also note that markets as tools for valuation and coordination rely very specifically on money as a signal for the desirability of a measure or a product, not the numbers of individual agents, for instance, as a political process does. None of this is to say that economists using top-down perspectives as their analytical framework would not be sensitive to the issues just mentioned. However, the reliance on a market reference framework, and the assumptions about the proper functioning of an economic sphere that such framework rests on, result in a very specific approach that the bottom-up analytical structures cannot righty replicate.

IV

Markets are always constituted by a set of rules and norms, and typically by informal conventions and understandings that follow from local or regional customs as well. They are not natural states or neutral reference points that exist naturally and that are tempered with at one's own peril. Even the perfect market setup for the reference point is a set of rules, norms, and laws, if only implicitly acknowledged at times. What is assumed there is that one combination of factors giving structure to an exchange arena exists that leads to a particular set of, desired, results, namely, the reflection of the value of goods in the prices at which these goods are exchanged in an environment where no individual agent has an influence on the outcome. How such a combination of rules looks, cannot be derived based on the considerations informing top-down analyses, however.

Rules are in place to define obligations of all parties to transactions and thus offer a degree of stability and security for market participants. They try to allocate costs and responsibilities, liabilities, and obligations. There is more than one possible combination of all of these for any one exchange arena. Changes in rules and norms lead to changes in the distribution of costs and risks associated with economic activities. They do not automatically lead to the cessation of activities. Market activities can continue under a range of different cost and benefit distributions. Which one is the best one, cannot properly be determined, as there is no neutral reference point that is given by a natural outcome against which the impact of rules and norms could be evaluated. And even efficient outcomes will show very different distribution patterns, depending on property right allocations, for instance.

How one specific structure would represent a superior one to any other conceivable combination of rules and norms under such different possible emphases remains unclear. Trade-offs between different interests will be far more likely, in fact, and not necessarily resolved satisfactorily, much less optimally, by prices alone, as we will see momentarily. Put differently, how to constitute markets and support their functioning for achieving societal objectives is a critical question in which the balancing of the different interests involved is a major factor to consider. How related questions are answered depends on believes about economic issues and the focus adopted in the question, as well as in the framework set up to answer it. A first step towards providing a more general answer relies on an understanding of the exchange arena in question.

3.2 Different Markets and Allocation, Effectiveness, and Change

I

The assessment of market outcomes against the background of the assumption of an existing perfect market solution that can be found, even if only constructed as a counterfactual, for every market, defines the first scenario to consider here. The resulting reference point is drawn on for assessing and addressing market outcomes and perceived problems. The focus here is a socially desirable resource allocation without preference or influence of any of the involved groups or agents. Distortions are reflected in resource allocations that favor selected groups or individuals. They are signaled by economic profits being realized. The assumption driving research and policy recommendations under this perspective is that the basic considerations forming this perspective can be applied to every situation of interest in economic analyses.

Undisturbed market exchanges are the ideal when approaching economic realities that are found wanting. Even if they cannot be directly applied to the situation under investigation, they nevertheless provide the reference point for orientation when setting up regulations or other measures for improving outcomes. What the substance of the exchanges constituting market activity is is irrelevant in this view. The markets for basic primary goods, consumption goods, investment goods, labor, financial products, or others, all follow the same patterns and can be analyzed based on the same construction of the reference point for assessing their results and addressing their problems. Economic activity can only gain from being undertaken with a market mindset guiding individual decisions. For the wider set of implications, it has to be assumed here that scarcity trumps all other potential issues.

Analytically, the market model is set up to allow extensions in every direction, under the assumption that single effects emerging from influences on economic activities can be analyzed in isolation from each other. Market results converge to an equilibrium again after a disturbance, allowing to identify properties of the new equilibrium in comparison to the prior one. This in turn is supposed to allow the identification of the direction into which such disturbances can be expected to move economic results in a general manner.

Taking this reference point as valid, a number of routes open up for analyses (see Section 2.3 as well). First, in situations in which agents can wield an influence in the economic sphere distortions they cause can be quantified with the reference point in mind. Second, in situations in which agents' actions have an impact on others that does not clearly assign costs or benefits to them, distortions arise that result in an allocation of resources that is suboptimal. Taking influence on the price-quantity space, through taxes or subsidies, for instance, may remedy this situation. A clearer allocation of property rights may prove advantageous as well, for trying to assign prices to activities and drawing previously excluded areas into the realm of transactions, among other things to avoid a socialization of costs. In other words, incentives are to be formulated to induce behavior 'as if' individuals were in fact interacting in a perfect market arena. Third, in situations in which agents do not have access to information in equal ways, so that not everyone interested and involved in a transaction stands on the same foundation, agents with an advantage in access to relevant information can bend results in their favor. As long as their transaction partners agree to participate in market exchanges and not let the market collapse entirely, that is. If information problems stand to have a noticeable impact on transactions and exchanges, how to set up contracts addressing potentially arising issues becomes a critical aspect to consider.

The objective in any case is to set up structures that lead to an approximation of the free-market reference result, taking every aspect of interactions properly into account, either by influencing the prices individuals face, or by setting rules in place that lead them to behave as if they were moving in a free-market setting. The identification of issues that may prevent the reaching of the perfect market solution in a given situation is a critical focus here.

II

To describe market functioning in this setting, it is assumed that demand falls when prices rise, and that potential supply increases with rising prices, in all relevant markets, and at least in the relevant range of possible outcomes. Some exceptions are acknowledged, but discarded as fringe areas of minor or minuscule importance. Price signal go to consumers or producers to adjust their demand or output levels in response to disequilibrium prices. These signals can be identified in all markets. They derive from the utility, and hence the value, of the object of acquisition. This can change over time, but at any given moment provides an anchor for the equilibrium framework to function. In the aggregation of individuals' wishes, the assumption is introduced that supply and demand intersect at exactly one point, the equilibrium price-quantity constellation. Every divergence from this equilibrium is assumed to trigger a process bringing the agents in the market back to the equilibrium constellation. Overhangs in demand are perceived by producers as possibilities for price increases, which are implemented until the surplus demand has vanished as people reduce the amount they desire to purchase in response to the price increase (analogous for the other sensible imbalances in this view). If producers overcharge, others can undercut them as long as a profit potential remains. In equilibrium, no undue profits are realized. Prices send signals regarding either the equilibrium constellation attained, or divergences from that equilibrium as supply and demand adjust. These laws of supply and demand are a crucial aspect to the analyses here, as they provide the general laws of motion in markets even if faced with distortions – negative feedback between prices and quantities leads market outcomes to their equilibrium state.

The overall analytical system set in place thus provides the frame for thinking about economic activities. 'The market' will make it right, if sometimes with a little nudge for the people in it by tweaking the framework that structures a specific market. People are producing optimal outcomes by virtue of the laws of supply and demand in a competitive system that keeps them from exercising undue influence, and by virtue of their informed self-interest that prevents them from entering exchanges they will find disadvantageous to themselves. All of these influences, and all actions, are shaped or constrained, depending, by the single equilibrium in the part of the economic system under consideration.

However, the laws of supply and demand have so far only been formulated in the un-complex reference framework. The assumption that they will be equally valid in more complex settings is not a priori justified simply because we can find some settings in which they appear to hold at times. That the price-quantity relations in demand and supply hold as a rule of thumb in a number of markets we are familiar with does not constitute proof for their general validity; much less does such an observation amount to support for the general validity of an equilibrium notion as the foundation for our market-understanding. Different markets may be viewed differently in more complex settings. In any case, we can note that complexity reduction has to be taken to an extreme in order to be able to formulate the general laws of supply and demand for markets.

Math has helped a lot for understanding just how much of a reduction of complexity is necessary, in ways that verbal arguments cannot travel (also see Chapter 2). If agents are not identical, already the perfectly calculating individuals of the reference model can produce systemic effects that are outside the scope of forecasts, as then the resultant complexity of their interaction system bears down on them. In complex systems, the interplay of individuals can father effects that no one foresaw nor intended. Particularly good outcomes are no longer guaranteed. Additional tools are required here for stabilizing such systems to the degree that individuals can pursue objectives in meaningful and intentional ways.

III

When we approach the individual agents without market mechanics to automatically offer a corrective constraint, aspects start playing a role that are excluded as inconsequential in the reference point formulation, and seen as obstacles easily overcome by extending the reach of markets or the proper layout of the rules structuring exchanges in markets. Limitations of agents are reflected in their strategies for behavior. Supporting these behaviors, we saw heuristics, customs, habits, rules of thumb, and habitual expectations, as well as social rules, among others, moving to a more prominent position for understanding market activities, and economic activities more in general, supporting interactions and providing stability. From these behavior patterns, specific market environments emerge. The influence of institutions is manifest in anchoring perceptions, concerning prices and relative prices, for instance, but also delimiting the sphere of the desirable as well as the acceptable and thereby shaping behaviors in social environments. Tools that may spell unwarranted interventions in the case of the perfect market reference model may become not only acceptable but effectively very useful, and in some cases even needed, for stability and continued activity in more complex settings. When the market environment itself cannot automatically correct potential mistakes, the interpretation of market interactions offers information to the agents.

More complicated patterns in markets and market functioning arise as systemic effects are not excluded by assumption here. How these may manifest will depend on the form of markets, and the goods traded, so we will have to hold off on those until focusing on individual markets more specifically.

Uncertainty plays a part for a number of alternative perspectives on economic issues. Uncertainty has an impact on strategies aiming at planning and control, but is also reflecting on the interpretation of signals from economic activities, whether they come from individual actions or from aggregate indicators, like prices. Prices provide information beyond allocation, comparability, or sustainability of operations. They are carrying signals not only for the agents, by drawing attention to what others may be doing, but from the agents, in communication with their social environments. The interpretation of these signals, not as proper value, or derivation therefrom, but as shaped in a continuous process can be an influential guide to behavioral decisions. Such signals can arise in different areas of relevance for individuals and may refer to status considerations but may also confer information about other agents' expectations. Where the focus lies depends partly on what agents seek from a specific good – what is actually acquired by purchasing a good and how that relates to signals sent through market activities and prices (such as immediate consumption potential, status signals, or the generation of future cash-flows, among others). Negative feedback is not necessarily always given. Positive feedback can at times be part of the usual functioning of markets.

The characteristics of the acquisitions themselves may be leading to different exchange arenas, then, in terms of their functioning. When the focus lies on market prices as the principal carriers of information, price changes may trigger different kinds of reactions, depending on the signal sought in a price or the motivation for a specific acquisition. The sum of these reactions, in turn, may trigger different effects on the aggregate level of the market under consideration, exacerbating the initial impulse or mellowing it. Which effects result may well depend on the general context embedding a specific market at a given point in time, and thereby be subject to moods, as well as fads or fashion, or the technological environment, and thus also change over time.

We may observe such trends, for instance, if prices are taken to include signals about agents and their expectations, so that changes in prices may be seen to hold information about agents' assessments of future possibilities. One very important consequence for some goods is that in this case, rising prices may lead to an increase in demand. For example, investment goods are required for production, and rising prices for them may be taken to mean optimistic assessments for resulting goods and hence draw more demand for them (see below). Financial market products granting rights to future streams of income may see increases in demand following price rises for the same reason. Eventually, price rises may be taken to indicate future price rises to come, and draw even further activity. There is no fundamentally correct price, here, but a steadily changing signal reflecting market activity and expectations. Such an example signifies a fundamental and systematic divergence from the supply and demand setting laid out in the reference framework. The supposed market laws bringing individual self-interest and group-interest to be produced through the same individualistic actions do not exist here. Even if we were to maintain the slopes of supply and demand schedules, they would be constantly shifting in response to changes in expectations. Their shapes would not be able to offer any explanatory potential, as that would have to center on the relation between expectations, their changes, and their impacts on market outcomes.

3.3 Different Products and Different Markets

I

The characteristics of some goods are immediately observable so that people interested in a purchase can usually form an accurate assessment of their quality and state, especially when they can be used or consumed in a short time span. They are comparable and their characteristics have been experienced over time and can be assessed. Transactions involving their purchase are taken on the spot, money for product, and habitually entered into and executed without further steps accompanying the transaction. Agents have learned about the goods and have a reasonable understanding for assessing their quality, we may presume. In this context we need to distinguish two kinds of experiences with goods. The first is the one just referred to as even when things are observable and in the open, the assessment of what is seen will be easier once some ideas have been formed, in direct contact or with similar products. For routine goods the experience is in the recognition of potential problems with the purchase. There are also goods that are called experience goods, in which the term refers to learning about the good in question through its utilization, building knowledge about a specific good over time. Already the longer term use that they are designed for suggests that we usually do not make many new purchases of those types of goods in a lifetime. Guarantees and additional information, for instance from other users, may be more important for these types of goods. Information advantages for producers, who may be assumed to know more about the actual quality of their products may be countered to some degree thereby. Where experience goods can have a direct impact on users' health, such as where safety features of cars may be concerned, or medication, for instance, more direct regulation of minimum requirements formulated with regard to standards for a product may be appropriate.

Products included in the quick and relatively easy-to-assess category are, for instance, primary goods. We need to note, however, that with large-scale production of foodstuffs, our distance to the producers has grown and the product itself can have attributes that we cannot observe nor evaluate immediately. Things such as pesticide use in production may be unobservable, and knowledge about the effects of pesticides on the consumer side may be limited. The same may be true for the use of preservatives, artificial flavors, or genetically manipulated products, for instance, without even starting about products that were made from meat once upon a time. Even the standard examples of goods drawn on in the equilibrium perspective have thus been moving in the direction of the majority of goods in modern economies, namely, away from a framework to which the equilibrium view may have much of a contribution to offer, and towards industrial production.

For these goods, therefore, as we may remind ourselves, our capacity for accurately assessing what we acquire may actually have diminished over time, especially also regarding potential long-run effects they may have. So, the other way around, we may say that over time, we have become more dependent on measures to supplement relationships within a given social network, as we cannot individually observe what goes into produce production, meat production, or the production of basic plastic-based toys, etc. The options have broadened for producers, and the distance between producers and consumers has increased. The combination of these two things may lend itself especially pronouncedly to implementing changes with a view on profits, where earlier the relation to the customer and quality expectations put stricter limits to attempts at cost reduction. A mindset tending to interpret profits as a sign of quality of producers, embedded in the notion of markets as particularly suitable solution mechanisms for addressing societal problems may thus enhance a short-term focus of decisions.

In the constitution of 'free markets', where does that leave us? Information availability is one thing, its interpretation is the next. What do we know about the potential effects of some chemical or another? When someone issues warnings, what are these based on, and which interests are involved in their formulation? How far can we allow business interests to play a role, when effects of their products may be unclear? When to start alerting people to possible effects consumption of a good may have, on them or their environment? Do you block products until you are reasonably certain that they are not harmful, or do you permit products until it has become clear that they cause harm? Put in more general terms, how is the risk related to products distributed? Does that change if we assess it in terms of monetary cost or profits foregone? How far can we trust a private, for-profit company in matters that touch upon the safety of customers, or other affected parties, on the one hand, and the interests of the companies in a different manner, on the other? When bottom lines rule, can companies be trusted to improve safety measures, at a cost, or will they settle for less costly compensation? Denying claims may be a sound business decision for an insurance company, for instance, in another instant where the customers (as source of revenue and cost factor) might not find out until long after the purchase of a product whether it keeps what it promises. Safety, as can be noted, may also mean something like a reduction of unnecessary exposure to negative effects from financial sector activity, for instance. Where a price mechanism can be relied on, it may offer a first orientation and guidance. Where we may have reason to doubt price signals, we will have to develop more concise and more complicated measures to address issues that may come about from market interactions and related activities.

II

Besides the usefulness of consumption goods for satisfying a need, want, or desire, they allow to send signals, and thus address social need, want, and desire as well. The willingness and the ability to spend resources can be employed for strengthening one's representation of the self to the outside world, depending on what signals are perceived and accepted by the relevant peer-group. More generally, providing offers to people that respond to their need to partake in social relations, and meet the standards required by their peer group is a core competence to be developed for marketing products, from children's toys to daddies' cars, mommies' spa of choice, or the vacation spot opted for. Which triggers to our attention and suitable behavioral patterns and heuristics may be most fruitfully targeted is then the next step to figure out.

In combination with characteristics on the production side – typically falling unit costs with increasing production volume so that larger producers enjoy a cost advantage over smaller ones, another aspect that unhinges the reference framework – market power becomes a very real option. This market power refers to issues beyond the picking of a profit-friendly price quantity combination in markets and includes the creation of demand by shaping people's, including children's, wishes and guiding their attention. If a producer can establish her products as sending a specific signal to others, a potential market has opened up. Already very basic products – toys, for instance – can come with status signals attached, for instance. A 'must have', in order to keep up with the peer group is well within range for producers to establish, where the pressure may very well be exerted by the kids who use the toys. Consumer targeting is very possible here, as well, of course – in modern economies, 'invention is the mother of necessity'. 'Educational toys' may offer one example, as rebranded basic toys sold at increased profit margins to the parent who feels the need to have provided everything materially possible for a successful career path for junior, possibly with the attached boon of letting the world know about one's ability and foresight through the purchase. Aspects other than the price itself can be borne in mind when devising a communication strategy around the category and specific product, including the communicational value of the goods themselves, also and especially with regard to the presentation of the buyer to the outside world. Offering something that allows a person to see herself as being a 'good parent' may be a very fruitful inroad to market creation. An elevated price may not be the worst route to go, there, either, especially if combined with an, at least implicit, promise of giving junior an edge over other kids later in life, avoiding competition not only by limiting general access to decent schools, but furthering the distance more through additional resources poured into the little one.

Additional aspects of trends and fashions are mutual reinforcements of behavior and feedback loops between agents. If such issues influence demand for products, then there is no market behavior as that which is assumed under the law of demand. Demand for a product is no simple negative function of its price, but a function of its social environment, with different possible shapes.

III

Among the characteristics of goods, the time horizon under which they are acquired can be a reason for some adjustments to markets and our view of them, too. Additionally, as soon as we allow real time to play a part, future scenarios and conditions entail unknown unknowns, agents act under uncertainty.

We have already come across aspects of real time when considering information asymmetries, that is, before uncertainty plays a noticeable role in an analysis, so that only risk needs to be considered. Information asymmetries referred to differences in the knowledge about the object of exchange, such as a car. Guarantees and other signals to a commitment to the items sold and the willingness of support over time can be put in place for addressing some issues that emerge. Without additional support, from inside as well as outside of the market sphere with an influence on the exchange relations to amend potential problems, markets as exchange arenas cannot function in many cases, at least not very well. Markets are in need of additional structures in order to get suppliers and customers to actually enter a specific exchange arena. Where formal rules and norms fail to provide the required space, informal provisions can take their place, but there are never any unstructured exchange arenas.

More generally, and complementing the aspect of information provision in the example of foodstuffs, this underlines that real-world market activities are embedded in a network of structures that are needed to enable their use, as markets' constitution, working, and expansion. How well market exchanges can be employed in a set of problem-solving devices depends on the way this embedding is undertaken, including the rules that shape the shares of risks and costs that different groups have to bear. These groups may be those engaging in exchanges, as supply- or demand-side, but may also include third parties who do not engage in at least that particular market. For large-scale food producers, industrially produced meat may be more profitable than ways of production that are resulting in fewer health issues, for the consumer directly, and society at large, if you think of the use of antibiotics and the negative impact that has had, for instance.

Changes in frameworks setting up exchange arenas typically result in changes in the distribution of risk and cost, without disrupting the exchange arenas entirely, but shifting balances and possibly affecting volumes. That is to say, there is no single solution for making an exchange arena functional, and how a specific market is defined can differ from economy to economy. Risk related to activities in markets and the distribution of related costs can always be contentious points among the interest groups involved. Most of the times, arguments for a withdrawal of government from certain sectors mean a reregulation that allows to increase the influence of selected private groups, and thus a 'liberalization' for a selected few who in turn can increase their weight when it comes to negotiating, or imposing, changes in the distribution of risks and gains from economic activities. The 'freer' exchange arenas become, in current common parlance, the more power is typically shifted to producers or the financial sector.

Once complexity reduction is not driven to the extreme, it is no longer possible to create a 'market' concept that can cure all ills. All perspectives recognize that exchanges need embedding in supportive structures. These structures influence the distribution of costs and benefits related to specific activities. A range that both parties to exchanges are willing to accept offers a lot of possible combinations to pick from. Different interests will be reflected differently.

Also, aspects may be left out that refer to individuals who are not part of the exchange arena in question. In such a case, for instance, companies may be profitable because they do not have to account for all the cost and potentially damages that they may, in fact, cause. How far societies are willing to tolerate such situations – for the sake of the jobs that are offered, for instance – cannot be answered for them, and will have to make recourse to values, to ethical and moral considerations. In some circumstances, extensions of private business activities may be the result of a more permissive treatment of socialized costs. While every perspective can offer some contribution to an answer to such questions, how far market mechanisms are relied on, differs, and has to differ because the information that is transmitted through transactions is assessed differently.

IV

Real time also has an impact on decisions in exchanges of goods and services acquired to be a part of production processes. For the production of goods, expectations about future sales-conditions under uncertainty are a significant contributor to the motivation to pursue specific avenues of activity. In the case of financial products, which transfer the rights to future streams of cash-flows, similar considerations can be formulated.

Observations in markets may be seen to offer indications of others' assessments of the potential of products or sectors. If a positive outlook triggers increased activity, this may be assumed to be reflected in an increasing demand for investments, physical or other. Trade volumes as well as price movements can be seen as carrying information about others' expectations. If we factor in real time, and related problems of limited information availability and uncertainty, the signal that prices themselves include can gain in importance, therefore. Prices do not just refer to the valuation of products, whatever their foundation, but carry information about outlook and expectations. Changes in prices can trigger further activities, and rising prices may lead to increased activities and transactions, whereas falling prices can lead to reductions in activity. Demand may move with the price movements, not against them.

Note that the terminology of a 'bubble' in markets refers to such a dynamic as well; however, and this is the interesting aspect here, with a reference value in mind that derives from the assumption that papers traded have a fundamental or real value. The fundamental value is given by discounted future profit flows. A departure of trading prices and real value is the result of irrational behavior then, leading to a deviation from correct prices, for instance, driven by a bout of optimism that carries people off, or an increased presence of stupid people in an exchange arena, which at the end of the day offers the two aspects drawn on when financial market crises are 'explained', and can be identified as such by recourse to the reference point model. In a 'rational bubble', resulting from everybody following a trend because they can make money doing so while it lasts, everybody is being aware that it will not last forever. You just hope you're not the one stuck with the hot potato in the end – which more often than not does not refer to the actual traders who have their fees siphoned off other people's funds that are actually taking a hit from collapsing prices.

However, if exchange arenas function differently, then there is no reason to interpret a bubble as a deviation from a proper valuation. Price movements may then simply be an outcome of individuals' exchange activities. Fundamentals and proper prices cannot be determined, and therefore have no particular analytical meaning, as they are deprived of logical content. This is not to deny that focal points for prices and relative price relations exist that can influence agents' expectations, for instance, derived from long-term averages in specific market segments, or share indices, or reflecting custom and habits where prices of physical goods are concerned. Such measures are not to be confused with a reflection of fundamental or real value, however. They may provide a focal point and thereby shape expectations of agents, whose behavior confirms them as temporary resting points for the system, and reference points for analyses. But they can change, and so prices can move without being drawn back to some fundamental value position. While temporary deviations from long-term averages may be a sign of instability to emerge, that is not the result of a deviation from proper prices, but of other effects, such as changes in the risk incurred by agents, knowingly or unknowingly, as we will momentarily see. How much informational value a long-term average itself holds may differ from situation to situation and context to context as well, then.

Market characteristics no longer bear any pronounced similarity to those set out in the reference point formulation. The integration of a number of aspects that are not commensurable to the reference framework leads to a different picture of the functioning of related markets, and may change the role that markets can play as problem-solving devices. Behavior in the emerging market environments does not necessarily lead to socially desirable outcomes. As one example, reversals of price developments, in financial markets typically rather quickly once they have started, can lead to widespread disadvantageous effects, for agents in financial markets, but also more broadly, as financial market developments can have an impact on economic activity in general. Physical investments, in production goods, can lead to overcapacities and reversals of expectations once these capacities are fully developed and available. A first impact would be on employment. Furthermore, as investments tend to be financed through debt, and overcapacities can make the amortization of investments more difficult to realize, such developments may introduce problems as well, in this case from the producing sector, with an impact on the financial sector that made loans available. We will take this up again in Chapters 4 and 5. Such possibilities are irrelevant only if we discard them from the outset.

3.4 Specific Markets: Labor

I

Turning to a couple of examples for specific markets over the next pages, we will look at labor markets and financial markets including particulars such as foreign exchange markets and will also consider approaches to questions of foreign trade.

In general, in the top-down perspectives, the value that every unit (say, hour) of labor adds to production is known. Wages reflect that value-added, or, at least, the current best aggregate assessment. As, in the reference point, every market is in equilibrium, by extension that means that there are no gainful employment opportunities that remain open; and no demand for labor that is not filled. Every worker earns what they contribute to the process of adding value in production. If profitable production options were open, wages could be raised to attract personnel. There is no particular negotiating strength on either employer or employee side, if laborers are unhappy, they can switch jobs without problem. Employers know this, and for protecting their income have no choice but to offer decent treatment to labor. If unions enter the picture, they distort market outcomes to the advantage of their members (insiders) over nonmembers (outsiders) who have to stay unemployed – labor hurts its brethren by distorting market forces. Another option for interpreting persistent real-world unemployment, as a sign for wages that are too high, is to assume that employers voluntarily pay higher wages than they would have to, because of issues with monitoring the efforts that workers actually put into work. Assuming that perfect monitoring is not possible, paying workers more than the equilibrium wage means that they have more, or actually something, to lose in case they get caught slacking off.

II

One may say that labor is not a good like any other. It is not produced, but drawn into the economic sphere. Two aspects stand out in particular. Labor is not separable from the laborer. The laborer has needs, selling her or his labor power allows gaining access to the means for meeting those needs. The second point is that labor, is a remunerated activity in the production of some kind of good, intermediate or final. The demand for labor may not be given independently of the environment, but rather depend on the overall economic situation, demand patterns, and the expectations of those making the decision to hire people regarding developments in those areas (we will take related issues of aggregate economic demand and unemployment up in Chapters 4 and 5). In this case, we have a rather pronounced example of demand and supply decisions that are not independent of each other. If they are not independent of each other, even if equilibria existed, a trend from measures would not be clearly identifiable. For all the models considered under the perspective of an isolation of individual effects of measures, demand and supply have to remain independent. If both react to the same impulse, a clear-cut derivation of effects will, as a rule, no longer be possible. The overall change in the particular market would depend on the relative strengths of demand and supply reaction, which may not be equal throughout all wage-work, or more in general price-quantity, combinations. In that case, effects could well differ depending on where in the system a labor market found itself before a change.

Individuals' need to participate in the labor market means that, regarding considerations of market functioning, the assumption of a labor supply curve that is constantly upward sloping – more labor is offered as wages increase – is not entirely tenable. Equivalently, given the reality of need, that labor supply was always reduced with falling prices is then not a reasonable assumption (and in fact does not find support in empirical studies). Below a certain wage level, the offer may be increased in order to maintain a minimum, for instance socially defined, consumption level. In fact, it is entirely conceivable that the interplay of agents makes the situation worse for each of them once that point has been reached: feedback mechanisms in which low wages increase hours worked may lead to more competition among labor and may drive wages down further. Likewise, for high wage levels, the offer may be reduced in order to be able to enjoy leisure time. If labor demand was describable according to the reference framework view, meaning that more labor was hired the lower the wage rate, the supply-side considerations alone would still mean multiple equilibria in labor markets that no market mechanism could distinguish. Which outcome results depends on the embedding of labor market relations, in this case.

The other aspect raised regarding the position of labor refers to the fact that, as labor remuneration leads to demand in other markets, the derived demand for labor makes it entirely conceivable that, at least over a certain range, increasing wages and increasing demand for labor go hand in hand. Either point, for the demand or supply of labor, means that labor markets, or segments, displaying such characteristics can show various resting positions, at high wages and medium workday durations just as at low wages and long workdays, or in case of negative expectations on the supply-side, low wages and short workdays, for instance. But there is no market criterion according to which preference should be given to one over another outcome. Working conditions, distributional aspects decided in, and negotiating power granted from the political sphere will contribute to shaping outcomes, and may well be instrumental to improving a situation, if higher wages and fewer hours were to be seen as such, for instance. Attitudes shape the situation, not disembodied market forces. However, given that for global companies the demand potential in any one market they service may be of lesser importance, it may be less likely that companies are willing to pay higher wages, benefiting the community as a whole in various ways, if demand for the product can be sought elsewhere. Of course, this only goes so far, as someone somewhere will have to be able to purchase what is offered.

It may also be important to note that typically, by entering a labor contract, the control of the employer reaches additional aspects of a person's life, and decisions about nonwork related activities. As labor force is rented and labor is tied to a person with needs, and delivered by that person, an enhanced negotiating power – or at least its potential – is gained by the employers. The fall-back option of an entire retreat from modern consumption and societies is not something that most people will seriously consider, or can, at the latest once they have to support a family. A going wage rate – for certain sectors, at least – may simply be a reflection of negotiating power of employers. Interpreting such a situation as the outcome of freely interplaying supply and demand sides in well-behaved markets puts an analytical and interpretative framework to work that abstracts from such issues and thus remains blind to them and their implications. A threat-scenario of a situation a lot worse than employment conditions holds, in case of unemployment, may in the extreme then be interpreted as the natural outcome of markets in which individuals enter freely into contractual relations. We had referred to vulnerability and insecurity in economic matters already. Measures taken by a community to help support its members in case a problematic economic situation manifests reduce their insecurity. If such measures are shunned, the negotiating position for the affected further deteriorates.

3.5 Specific Markets: Finance

I

A second area for markets that is of particular interest is related to financial products and money. Beyond credit and loans, more in general, financial sector activity entails the trading of papers granting rights to future streams of income in different shapes and forms. All advances in financial sector activity revolve around two, related, issues, namely, the spread of the risk of particular activities and possibilities to increase the leverage in investments. We will address these issues in more detail below in this section. We will also include considerations concerning foreign exchange markets in this section. Traditionally connected to trade-flows, financial investment-driven foreign exchange demand has dwarfed trade-related demand for quite a while now.

The general role of financial markets that results stems from the related issues of making monetary capital available for financing investments, enabling larger investments than possible for individual agents, or permitting to smooth over momentary shortfalls of revenue, and from spreading the risk of such investments to larger numbers of agents. On the other market side, access to future streams of income is acquired. Increasingly, this covers the resale of rights to income streams, from bonds, shares, mortgages, etc., or more complicated papers drawing a number of such income streams together. The prices for financial products are therefore assumed to relate to expectations about the development of these income streams. How loose or tight the connection is interpreted to be may differ. What information prices can offer in regard to financial sector products is accordingly evaluated differently under different perspectives.

Making monetary funds available and spreading risk is easily enough illustrated. Say, ten people lend money to ten debtors. If each lends to one specific debtor, the risk of not being paid back and losing the entire loan is carried by that one person. If the creditors pool their funds and have rights to shares in the cash-flows the payments by the debtors make up, even if one of them cannot repay their loan, the lenders are pretty well covered. Structures may get more involved, but overall, this is what it comes down to. As long as the risks of nonpayment are not correlated, pooling funds and lending to larger numbers reduces overall risks for lenders. This noncorrelation is a core assumption of dominant approaches to financial market analyses. Whether it can safely be made as a general rule is by no means clear, though, to say the least. If risks turn out to be correlated, their reduction by pooling funds is not necessarily as effective as it is for uncorrelated risk. In terms of the example, say, the ten borrowers from above buy houses in the same neighborhood. They work for the same employer. The employer closes shop, they are out of work and cannot service their loans. At the same time, the ten houses becoming available at once, in an environment where a major employer apparently just decided to discontinue operations, which at least potentially lets house prices drop, reducing their value of collateral for the loans granted. If new buyers can be found at all, that is.

With a banking sector, as the intermediary between lenders and borrowers in that scenario, the picture changes; slightly if we assume, with the benchmark model, that banks funnel funds from depositors to borrowers to finance those guys' investment needs. As an additional layer, banks buffer their depositors from losses. It is easier to pool savings, they are in a better position to assess risks of lending operations and provide a simplified point of access for taking a credit. Operations can spread further. As we will see in more detail below, in Chapter 4, the functioning of banks is not necessarily properly described in these terms, however. Collecting money from depositors and making funds available to debtors are separate operations, there. Banks offer a promise to convert funds into government money, legal tender, when they lend. They can draw on central bank borrowing for adjusting their accounts and meeting obligations. Their lending creates deposits or changes in deposit balances. That means, in modern economies, banks create money through their operations. The constraints they face differ, then, from those where the amount of deposits they have collected sets a limit to the amount they are able to lend.

In either case, banks have a large pool of investments to spread the risk they are exposed to by making investment funds available. The risk of nonpayment exists independently of whom the banks have obligations to for the funds lent. They evaluate risks and make lending decisions, earning a fee for their troubles. The debt they owe is short term (people's deposits) and their lending is long term (credit, mortgages, loans). This temporal mismatch is the fundamental problem of banks, whether commercial or investment. Central bank funds help banks tide over tight spots, should they find themselves in those. This holds in all perspectives on banks and the financial sector. The divergence in the timeframes between obligations and returns introduces a layer of difficulty for maintaining operations, as the belief that banks may not be able to service their short-term obligations can lead to behavior that forces them into problems. Policies aiming at the financial sector are built around permitting smooth flows of funds, stopgaps to reduce risks and reassure creditors, and a general stabilization of that sector in economies. For instance, banks are typically required to hold reserves to cover short-term demand for money from them, in order to prevent depositors panicking. Central bank lending in times of distress is a crucial feature for stabilizing banks, to help tide over liquidity issues before they can turn into solvency problems.

The larger financial sector offers further ways for spreading risk and increasing leverage, by drawing on the transactions of the banking sector, setting up papers that tap into the revenue stream originating from banks' activities. Again, leveraging investments and spreading risk, or hedging, are the drivers we can identify behind activities. Arbitrage and speculation are expressions of these. If price divergences exist in different markets trading the same products (Frankfurt stock exchange, Tokyo stock exchange, New York SE, etc.) arbitrage opportunities arise that are pursued to bring prices back in line. Arbitrage refers to actions that are carried out in a very short time span – current divergences in prices are exploited. This is not the same as speculation, which is carried out with a view on expected future price developments. This distinction is often blurred.

II

The reference point position is, again, relatively briefly explained. Prices in financial markets reflect all available information and thus properly reflect current assessments and valuations of assets. Returns on investments converge, as agents seek the most profitable opportunities, thus bidding up their prices as long as there is an extra return to expect. Part of financial transactions is the risk that a debtor cannot meet obligations from agreements. Interest payments reflect this. Any difference in real interest rates covers differences in the risk attached to an investment vehicle, as more risky endeavors reimburse lenders, or investors, by offers of higher interest payments. The other interest component is a reimbursement for making the funds available in the first place. Overall expected returns, returns adjusted for the risk undergone, are equal for all investments.

In a static perspective, an equilibrium price exists that matches supply and demand for financial papers, as claims to future cash-flows. People who want to acquire such claims and people who need to borrow against future income are brought together, and, as always, both sides of the transaction gain and get something they want.

Beyond the static perspective, prices move randomly when new events that have an impact on them become known and change asset valuations. Information that becomes available was not known before; it could not have been included in the pricing of a financial product. As information may affect earnings prospects positively or negatively, and thus increase or reduce the value of future cash-flows tied to said product, price movements over time cannot be foreseen. You cannot beat the market in a structured manner, therefore, and generate higher returns than are attained there on average. You may speculate, though. People who do earn above average returns for a while, do so because they have been lucky. Others were not, so some lie below average. You cannot know in advance who the lucky ones are, however. A successful investment portfolio management of the past does not seamlessly translate into the future.

For integrating this notion into model formulations, it is additionally assumed that information that is relevant becomes available arbitrarily, and may signal positive or negative earnings prospects. Information changes are assumed to be distributed in a way so that price changes, responding to new information, follow a normal distribution – very many small changes, few large ones, very few extreme ones. The same is assumed for the movement of indices describing the aggregate movement of selected shares. However, price movements in real-world stock-markets are much, much more extreme than this modeling approach permits. Events like Black Friday, Black Monday, the dot.com-bubble bursting, or the subprime crisis and similar occurrences and their effects in financial markets should not happen once every decade, or so.

III

Particularly important among the assumption behind this approach to financial markets is that single events in an economy are independent of one another and that agents take their decisions independently of one another. If events are not, then a trigger will potentially lead to a cascade of follow-up events that may even reinforce each other's momentum. Valuations and risk assessment can become fiendishly difficult, if possible at all. If decisions are not independent of each other, feedback loops between agents' actions and other nonlinear dynamics outside the models' scope will have to be acknowledged. Where guesses about future cash-flows and thus proper prices are taken independently of each other, a good compromise among all interests and valuations can result. As soon as mutual influences enter the fray, such an outcome cannot be relied on any longer. If agents follow trends they observe in other agents' actions, positive feedback can become a normal aspect of market functioning.

Where debtor and creditor are involved, the debtor has payment obligations to the creditor. These involve interest payments creating the return to keep the creditor in business. When the debtor runs into trouble, the creditor loses an asset, reducing future cash-flows. If enough debtors run into trouble, the creditor may face problems as well. What 'enough' means cannot be defined before something happens, unfortunately. The tricky part is that the perception of other agents shapes the development of the mismatch in the timeframes between own obligations to others and others' obligation to oneself. If other agents, for whatever reason, develop doubts about the ability of a specific agent to continue meeting her obligations, they can act in a way that fosters the materialization of problems, not out of bad will but out of the desire to protect their own assets. Given the nature of financial sector transactions that link debtors and creditors, depending on the initial impetus bringing about the problems and the links between different agents, the structure of relations itself can foster larger scale trouble.

An additional source of momentum for the spread of problems because of the linkages of agents in financial markets, results from the sale of assets that may pick up once agents start running into balance sheet trouble. If increased sales activities lead to a price reduction, which is an entirely reasonable development in an environment where fire sales have started, then other agents may run into trouble as their asset values decline. Notice that the price changes here are not at all due to an assessment of the business side of the papers sold but may be solely due to liquidity concerns of the seller. The same is true for bonds or more complicated bundles of different papers granting access to cash-flows.

At a time where a reliable price signal would be particularly helpful, it is most likely that it will not be carrying easily identifiable meaningful information about assets, but rather respond to market conditions and the state of their current owners.

Price declines signify dropping asset values, with potential balance sheet problems resulting. When assets decline in price, this may cause trouble if the obligations held are not affected; something entirely possible, as these processes are unrelated. There may thus develop pressure to reduce obligations. That may require cash, which may require the sales of assets, which can contribute to a downward dynamic in markets, especially if it eventually begins to shape the general mood in the financial sector. It may become increasingly difficult to meet short-term obligations, when assets cannot be sold for the price at which they have previously been valued.

We might say that the structure of relations leads to a systemic or sectoral risk exposure. This level of exposure emerges from the connections of the agents. It is not something that the analysis of an individual agent could help understand, much less forecast. Such emerging properties are characteristics of complex systems, in general. Bottom-up analytical perspectives allow to acknowledge them.

The independence of prices and price movements in such environments cannot simply be taken as a given, as for instance the development in housing markets and related financial market products has just shown again. Why such independence should be the rule, outside the reference model world, has not been established. Keeping regulators' hands off a market in which those aspects matter for the price movements observed will come at the danger of drastic and quick revaluations and price changes, typically downward. An understanding of the system financial sector, on the other hand, may improve our chances to keep the system as a whole outside the areas in which trajectories that can damage the wider economic sphere noticeably become more likely.

IV

Bottom-up perspectives on financial markets thus take issue with simplifying the analytical framework to the point where an independence of agents, decisions, and individual price movements is assumed as the foundation for analyses. Instead, they are allowing for connections between agents which introduces options for capturing herd behavior, fire sales, and a number of other aspects, in financial markets in a coherent manner within the framework for analyses, and not as something like the sudden emergence of idiots who have an impact on prices in the perfect market world. This perspective also permits systemic effects to play a part, and be a part of the analytical framework. Typically included is the recognition of uncertainty as a factor in decisions. There is no reason to suspect that agents' activities would actually lead to a convergence of market price onto any particular price. The movements of short-term periods make for the price dynamic. There is no corrective long run pull or push, there is a sequence of short-term changes that move in tandem with expectations and the interpretations of observations in a certain environment, and informed by a certain worldview. That is not to say that prices everywhere might fluctuate wildly, though. Custom and habit, expectations and supply conditions, among others, all influence and limit the range of price movements, for most goods, at most times.

Periodic stability and long-term trends that we describe in markets are thus still possible under a perspective permitting complexity. They result from expectations that contribute to stability, as they may provide focal points for agents in the form of an orientation on long-term averages as a heuristic, for instance, or may be due to effects that result from different types of strategies pursued by agents. Such influences may limit price movements within a certain range, at least for non-negligible periods of time. This does not have to mean that everywhere in the system, stability results, nor does it mean that the system characteristics have to remain fixed over time. A reduction in the diversity of strategies can, even if oriented on the same focal points, result in more pronounced price movements as such strategies can trigger actions that are reinforcing trends once they have taken hold. Systemic characteristics may mean that once a certain area is reached – say, described by the joint risk-exposure of the agents involved – self-reinforcing, as opposed to stabilizing, dynamics become more likely. As they are rooted in general strategies pursued by agents in financial markets, resulting feedback loops can be seen as a different mechanism leading to larger price movements than a generally optimistic outlook of agents. There is nothing about the price movements and the dynamics behind them that would qualify them as aberrations from what might be expected in the described environment. They are a normal part of the range potential market dynamics.

As uncertainty plays a part, prices themselves can be seen as signals in those markets, with rising prices as signs for a positive outlook on the part of a sufficient number of agents. This positive outlook itself can be reflected in subsequent market activity, leading to further optimistic assessments (or the reverse, in case of a negative outlook). This may result in, at least temporarily, self-reinforcing movements of prices in financial markets. Furthermore, the same variables are influencing supply and demand in financial markets, in terms of expectations and in terms of relative prices of related assets. The two market-sides are not independent of each other. Market activity creates market movements, and expectations, observations, and interpretations shape those movements by influencing the direction of subsequent activity.

So under uncertainty, beyond risk, expectations and positive feedback mechanisms can become a crucial part of financial markets and their functioning. We do not have to treat these as aberrations or temporary disturbances of the force, but may see them as reflections and outcomes of normal human behavior, and therefore a part of normal market economies and their financial sectors.

Price movements that are driven by expectations are parts of markets, and market prices a reflection of the mood of market participants. The market environment is shaped by these moods and perceptions with related expectations. As we have seen in Chapter 2, an environment can have an influence on what actually constitutes a promising course of action, and in financial markets the environment plays a pronounced role for the possibilities for success for individual agents. If everybody is optimistic about the perspectives in the financial sphere, and is willing to buy financial products, going against the trend may not be the recipe for success in a relevant timeframe. Even if prices have reached levels at which a noticeable reversal is likely to happen, it is not known when that may come about and the moods of people investing may well sustain high prices for a while, and for a long time after the funds of those betting against the trend have run out. We may note here already, taking the issue back up in more detail below, that a stabilizing role for speculators, as is at times argued, should be viewed with many reservations.

V

For the general functioning of financial markets, the systemic level of relations between factors matters. The combination of the strategy environment shaping advantageous behavior options, people's moods, and possibly resulting feedback loops can lead to distinct patterns in price movements over time. These patterns also indicate that regulation does have an influence and can prevent very pronounced downward movements from happening, thus stabilizing the overall economy, even if high short-term profits for some individuals are no longer in reach in that case.

The impact that mood and expectations have is assumed to operate through the risk attitude of the agents in financial markets. Rights to future cash-flows are what is traded in those markets. For realizing investments, debt financing is not uncommon. In low risk approaches, the expected returns from investments are sufficient for servicing interest obligations as well as repaying principal. More risky endeavors focus on projects in which expected cash-flows are only enough to cover interest obligations. Even more risky ones do not even generate the cash-flow for servicing interest payments and are undertaken solely in the expectation of increasing prices. Over time, in an economy in which a positive mood has taken hold and persists, a shift towards higher risk investments and investment financing is observed. The risk positions for individual agents become potentially more problematic due to the higher leverage in their investments, and, with that, eventually, a point may be reached at which risk is spread through the financial sector to where the sector itself becomes very vulnerable to deteriorating prices. But, at first, if positive expectations are reflected in increasing prices, speculative investments can pay off, and handsomely. Further, in an environment in which activity and its success is more narrowly evaluated by short-term profit margins than in any other economic sector, a failure to participate may quickly result in being presented with the offer to consider new career paths. As long as agents are permitted to pursue high risk activities in financial markets, there is always the potential for drastic downward spirals when attitudes change. How far their effects can reach depends on the regulatory structures in place.

VI

The risk related to specific products does not remain given over time. It changes with the developments in the financial markets. Furthermore, it changes with developments outside the financial sector, as the revenue stream financial products tap into is generated in the real economy. Risk exposure by individual agents, to some degree also reflecting the risk exposure at a systemic level, can thus be expected to change over time, in reaction to developments in the financial sector or in other economic arenas as well. Changes resulting from a changed risk exposure at the systemic level may be difficult to foresee or even generally anticipate, especially if financial products are involved with which only limited experience exists. Even though, the fact that what is labeled innovation in finance simply consists of new ways to package risk and leverage investments should be enough of an indicator to be cautious. You cannot make risk disappear in an environment like that of financial markets, and increased leverage just means a higher risk of liquidity and solvency issues.

The risk of individual investment activities is transmitted into the economic system particularly quickly if investments are debt-financed, i.e., leveraged. The higher the debt share in an investment, the higher the leverage in this investment. For every debtor there is also a creditor who may eventually run into financial problems as well, if too many debtors face liquidity constraints or solvency issues. Leveraging investments is a tremendously attractive tool for increasing returns on investment, and as long as it works, very profitable. When it stops working, the losses typically incurred are much more damaging than the profits helpful, however. A cumulated risk exposure of the individuals in those markets may push the financial sector into a new phase, making it much more vulnerable to adverse effects.

If you leverage an investment, you borrow money that you invest, your lever. The attractiveness of leveraging investments results from a simple relation: your expected returns are higher than the interest rate you pay on your borrowed funds. The difference is yours to keep. To keep the numbers simple: you have a million dollars and an investment opportunity promising a return of ten percent. Now, you decide to use your million dollars as collateral in a loan and borrow another nine million dollars. The interest rate for that loan is five percent. You invest the ten million that you now have in the ten percent project. All goes well, so after a year you have 11 million dollars. You repay the loan, nine million, and the interest payment that runs to 450,000 dollars (five percent of nine million). That leaves you with a profit of 550,000 dollars, instead of 100,000 without the lever, or, a return of 55% instead of ten.

Now, say things do not go well, instead of gaining ten percent, your investment loses ten percent in value. At the end of the year you are left with nine million dollars. You can repay your loan, but still owe the 450,000 in interest payments, and your money is gone. Through the lever, your rate of return can be increased quite handsomely. However, by the same mechanisms, losses will hit hard.

We can also see here an example for how the structure of the relations between agents may play a crucial role in the functioning of parts of an economy. Specifically, for financial sectors, 'too big to fail' is only one aspect that regulators have to bear in mind. 'Too connected to fail' is likely to be as important. Long-term capital management (LTCM), the hedge fund that went bust in 1998, and purportedly brought the financial system to the very verge of collapse, was not that large in terms of capitalization. It was connected to main players and nobody knew which risks were hidden in which balance sheet, however (as was the case when the interbank market ground to a halt in 2007/08 as well, for instance). Besides a desirable regulatory focus on preventing financial markets from entering into a high risk-exposure state, transparency about connections between different agents would make adverse effects on the rest of societies less likely.

VII

We will also have a brief look at foreign exchange markets. Exchange rates give the cost of one currency in terms of another one. They should reflect the earnings potential in different economies, from different investment opportunities and in relation to the potential in other economies. Thereby, they integrate weighted expectations about short term costs and benefits and long term costs and benefits of cross-border investments in one way or another. At the same time, they influence the distribution of these costs and benefits, between different sectors in an economy, for instance, and should reflect this dimension in some way as well. If assessments about a proper rate were taken independently of one another, then even a best possible assessment balancing all interests might result. If agents are influencing others' decisions, no such outcome can be expected, however.

In the reference framework, the exchange rate mirrors differences in the price levels in different countries and simply serves to translate the price in one currency into that in another currency. Distortions may arise from costs of transportation, for instance, but the general tendency is clear: money has no influence on value but simply translates values, as reflected in prices. Different monetary units require an additional translation, the price of monetary units in terms of other monetary units – the exchange rate. Market forces bring the adjustments of price levels expressed in different currencies about. If there are price differences, these will be reflected in demand, which in turn leads to an adjustment of prices until it is no longer advantageous to buy in either one or the other economy, as agents are indifferent between them.

Real-world exchange rate movements suggest that this view on exchange rate formations falls short of capturing the main contributing factors, at least for the short-term movements we observe. A core extension to this basic mechanism therefore factors in the role of financial flows. These dwarf trade in goods and services nowadays; even though, in the reference framework, they should still be determined by productive potential, as they ultimately draw on cash-flows generated in the real sector of an economy. Still, returns to financial products are a main factor for cross-border activities. Prices for these products, and the interest earned on them, are more important for short-term exchange rate movements than trade-flows. The real side of the economy, goods production, adjusts, but more slowly. Over shorter time-periods, therefore, a divergence of the exchange rate from its assumedly existing true value is possible, and frequently observed. Again, we are in the reference perspective here. Expected exchange rate changes and interest rate differences lead to expected returns on investment in the domestic currency of a potential investor. These can be compared to expected returns from domestic investments. Depending on the outcome of such comparisons, investment funds may flow across borders, changing supply and demand in currency markets, and bringing expected returns in line. Expectations are, rhetorically, a core part of this extension. However, expectations are limited to assuming a reversal of the economy to its equilibrium position. Which is in fact a certainty, as this is exactly what it does in the model, and has to do qua the set-up of the system. Expectations in the sense that they would reflect uncertainty about the future have no role to play here.

Again, in the long-run, adjustments to a global equilibrium are expected to hold so that the goods market will be in equilibrium at the exchange rate that equalizes the price levels in different economies. The usefulness of goods as assessed by agents remains at the heart of determining the systems' outcomes. This global equilibrium, even as temporary divergences are permitted, remains the driver of the changes we observe (more on this in Chapter 4). Even as expectations are built into descriptions, these are formulated to bring the new equilibrium level about. Agents know where the system should be headed, expect it to head in that direction, and adjust behavior accordingly to take it there.

What is recognized is that differences in time horizons of agents may have a detrimental impact on the observed exchange rate. An example that may illustrate some related issues is the so-called Dutch disease. Having discovered natural resources, namely, oil and gas, in the Netherlands, trade flows out of the country were soon dominated by the impact of oil and gas. This produced exchange rate effects that harmed other export industries. Given the nature of technology, as a combination of skill and equipment, the damage done to other industries can then not only produce short-term distortions, tension, and friction, but may actually weaken the long-term prospects of an economy as skill and knowledge in momentarily uneconomic sectors is lost. This is not an effect of a sudden loss of attractiveness of goods or production capabilities in the economy, or a relative loss of technological competence vis-à-vis its competitors, but is purely due to monetary effects from exchange rate movements dominated by narrow and short-term considerations, in this case. (Which also provides an example for an impact of monetary values on real structures, something that is incompatible with the reference perspective, in which real values are given and money simply reflects relative values and eases transactions.)

VIII

Currently, financial flows are the main influence on exchange rate movements. Expectations concerning exchange rate movements and interest rate differences are the principal influence factors shaping decisions for currency purchases.

Expectations under uncertainty can lead agents to act in a way that produces self-fulfilling developments. For instance, expectations about a depreciation of a currency should lead to increased sales of it, in order to protect returns, or avoid future losses, which can easily trigger the depreciation that was expected. These expectations are drivers of price movements. Without systemic constraints in the form of an equilibrium, they can produce ongoing movements in economies. Some of these, in turn, may be reflected in imbalances in the accounts utilized for recording economic activities. For the economy providing the global reserve currency, currently the United States, this may produce some additional effects that an equilibrium framework has difficulties incorporating (see Chapter 4). Exchange rate expectations themselves will drive actions. Self-reinforcing trends following self-fulfilling expectations and related actions result.

That such fluctuations affect exchange rates and that self-reinforcing trends are not unlikely can be glimpsed when actual exchange rate developments over longer time spans are considered. There is already a noticeable short-term volatility, leading to rather pronounced movements over medium ranges, say, three to five years. Typically, nothing fundamental changes that regularly (as an example pull up German Mark – USD after the end of the Bretton Wodds arrangements and then Euro – USD long-term trends, for instance). Still, there is typically something happening, so that for instance for the impact of new bits of information on price movements, its availability can be bent and interpreted this way or that if a specific interpretative framework is to be maintained. The stock-market reports before the evening news that you find the world over are similar exercises in story-telling. For an illusion of understanding, some cause is pinpointed, and the 'market's' response noted and 'interpreted'.

In foreign exchange markets, the lack of an independence of supply and demand decisions may be particularly obvious. Demand for foreign currency is due to trade relations that require reimbursing the transaction partner in her currency, and investment activities that cross borders, in real structures as well as financial markets. Demand thus can be expected to depend on relative prices in economies, and expectations about changes of these, relative returns for different investment outlets, including relative inflation rates, and desires to protect against losses incurred through disadvantageous developments, among others. These same factors influence supply decisions. As supply and demand are not independent, there cannot be a unique equilibrium to deduce influence patterns, or set a correct price, for that matter (see the previous section).

As trade flows and related currency requirements are dwarfed by financial market operations, expectations about relative returns of financial activities may be assumed to play a particularly pronounced role for exchange rate developments. Feedback loops and reinforcing expectations are particularly possible, here, then. Abstracting from those by assuming a single and stable equilibrium value for currency prices towards which exchange rates would trend may then leave out critical aspects of this market. How outcomes are to be evaluated in such markets is not easy to argue for, absent a reference point, however. The turbulence that unregulated exchange markets subject producers in real-world activities to may introduce an untowardly pronounced disadvantage. Futures etc. can provide some protection against erratic price movements in exchange markets, for sure and for a while, at least, but that shifts efforts to producing companies that they do not need to incur in case of a commitment to stabilizing exchange rates (which is not entirely unproblematic, either, however, as we will see in Chapter 4). Again, we see that changes in regulatory structures and capital controls shift costs and efforts to different agents, in this case between those involved in cross-border operations.

3.6 Specific Markets: Trade Relations

The final aspect to turn to, focusing on specific markets for the moment, is concerned with trade relations, that is, the flows of goods and services across borders. Even though no particular goods market is considered, trade in and of itself merits some separate considerations. Questions typically asked revolve around the way the members of an economy participate in such cross-border transactions, and whether more harm or good comes from these, whether trade in general or specialization patterns, reflected in changes in trade structures, that might result from trade relationships are concerned. The advantage of an access to a broader selection of goods, and goods that lie beyond the capacities of a particular economy to produce, is easily pointed out. However, as different levels of technological capacities and other standards, such as social or labor, are involved, the impact that trade relations may have on the members of economies, and their economic potential as a whole, draws attention.

I

In the tradition of the benchmark model, the basic arguments regarding the general issue of trade are rather simple: exchanges always benefit both sides of the transaction as long as nobody is forced to partake. Hence, every transaction creates some benefit for the parties involved. Trade as a term captures a number of such transactions, namely those in which the partners to transactions reside in different economies. Hence, trade has got to be beneficial as well, at the least at the individual level of the agents involved.

Additional aspects can be raised, as well. Cross-border transactions have the potential to expand the range of choice available in the economic sphere thereby conferring additional benefits beyond the more limited range within a country. The high levels of trade between economies exchanging products in the same product class is typically looked at as driven by the scope of choice that is offered thereby, and which people like. The harmonious view on economic systems embedded in that framework gives the direction for the answer, therefore. The potential of economic gains on the national level, as the sum of all the individual beneficial transactions, in a static environment is stressed.

That individual groups and sectors can lose out from changes in trade relations is a main result from analyses as well. Still, if the analysis shows that the economy as a whole can gain from trade, the issue is laid to rest referring to the need to negotiate the distribution of those gains, including the reimbursement of those whose position is likely to worsen following the opening of an economy to trade relations. (Such redistribution would later be labelled an inefficient interference with the market, however.)

II

More interest has been generated by questions of specialization patterns that follow the establishment of trade relations. Do what you are relatively, or comparatively, good at, is the answer to this. The fundamental issue continues to be the allocation of real resources, such as labor, in production processes. Labor is limitedly available everywhere. No one can produce everything they and the entire rest may need, even if one were to excel at every single production process beyond what can be attained by the rest. A concentration on some production processes will be necessary in order to put the available resources to their best possible use.

One of the most revered answers to questions of trade was formulated very early on in modern economics. It is not particularly intuitive, which almost certainly lent it additional appeal. It is, more importantly, though, a core example for the arrival at interesting results based on the first principles approach.

The core additional assumption it rests on is that neither technology nor resources can move across borders. Only products can. Production inputs cannot move towards the advantageous structures where they might be employed more gainfully. Likewise, advantageous structures cannot be set up anywhere else, because technology cannot cross borders. Trade patterns should follow so-called comparative advantages, then.

If you are better than the rest of the world at making cars, but a lot better at making microchips, than microchips it should be for you. At the same time, idle resources would be wasted. So, stopping production because someone somewhere else is more effective in things in absolute terms would not benefit the system. Hence, your trading partner, worse in their abilities on both counts, but less pronouncedly so when it comes to cars, should focus on the production of cars. Again, one economy cannot produce to cover the needs of everyone and it does not make sense to let resources anywhere go to waste.

For another modeling approach in this line of thinking, technology transfers are allowed in addition to the trade in products. Resource endowments are fixed, though. Differences in resource endowments spell a different relative price structure in the economies under scrutiny. Even though the technology may be the same everywhere, the differences in resource endowments and resulting differences in resources' relative prices in different economies mean that technologies are employed more or less profitably in different economies.

In this case, we assume that specialization patterns follow relative prices. Abundance of a production factor leads to low relative prices of those factors. In consequence, they will be drawn on heavily in production processes, which will therefore be capital-intensive, labour-intensive, etc., in different economies. In other words, a lot of arable land leads to a presence in agriculture, large forests bring paper, building materials, furniture, human capital in the shape of knowledge about chemical processes in production result in a heavy presence in the chemical industry, etc. Note the static underpinnings again.

In the first approach, technological conditions shape the labor requirements in production and thereby the costs of production. Based on comparisons of relative prices of products, we arrive at the best possible specialization patterns for the economies involved. In the second case the resource endowment shapes relative prices for inputs, influencing where a given technology can be employed most profitably. Specialization patterns responding to these price patterns will develop once trade relations are entered into. As every economy can then commit its resources to what it can produce in relative abundance, overall production levels will increase in both cases.

Recommendations for where to focus one's economy are invariably focused on such status quo based outlooks in these static formulations. Do what you are already good at. Dynamics for change cannot be integrated into the perspective and fostering them would be inefficient, as this would divert resources to processes where, at that point, they would be more unproductively employed. In consequence, no country that has followed policy prescriptions in the afore-stated vain has ever seen substantial structural changes and a transition to higher value-added and more technologically advanced activities in its economy materialize. On the contrary, the countries that have seen such changes have all actively fostered the development of structures that were under-represented or inexistent at the outset of their development processes.

III

In a more open understanding of an economic system, allowing to integrate longer term benefits from trade, such as access to knowledge, or disadvantages from trade such as overbearing competition that hinders the development of technological capabilities, or the potential for a race to the bottom in labor standards and reimbursements due to the shift in negotiating power between companies and workers, an unqualified embrace of trade flows cannot be given, even though the general assessment of the potential for an overall positive impact is widely shared. Still, a momentary snapshot of assumed gains and losses in monetary terms is not enough to complete the picture of trade relations offered.

IV

As production technology is at the heart of the results above, in one way or another, a closer look at the nature of technology can potentially offer additional insights. This will allow to address the process of technological change, and productivity increases in production. We will reserve the last aspect for Chapter 4, when we discuss concepts addressing economic growth and its sources. Technology and its change, in relation to trade, we will take up in the following.

As noted, in the reference perspective, for one angle on trade-related questions technology is assumed to be given and distinct in each economy, for another angle technology is mobile and accessible in the same way everywhere. Resource endowments are fixed for both views. Technology refers to the techniques that transfer inputs into products. Technological advance signifies a reduction in unit costs of production, and hence easily identifiable improvement. Relatedly, investment in machinery brings technology to wherever the machine has been set up. Access to sufficient monetary funds to finance investments is the key to improving economic conditions, through the more effective conversion of inputs into outputs. Accordingly, capital can signify monetary capital as well as physical capital, and capital is what is needed for upgrading technologically.

We can also introduce technology into the analytical framework as the combination of skill and equipment, its change being understood as emerging problem-solving potential. It is neither only one nor only the other and cannot be reduced to either one. Activity becomes an act of skill if it applies tools, something becomes a tool if it is utilized in an act of skill. Resources are created in the process of technological change, as problem-solving capacities expand to integrate more matter than was possible before. Technology cannot easily be approximated by a capital term and cannot be reduced to an index number in one unit of measure.

Human curiosity and learning drive changes in technology. Curiosity and learning also lie behind the ability to participate in structures of a certain technological sophistication. Skill has to be acquired. In consequence, technology cannot be used equally effectively everywhere you might feel moved to make machines available. Upgrading production structures does not simply require access to monetary funds. It requires supportive structures to be in place to facilitate production and distribution, as well as complementary factors, such as a pool of potential employees to staff not only a production site, but possibly also the office jobs around production, for instance. Most importantly, it requires a framework of institutions that allows to operate technology, experiment and learn, and transmit and disseminate knowledge and skills.

Recombining skills and equipment is, in some way or another, the shape that change takes; more generally, we may speak of a recombination of ideas. This conception of technology embodies dynamics of change at its core, therefore. The potential for change, at a given point in time, depends on what has been mastered and is applied, at that time. Improvement depends on learning, in processes utilized already, or for introducing something entirely new. The capacity that has been reached is crucial for what else can be achieved.

Here is where contact to other economies and their techniques and technology can be beneficial. Instead of having to find something again that is known already, technology may be adaptable to local conditions. The embeddedness into a larger system permits an exchange of ideas and fosters the exposure to structures that may offer new impulses for solving particular problems. Drivers of change do not respond to monetary incentives alone. Within processes, material equipment has to be compatible with existing technology. If you cannot connect to existing processes, novelty is usually of little use. The path dependency of technological change can be reduced to fewer paths that are open for pursuit, and the options for those further down the ladder may be more limited, still.

Compatibility with existing institutional structures is also required for the ability to introduce new technologies, at an acceptable level of effectiveness, at least. Institutions, as you will recall, are the rules and norms that maintain social structure in a society, or group, structuring the relations of agents by constraining and at the same time enabling their interactions. A frictionless transfer of technology from one society to another may prove problematic at a given point in time, if values and social structures differ. On the other hand, exposure to different technological regimes may be supporting the overcoming of ceremonial structures and help an opening towards more instrumental institutional settings. The contact with other worldviews in general can have that effect, of course.

Another effect that emerges in this perspective is the fact that the value, of products as well as ideas and technologies, depends on the environment within which they are conceived and dealt with, yet again. Contact and exchange has to be structured then, viewing the protection of the livelihood of workers, without a detrimental protection of the interests of companies to maintain inferior structures behind a barrier to permit this. Technological upgrading requires structures in place to support the integration of new ideas. Neither throwing the borders open and potentially harming structures in place nor closing them down and petrifying existing interests' influence can be the sole guide forward.

Hence, with the potential to increase the spread of knowledge, improve material conditions, but also stimulate ongoing institutional change, relations between different groups, in this instance motivated by trade-flows, can be very beneficial. They do not have to be, however. Technological capacity takes time to acquire and without support it can prove impossible in the face of more advanced competitors. Economic relations can then be one aspect to enhance control of some economies over others, by barring their technological upgrading while profiting from additional market access. The potential to stimulate advances will have to be carefully supported, therefore.

3.7 How to Utilize Markets for Societies

I

Principal questions in economics revolve around the exchange arenas in which transaction are carried out, markets. In modern economies, these transactions provide access to the means and the goods required to sustain the livelihood of agents, and beyond that, cover wants and needs that result from their nature as social beings. For the other market side, they permit the continuation of activities that are undertaken with a view on the realization of profits, usually as a means to achieve other ends. On a societal level, markets are tasked with fostering an effective resource allocation and utilization in production processes, and ongoing technological improvements, based on the information they make available for agents via prices and changes in prices.

An increasing division of labor has allowed specialization and thereby productivity increases in production, and enabled the shift towards increasingly market-based exchanges. The rising remuneration of workers has created potential demand for the products made available, thus making specialization worthwhile. Need creates demand for basic goods, and we find outlets for curiosity, support for activities, and want that is stimulated with a view on social positioning in the demand for other goods. Motivations in and approaches to market exchanges have continued to shift as production and the creation of wants have become the main motors of economic activity. The shifts and developments in social values that accompany the changes of markets in a circular and cumulative causation pattern are a necessary part of the process of change we can observe over the last couple of centuries. Beyond the aspects referred to at the beginning of this paragraph, market activities themselves may send further signals and information, therefore.

How markets function thus has a direct impact on the well-being of the agents in an economy. What can be achieved through the organization of markets in pursuit of societal objectives, how to increase the potential to meet individuals' wants and needs, is a principal area of concern for economists, therefore. What potential hazards might come from relying on markets for achieving certain objectives, has to be addressed as well, though, at the latest once policies are considered. The different perspectives we have seen in this chapter, emerging from different approaches to dealing with the complexities of real-world market environments, offer different insights into particular aspects of markets, and sometimes different perspectives on more generic issues connected to market functioning. How markets function has been our concern, here. How our understanding of their functioning informs policy perspectives to foster the objectives societies pursue when relying on markets will be taken up in Chapter 5.

II

A starting point for us in this chapter was the question whether all markets are the same, in that they function in the same manner and can therefore all be analyzed using the same modeling framework, or whether there are differences in aspects of markets that result in, possibly significant, differences in their functioning. Following the distinction of top-down and bottom-up approaches in Chapter 2, we can find these reflected here as well. Markets are given by definition, or they emerge from individual interactions. In the latter case, shaped by individual behaviors, we expect to see differences in different markets. The goods that are traded have different characteristics, which can influence individuals' behavior. Such influence, in turn, can be reflected in the market dynamics we observe. Still, the current benchmark for economic thought is given by the postulation of the basic reference point, which guides people's thoughts about economics and economic matters to a significant degree in a number of societies. Perspectives and tools matter in analyses, but to some degree, the tools shape the perspective.

The 'laws of supply and demand' serve as the main tools for developing an understanding of this reference market, assumed to describe the 'normal' functioning of markets. There are, to be sure, some admitted exceptions, but these tend to be relegated to fringe markets, not particularly relevant for modern societies, or the prerogative of people who have more money than they know what to do with.

If this approach to market exchanges serves to capture enough of an economic reality to afford us an approximate understanding of transactions and their structures, then only superficially diverse issues remain in answers to questions of economic impact. The markets for nuts and berries, markets for smartphones, markets for cars, markets for financial products, or the market for labor will all be subject to the same general dynamics and, hence, can indeed be analyzed employing the same framework. Distortions in outcomes can be identified and addressed relying on market laws, giving people the proper monetary motivation to align individual action and social interest.

III

Assuming a bottom-up perspective, thus opening space for strategic behavior by agents, and the effects that open processes and uncertainty can have on behavior, for instance, does not result in negligible differences in results. Rather, fundamentally different perspectives and evaluations of potential and outcomes emerge. Allowing the possibility that individuals are not identical relegates the 'laws' of supply and demand to rules of thumb for some selected markets, for instance. The markets where they may not be expected to hold, furthermore, tend to be at the very heart of activity in modern economies and not limited to the fringes of individual activity.

Focusing on market functioning, to integrate the aspect of an ongoing process that is shaped by individual decisions, among other things means that agents cannot plan ahead being fully aware of what may come, but have to act under uncertainty. Once uncertainty is integrated into analyses, their scope and interpretations change. Where a price change in a perfectly competitive market relays information about the divergence from its equilibrium, under uncertainty it may be seen to offer information about others' assessments of future possibilities and developments. Agents can also react directly to others' actions, not only to the aggregate price vector they perceive. Temporary positive feedback loops become a logical possibility, and changes of the situation within markets become a natural part of market activities. Value can be created in transactions and may not be a given characteristic of goods. Price movements are then not deviations from some fundamental value but a natural part of market activity where individuals act under uncertainty. Markets in complex environments may be characterized by swings and movements as part of their normal functioning. Limiting the impact these effects have has been a long-pursued route of individual and collective action in market societies, in order to offer some protection against the volatility that individuals face in turbulent market environments. Of course, there can be reasons for price movements that are related to supply or demand conditions, or rather, changes, therein. But these are not the only possible causes. Furthermore, custom and habit may limit price movements for certain goods, but that is not the same as a given value binding the price for every good.

IV

The proactive nature of individuals who shape their environments means that a functioning of markets in terms of laws of demand and supply may not be feasible, and that therefore the economic laws derived in reference to the equilibrium established simply do not exist. That the laws of economics are man-made has been pointed out repeatedly, that they may in fact be made on a piece of paper, and mostly confined to said piece of paper, is not always stressed, however.

Regarding the utilization of markets in support of societal objectives, more careful considerations will be required if we consider the bottom-up perspectives. Changes in market functioning over time will have to be considered, in combination with an instability that can result. The exercise of power is still very possible, and if nothing else, then at least the labor market will require specific consideration. We may also stress that in an environment in which status is sought, market-based activity cannot lead to an overall advantageous outcome for all individuals involved. Within a transaction that is very well possible, but overall, for everyone moving in said environment, status-changes are zero-sum changes, as we cannot all move up the status-ladder at the same time. Actors may be negatively affected by others' actions. This may provide yet another impulse for ongoing changes. At the same time, developing consumption potential moves the aspiration level of individuals, so that at some point, additional welfare gains from consumption for well-being are unlikely to come forth, as the desire to keep up with observations about surrounding levels of consumption drives decisions, and the relative position will eventually likely matter more than an absolute level that may have been reached. Finally, where status concerns play a part, measures that promise absolute gains may be thwarted if influential agents suspect that they may threaten relative losses.

References

For the full list of references, see the bibliography at the end of the text.

Akerlof, George A., and Robert Shiller (2015) Phishing for Phools: The Economics of Manipulation and Deception. Princeton University Press, Princeton et al.

The authors explore the consequences of the insight that market interactions do not necessarily lead to improvements for everyone involved in transactions, because our decision-making allows consumers to be deceived and manipulated by producers and sellers of goods.

Arthur, W Brian (2014) Complexity and the Economy. Oxford University Press, Oxford et al.

This book offers a collection of papers by one of the first economists to explore in a formalized manner the implications that an approach to economies as complex systems have.

Beinhocker, Eric (2006) The Origins of Wealth: Evolution, Complexity, and the Radical Remaking of Economics. Harvard Business School Press, Boston

The author integrates a large number of concepts and approaches to evolutionary and complexity economics to provide the foundation for rethinking what we thought we knew about economics.

Bhagwati, Jagdish (2002) Free Trade Today. Princeton University Press, Princeton and Oxford.

The author presents an overview of arguments for free trade policies.

Bowles, Samuel (2006) Microeconomics: Behavior, Institutions, and Evolution. Princeton University Press, Princeton et al.

The author analyzes how the interplay of individual preferences and economic environment shape the economic sphere and its ongoing change.

de Soto, Hernando (2000) The Mystery of Capital: Why Capitalism Triumphs in the West and Fails Everywhere Else. Basic Books New York

The author analyzes the importance of legal property rights for capitalist economic systems and their expansion.

Friedman, Milton (1962) Capitalism and Freedom. University of Chicago Press, Chicago

The author argues that uninterfered economic activity is a necessary building block for political freedom.

Galbraith, John K (1958) The Affluent Society. Houghton Mifflin Co., Boston

The author argues that in rich modern societies, the notion of scarcity is no longer the principle problem of economic activity to address, and analyzes the consequences that abundance has for economic activity.

Hayek, Friedrich von (1944) The Road to Serfdom. Routledge Press, London

The author presents his views on the political dangers of public sector planning in the economic sphere.

Hazlitt, Henry (1946) Economics in One Lesson: The Shortest and Surest Way to Understand Basic Economics. Harper Brothers, New York

The author argues that, no matter how well-intended, economic policies that try to improve a situation for a selected group in economies will eventually make the situation worse for everyone.

Kapp, Karl W. (2011) The Foundations of Institutional Economics (eds. Sebastian Berger and Rolf Steppacher). Routledge, London and New York

The author analyzes the role of institutions in economic systems.

Keen, Steve (2001) Debunking Economics, The Naked Emperor of the Social Sciences. Zed Books, London

The author presents a detailed discussion of short-comings and inconsistencies of standard economic theory.

Keynes, John Maynard (1936) General Theory of Employment, Interest, and Money. Macmillan and Co, London

The author develops a framework for understanding an economy, which may not return to full employment out of its own dynamics.

Kindleberger, Charles P. (1978) Manias, Panics, and Crashes: A History of Financial Crises. Basic Books, New York

The author presents and analyzes financial crises over the centuries.

Marshall, Alfred (1890) Principles of Economics. Macmillan and Co., London

The author presents, systematizes, and expands, the state of economic analyses at the time.

Metcalfe, J Stanley (1998) Evolutionary Economics and Creative Destruction. Routledge, London and New York

The author discusses competition as leading to an ongoing process of change.

Minsky, Hyman (1975) John Maynard Keynes. Columbia University Press, New York

The author offers an interpretation of Keynes' work that integrates a number of aspects of that work which are frequently neglected.

Minsky, Hyman (1986) Stabilizing an Unstable Economy. Yale University Press, New Haven

The author analyzes how dynamics in the financial sector can lead to instability in these, and how that can spill over to productive economic activity.

North, Douglass (1990) Institutions, Institutional Change, and Economic Performance. Cambridge University Press, Cambridge et al.

The author develops how institutions and their change impact economic performance.

Ormerod, Paul (2005) Why Most Things Fail – Evolution, Extinction, and Economics. Pantheon Books, New York

The author analyzes why failure is common in complex systems, and what economics and economic policy can learn from this fact.

Penrose, Edith T. (1959) The Theory of the Growth of the Firm. Basil Blackwell, Oxford

The author analyzes internal structures and the performance of firms.

Potts, Jason (2000) The New Evolutionary Microeconomics – Complexity, Competence and Adaptive Behavior. Edward Elgar, Cheltenham

The author develops an approach to microeconomic analyses that draws on various economic schools of thought and combines them with the analytical tools of complexity science.

Prasch, Robert E (2008) How Markets Work: Supply, Demand, and the Real World. Edward Elgar, Cheltenham

The author presents approaches for making sense of market functioning in real-world settings.

Schmookler, Andrew B (1993) The Illusion of Choice: How the Market Economy Shapes our Destiny. State University of New York Press, Albany

The author illustrates how a market-based approach to relations cannot provide good solutions in a number of areas of life, and how it affects our behavior where relations are organized using markets.

Scitovsky, Tibor (1976) The Joyless Economy – The Psychology of Human Satisfaction. Oxford University Press, Oxford et al.

The author applies current psychological knowledge to an analysis of consumer behavior.

Sen, Amartya (1970) Collective Choice and Social Welfare. Holden-Day, San Francisco

The author studies group decision-making and what conflicts may arise, drawing on economic theory and a number of disciplines beyond that where required.

Surowiecki, James (2004) The Wisdom of Crowds: Why the Many are Smarter than the Few and how Collective Wisdom Shapes Business, Economies, Societies, and Nations. Doubelday, New York

The author describes how large groups of people can make better forecasts than smaller ones, if the structures for aggregating their respective inputs are set up properly.

Veblen, Thorstein B (1899) The Theory of the Leisure Class: An Economic Study of Institutions. Macmillan, London and New York

The author analyzes the impact of social and economic structures on individual behavior and resulting dynamics of change in socioeconomic environments.

Veblen, Thorstein B (1904) The Theory of Business Enterprise. Charles Scribner's Sons, New York

The author analyzes the role of companies in modern economies.

4

Unemployment as Economic Crises

Market functioning and function, at the individual as well as at the social levels, and the other themes discussed in the preceding chapters provide one large area for economic analyses. The entire economy, i.e., the sum total of recorded economic activity within a modern nation state, is the other central area of such analyses. Specifically, the overall resource employment instead of the resource allocation to individual production processes, or the changes in the overall economy-wide price level instead of the price in a single market, are among the aspects of concern. In distinction to the microeconomic focus on individuals and markets, this area of analyses in economics is referred to as macroeconomics.

A way to distinguish perspectives on such entire economies is also based on the general assumptions about the nature of economic systems. Some economists work with homogeneous entities, while others disaggregate the whole and integrate different groups with a potential to tilt an outcome of a situation to their favor. Some work with an equilibrium framework, while others work with a view of economy as a constantly changing system. We can continue to think of the broad perspectives in terms of top-down and bottom-up formulations, with the overall economic system showing certain given characteristics in

H. Schwardt, *The Path to a Modern Economics*,
DOI 10.1007/978-3-319-52785-7_4

one case, or with characteristics emerging from the, potentially diverse, behaviors of agents.

A central issue that arises from the different sets of assumptions concerns crises in economies. We will label the under- and unemployment of resources on the economy level a crisis. Perspectives differ by whether they are allowing for crises to be a normal and expected part of an economic sphere, even a potentially perpetual state, or whether crises are limited to occurrences that result from disturbances from outside the economic sphere. Put differently, we can distinguish perspectives according to whether individual economic activities are supposed to add up to a desirable employment of available resources, if undisturbed, or allow for the tendency of individual activities to produce crises on the systemic level. As will no longer be surprising, for the formulation of a desirable reference outcome, we have to assume that result already at the outset. In contrast, analytical frameworks that integrate processes and uncertainty point to crises as a normal part of economic activities, without imposing those crises as assumptions.

Both complexity aspects referred to in Chapter 1, complexity within the analytical system and complexity from the open-system perspective, can be found here, having been dealt with in different ways. The approaches that are set up so as to assume harmony and equilibrium by eschewing complexity within their analytical frameworks have to rely on actors outside the system that can influence and distort it for crises to result. More often than not, government fills that role. We focus on identifying sources of disturbances and try to come up with ways to limit their prevalence and force of impact. On the other hand, we find that approaches that integrate some of the complex aspects of our reality into their analytical frameworks tend to arrive at settings in which crises are part and parcel of economic activity in modern economies. The issues of interest revolve around how to approach the economic system itself in order to stabilize it, and prevent or at least limit the crises it generates; or rather, the individuals that form it generate through their actions. Note that at the beginning, we will address approaches that focus on a short-term stabilization of economic activity. For the long-term expansion, we will see that some shifts in emphases may be required.

Of course, whichever framework someone relies on, it shapes people's thinking about economic issues and their interpretation of occurrences, including the direction into which a search for causes is directed. How to ensure the overall objectives that all researchers share – finding ways to promote individual liberty by removing economic hindrances that constrain individual action in economic matters, and maybe even beyond – requires markedly different actions under views informed by one perspective on economies over another.

We will, again, make the least complex approach our starting point and benchmark. This is, likewise again, not necessarily particularly instructive for an understanding of economic issues, but indispensable for an understanding of current economic rhetoric. We will find the same modeling strategy as in the benchmark models of Chapters 2 and 3, in that the focus is on attempts to identify individual isolated effects of changes on an economic system, in order to identify regularities of influences to draw on for more complicated analyses. Underlying this perspective continues the belief in economic rules, or even laws, that could be identified in simple frameworks and transferred to a complex reality.

Where the focus in the microeconomic benchmark market model lies on the effects of issues, such as market structures, information availability, or the effects of subsidies or taxes, and thus on resource allocation decisions in markets, the macroeconomic benchmark focuses on the effect of government or central bank measures on the overall resource utilization in an economy. Questions more specifically revolve around issues such as interest rate or price-level changes, or the potential to displace private spending by public spending as a result of public sector economic activities, and the effects these developments may have on employment. Not that such aspects would not matter in other analytical frameworks. However, there they are embedded differently.

A better understanding of the system will offer some insights into possibilities for alleviating economic crises. In the more complex modeling frameworks emerging in bottom-up formulations, a clear-cut answer to questions may not necessarily be identifiable. Instead, answers will have to be qualified – the wider economic, technological, social, and political situation has an impact on the way the system functions at a point or over a period in time.

The outcome at the macroeconomic level emerges from the interactions of individuals and interest groups. How they can assert themselves, and what outcome results, will differ. Furthermore, the state of the environment itself will have an impact on developments as they unfold. Hence, predictions are not as easy, and confidently underlined with simple numbers, but have to involve more cautious statements and a certain ambiguity toward possible outcomes within a given time frame. The other way around, a clear-cut and continuous relation between independent and dependent model components is not typically a core feature in models admitting crises possibilities. Current circumstances become a much more relevant factor of analyses, and these analyses' translation into real-world relevance. As in the smaller scale focus, the environment matters.

We will see various reasons why crises may develop from a lack of investment demand on the economy-level, sociopolitical influences, competition between companies leading to unemployment in some indirect manner, or irreconcilable contradictions between business interests and overall societal interests, among others. Acute crises typically go back to individual activities that lead to an overall structure which cannot continue on the path taken to that point, not infrequently related to a modern financial sector. Crises may also persist as a more or less constant background that people have grown used to. While political interference and backfiring policies can always be a cause for disruptions, in the bottom-up formulations, crises can also be traced back to normal behavior patterns of individuals in economic relations.

The final aspect addressed in this chapter is that of economic growth and development and structural change. The benchmark model proceeds by separating issues as much as possible, such as analyzing economic growth without an integration of change. Where the notion is integrated that it is the structural change that drives growth, the equilibrium approach is lost, as even a description posing as explanation, is not gainfully formulated within an equilibrium-framework in this case. Issues that draw on a different understanding of technology and systemic influences and relations, within an economic sphere and in relation to the rest of society, are brought into focus. An open-system formulation results that directs attention to a combination of economic and noneconomic factors that have shaped the development processes. How countries have grown richer is addressed in very different ways under different perspectives. (We have already briefly hinted at some aspects in Chapter 3, considering different views on issues of trade that may affect technological progress.)

4.1 Money and Inflation in Top-Down Perspectives

I

Different ways have been pursued to assess an entire economic entity. A basic reference point that serves as the starting point and foundation for more elaborate models is firmly rooted in an equilibrium framework: set up an analytical system that allows to identify individual effects of particular changes, interpreted as the natural, and constant outcome of, or at least constant tendency following the original cause. In this and the following section, we will focus on two varieties of such equilibrium models as our benchmarks, one dealing with inflation the other with unemployment as their main focus.

A number of extensions can be introduced building on this foundation, and somewhat more recent demands on economic modeling itself have been set to replace these basic models in research, if not in teaching or communication with the larger public. However, more intricate and more recent model formulations are set onto the same basic understanding of the economy as the simple benchmark models referred to in the following section. The basic story lines for macroeconomic models in the benchmark approach take microeconomic thought into account when it comes to a motivating narrative, and most importantly the markets behind the aggregate economic activity function like the microeconomic benchmark model. Furthermore, the specific macroeconomic assumptions that have a noticeable impact on the model results, from the nature of the equilibrium to the nature of money, are commensurable to the microeconomic benchmark framework. Therefore, the constraints set by the approach to complexity reduction remain the same, even as model structures get more involved, and the way that model-building has proceeded has overall led to a reproduction of the results attained in the models limiting themselves to an aggregate view of economic activity. The advances in modeling technique, on paper as well as through simulations, not the effects identified, have driven this trend.

Micro-foundations have, however, proven to be more successful in offering additional insights where the macro-environment has not been as constricted with a view on effects that may be emerging from micro-interactions as has perforce to be the case when working in an equilibrium framework. (Remember our discussions in Chapters 2 and 3 about the structural requirements that a general equilibrium imposes on interactions). We will nevertheless return to, briefly, discuss the variations introduced to the benchmark macroeconomic models through micro-foundations later in this chapter, once the structure of the basic approaches and the results they present have become clear.

II

One variety of the models to occupy us over the following pages starts out assuming that a measure of aggregate demand and aggregate supply can be formulated for the entire economy. These measures are furthermore assumed to work as representations of 'real' demand and supply, as opposed to nominal measures that would be based on prices. The reason is that this way a change in prices will not be reflected in the measures of supply and demand so that these may offer a view on economic activity proper and changes in it, allowing to discern changes in the price level after changes in economic activity. Whether such measure is in fact something that can be constructed in a meaningful way, to allow logical conclusions to be derived from analyses built around it, has been thoroughly critiqued. However, the models and their components stay in use. This is true even when it has been established and acknowledged that they are not defensible because they are logically incoherent; problems of aggregation of heterogeneous components occupy a principal rank among problematic issues here. An example is the growth theory built around functions which have been admitted to be flawed and logically inconsistent constructs by their principal proponents by the late 1960s, an admission that has been ignored in favor of their continued application in large parts of economic research ever since.

Anyway, the point here is to have a look at the perspectives developed and the results they are interpreted to produce. For this, we will have to accept the aggregate measures of supply and demand. Aggregate demand is assumed to be increasing, the lower a price index for the economy is found to be. As a consequence, the aggregate demand curve is given for the preferences of the individuals in our model economy, and can shift as a result of income changes, whether real or assumed by the agents.

A distinction is made on the supply side. In the long run, the level of output, as described by our aggregate measure, is determined by the state of technology in the economy. All production factors will be fully employed, and the capacity to convert the economy's endowment of nature's resources into economically relevant products gives the real output attainable. The equilibrium that results in the intersection of supply and demand is unique and stable, all underlying markets must therefore be perfectly competitive. Otherwise, possible changes in market structures will affect the amount produced in those markets, and thus the overall equilibrium measure of output. The position of the aggregate demand curve determines the price index-level at which output is sold. In the short run, however, supply is assumed to be expanded when the price level increases, or reduced when the price level falls. We will take this point up in more detail momentarily. If the three curves do not intersect in the same point – the equilibrium levels of output and price index – an adjustment has to take place to bring short-term output to converge onto the long-term output level again.

The price index is a composite of the prices in the different markets in the economy. As individuals' preferences are given, the relations between prices are fixed in equilibrium. Assume that one table is considered to be worth four chairs in this economy in equilibrium. Whether these are then priced at four monetary units for the table, and one for a chair, or 20 and five, respectively, or 100 and 25, does not change the underlying exchange relation. Four chairs are the equivalent of one table. Preferences, resource endowment, and ability to convert resources into products translate into those relative prices. Money is simply a means for transactions, it does not impact economic potential, or economically relevant activities other than facilitating them. This neutrality of money jointly with the lack of possibilities to create capacities and change equilibrium production becomes a core assumption for the identification of influence-patterns in the top-down perspectives.

By means of these assumptions, there is, therefore, a unique and stable long-run equilibrium level to which economic activity returns after a disturbance, or a shock. You may recall the distinction of use value and exchange value that we referred to in Chapter 2, and will see that this framework assumes that use value is, in fact, ultimately the sole motivator for individual economic actions.

The term shock is used for describing any kind of disturbance to core parameters or variables in the economy, and may be affecting consumer preferences, the level of technology, prices for imported inputs (e.g., oil), or may be due to public sector decisions, such as an expansion of the amount of money in an economy, among other factors. Analyses employing this modeling framework offer statements about the impact that disturbances have on the price level in an economy – are they inflationary, leading to an increase in the price level, or are they deflationary, leading to a fall in the price level. (Disinflation refers to a reduction of the positive level of inflation.) The nominal price level is the indicator for inflation, the relative prices that can be calculated by relating nominal prices are the real signal of the equilibrium-value of different goods in the economy.

III

The long-run equilibrium is not necessarily assumed to really ever be reached. It is a construct that serves to identify what trends an economy may experience following a so-called shock. As the stable attractor in the system, economic activity is drawn toward it. Regardless of the disturbance, the system will eventually find itself on a path leading back to its equilibrium state. Even if that equilibrium shifts over time at any given moment, the draw toward a specific equilibrium is experienced in the system. Even if additional changes occurred at the same time, or sequentially, the trend that each of them triggered would be clear from the identification in the model framework. Their overall impact would depend on their relative strengths. The assumption of an equilibrium level of economic activity is thus, again, crucial here.

IV

The effects of shocks, or policy measures for that matter, are traced following the changes in variables after a shock has led to a short-term divergence of economic activity from its equilibrium level. We will address policy concerns in more detail in the following Chapter 5. However, the models are set up mostly to discuss the impacts of such measures on the macroeconomic level, so that we will have to include the assessment of effects of policy measures from specific model-perspectives at this point in some cases, at least to some degree.

It is possible for shocks to have a short-term impact because even though money is neutral, consumers and workers can be confused and not immediately grasp the full impact that certain shocks will have, while producers (or the producer part of their representative-household-personality) will be aware of any developments immediately. Workers adapt their supply of labor in production processes because they momentarily perceive wrong price signals, and producers hire them because they know the real price relations. A temporary divergence from the equilibrium output level results. Note that the limiting factor in production is almost always, in fact, the labor force.

Depending on the nature of the shock, workers assume that goods are cheaper or more expensive than they really are, in terms of what they earn, and react to the resulting supposed change in real wages (nominal wages adjusted by the price level, as a measure of what the nominal wage can actually afford to buy) by expanding or reducing their labor supply. Hence, changes in demand that result from a wrong perception of true price levels can be met because labor supply is adjusted in parallel. Eventually, however, consumers–workers catch on to the changes in the economy and readjust their labor supply and spending decisions. Activity reverts to the equilibrium level, even though at a new nominal price level.

V

Policies are introduced in broad terms, as fiscal policy and monetary policy. Fiscal policy includes all measures that are expected to directly affect the real side of economic activity, through changes in spending on goods and services. This includes direct spending by government agencies as well as measures working through an impact on people's disposable income, i.e., changes in taxation. If government spending increases in equilibrium, no more resources can be drawn on for satisfying this spending. If government demand can be realized that means the private demand has to be reduced in order to free the capacities for servicing the government.

Monetary policy is supposed to affect real economic activity as well, if only in the short run, due to confusion about the actual inflation rate that leads parts of the economic agents to over- or underestimate their real wages. Thereby, in this particular approach, it indirectly influences individuals' spending and working decisions. In the case of fiscal as well as of monetary policies, expansionary measures, leading to temporary increases of activity beyond the equilibrium level, only cause inflation, and vice versa, for contractionary measures. The laws of supply and demand, with everything we have seen going into them in Chapters 2 and 3, make it so.

Another example for a shock is a technology shock. A technology shock is assessed through its impact on production prices; specifically, it is supposed to lower the cost of production. As a consequence of this kind of technological change, the equilibrium amount of output increases at the same time the prices drop. (Remember that we are looking for the impact of single changes here, so that the downward sloping demand schedule stays fixed, even as the long-run supply increases.) This conception of technology, though it may appear rather unique, is common to the benchmark framework.

VI

In a form that we will encounter repeatedly, the relation of the amount of money in an economy and the price level in that same economy is formulated in a simple linear relation – as the amount of money increases, so does, proportionally, the price level. The amount of money can be defined in numerous ways depending on what is most suitable for the question in hand, from very narrowly including cash and quasi-cash in checking accounts only to very broad, including rather illiquid long-term investments as well. The narrow amount of money is determined by the central bank in the currently discussed view. For determining the relation between amount of money and price level in an economy, then, also included are the real products of economic activity, at its fixed equilibrium level, and a constant describing how often a single unit of money is changing hands in a given time period. With those two components given by assumption, price level and amount of money remain to be determined, with the price level assumed as the dependent variable, and the amount of money as the independent. Within such a setting, every change in the amount of money is directly and proportionally reflected in the price level.

The reason is simple enough – the overall product is given by the equilibrium level that resource endowment and preference make attainable. Any signal for an increased demand that results from the increased amount of money in the economy cannot be met by increased production levels in the long run and, therefore, can only result in price increases. The transaction tool money becomes more abundant, so nominal exchange demands increase, allowing price rises, and an increased amount of money eventually only means inflation; or, as the standard moniker would have it, all inflation is a monetary phenomenon. Note that this statement and the implications derived rely heavily on the assumptions that have accompanied us over the preceding pages. In more complex systems, or in fact, also in rather simple systems that include a view on money that is closer to what we actually observe in modern economies, the statement quickly becomes voided of meaning, or, at best, a truism without claim to an explanatory content.

4.2 Longer Term Unemployment as a Possibility

I

The other main reference point for macroeconomic questions does not concern itself with the impact of measures or shocks on the price level, which is therefore fixed, but focuses on issues of resource employment on the level of the economy more directly. Various equilibria are possible and a state of underemployment may be persisting for longer periods of time without a natural tendency to revert to full employment. If individual activity in markets may not be able to revert onto a path toward full employment automatically is there something that can be done about it? Note that such a situation is excluded from the aforementioned analytical framework by assumption.

The view of economies as automatically returning to full employment has no tools to offer an explanation for a situation that appears to involve involuntary unemployment. Either, people are unemployed voluntarily, because they feel that wages are too low to give up free time, or something interferes with the return to full employment (typically read, unions or government, even though analytically, employers may as well if they can influence their market environments). Within the framework of natural equilibrium, the only factor of economic consequence that can cause a misallocation manifesting in involuntary unemployment is prices above the market-clearing level. Wages are too high. As voluntary unemployment on a massive scale, as well as massive interferences suddenly forcing unemployment, appeared to fly in the face of reason and good sense during the Great Depression – the idea of a sudden mass appeal to the adaptation of a walkabout in the American dust bowl did not convince many people outside conservative economics departments – alternative possibilities for explanations were explored. The outcome of the considerations that will concern us from here on will be, in one way or another, related to effects at the system level that individual agents may not foresee, desire, or plan, but can in any case not easily overcome once they make themselves felt.

Our first approach toward the question of potential longer term under- and unemployment of resources, and thus lasting crises, adopts some selected aspects that have been raised surrounding the Great Depression analyses. The selection has been made in a way to stay compatible to the microeconomic benchmark methods as much as possible.

II

The starting point is the observation that investment spending is the most volatile aspect of overall economic activity. For the purposes of setting up an analytical framework, the overall economic activities are separated to cover consumption spending, investment spending, government spending, and a trade component consisting of the difference between exports and imports. Consumption spending relates to items that are directly used by the consumer and investment spending relates to items that are employed for creating future income. Consumption spending depends on overall income. The trade component includes imports, as a loss of income, for money spent abroad, and exports, as an income gain, for money received from abroad for goods produced domestically.

This composition of income focuses on investment as the main driver behind the degree of resource utilization. The basic assumption is that the interest rate is set in the financial sector. Investment in productive equipment takes that interest rate as given and adjusts to the level desired at that rate. Now, a market-clearing interest rate in the financial sector may not be set at a level that would lead to the full employment of real resources. Real investment at said interest rate level may simply turn out to be too low for realizing that level of employment. The interesting aspects in the model perspective are thus the interest rate and the factors presumed to influence it, as well as real economic activities (production and consumption) and their relation to the interest rate.

The central issue here is that investment is forward looking, undertaken for creating cash flows in the future. Depending on the expectations about the future, investment activity may then increase or decrease. As a side effect, this is one opening for systemic effects – if enough individuals are optimistic and act accordingly, their joint spending can create the advantageous economic conditions every one of them may have been expecting. If they are cautious, reduced investment will create the economic environment they were worried about in the beginning.

The model formulation that we are concerned with at the moment does not allow scope to actually integrate such a narrative. It is set up to permit the comparison of different static situations. Each of these situations represents an equilibrium that the economy would not leave without an outside impetus to push it. Depending on the level of investment, a certain level of activity will be reached. Equilibria that include high activity–high output ones, as well as low activity–low output, are possible. Government spending is discretionary, and consumption spending depends on the income realized. In the an-economy-as-a-household perspective adopted here, national income determines national consumption spending.

The analyses around this framework address whether the economy can be moved from a low income outcome to a higher income outcome, without, as in the previous case, just producing a short-term overshooting of activity resulting in negative effects thereafter. The answer already lies in the assumptions, of course – different levels of activity in different equilibria that a market on its own cannot distinguish between mean that, by the nature of the equilibria here, some other factor can be drawn on to shift an economy from one equilibrium to another.

III

The financial sector here is a market for money. The supply of money is determined by the central bank. The demand for money depends on the income level in an economy. For a given level of income, the demand for money increases with a fall in the interest rate. In other words, as its price goes down, demand for it goes up. For a given demand schedule of money, the supply decision then determines the interest rate in the economy. Money is needed to engage in transactions on a continuing basis as a buffer should larger spending items come up, and as a speculative buffer against suspected shortfalls of future cash flows.

IV

At the interest rate that the money market has determined, a certain amount of savings and investment are desired by individual agents. Savings are today's foregone consumption, in exchange for tomorrow's consumption possibilities. The interest paid increases those consumption possibilities and thus reimburses agents for holding off on more immediate consumption spending. The demand for investment funds depends on the mood in the economy, the better the mood, the higher the demand at a given interest rate. Here, the investment demand is satisfied by the available funds from the savings of people.

Equilibrium is described as the interest rate and income combination at which savings desired, being offered as investment means, and investment desired are equal. Two aspects are very noteworthy for us at this point, namely the assumption that the money market determines the interest rate in the economy, and the fact that savings are seen as determining how much can in fact be invested in the economy.

Economy-wide, there are numerous combinations of interest rates and income, at which financial side and real side of the economy are in equilibrium. For a given situation (mood, inclination to save, level of government spending, etc.), only one combination of interest rate and income results in money market and goods market of the economy to be in equilibrium simultaneously. These are the resting points of interest, the static situations that inform the analyses of measures and shocks, providing the starting point for subsequent analyses of the effects of changes and shocks. For given prices, changes in income are translated into changes of employment. The focus of analyses is interest rate and income changes, as well as considerations regarding the composition of activity. The last aspect is concerned with a potential replacement of private spending by government spending, a crowding-out of private activity by the public agent. The effects are assessed in terms of the income they generate. A crowding-out of private investment will thus take the form of someone receiving their income from another source.

V

Different situations can provide the starting point for the comparative analyses that are possible within this framework. In a situation of unemployment, income is lower than it could be because investment is only inadequately forthcoming. Expectations about the potential of investment projects are too cautious to merit spending at the current interest rate.

A low-level equilibrium of economic activity means that resources lie idle. Equilibrium means that the system as we see it has no way to move to a higher level of activity on its own. However, idle resources mean that higher levels of activity can materialize. Policy measures can be taken to bring the idle resources into the economic sphere, i.e., to give work to unemployed labor. Any measure taken, fiscal or monetary, can count on an additional factor, if it has originally been successful in achieving the expansion of activity hoped for. That additional factor is a multiplier effect. If policy measures increase economic activity, it means that income increases. In a second step, therefore, consumption spending will increase, increasing income further. As, per assumption, not all income increases are consumed, but some will be saved, this additional consumption spending is smaller than the additional income received from the original impulse, and so on. Eventually, a new equilibrium of income and interest rate is reached. The overall effect of an expansionary measure can be quite a bit larger than the original momentum it was given, although, it does, of course, not have to be. When actually implementing policies, it does matter where the original measure was targeted.

Anyway, in a situation of unemployment, a fiscal measure can have a positive impact on economic activity, and increase it. However, the measure has to be financed, either by borrowing or by raising taxes. As the point of the fiscal measure(s) is to increase spending and induce increased productive activity, taking money away again by raising taxes at the same time, and so counteracting the original impulse, is not the wisest way to move forward. Deficit spending is the way to go. To finance a deficit, funds for that spending have to be borrowed. This borrowing happens by drawing on the available pool of savings in the economy. The effect this has depends on the situation in which the economy is.

If the economy operates at full potential – the assessment of the situation was wrong and there are, in fact, no idle resources – then private investment spending will simply be displaced by government spending. The displacement does not occur in the goods market, but through a reduced access to credit for private agents. The amount of savings is limited, and we assume that people prefer lending to government. At full potential, an increase in governments' borrowing requirements reduces the amount of savings available for private agent borrowing and thereby reduces private investment activity. At full potential, increases in government spending lead to a full crowding-out of private spending.

Below full potential, however, that is not the case. As previously idle resources are brought (back) into the economic sphere, income increases and with that available savings. Now, the initial increases in government borrowing and spending will still lead to an increase of the interest rate and a reduction in investment. It will, however, also result in an increase of income in the economy as the reduction in private activity only partially offsets the increase in government activity. The initial spending impulse's income increase means that more savings are available, so private investment may not be reduced by as much as the increase in government spending.

The only situation where a crowding-out does not occur is when investment spending is severely depressed. That is, if the mood is so cautious, negative, or bleak that private investment has hardly been forthcoming. No private activity will be crowded out by increases in government spending.

VI

For monetary policy, the approach is to lower the interest rate so as to stimulate investment spending. For a given income level, and a given demand schedule for money that follows from it, changes in the amount of money lead to changes in the interest rate. As with fiscal policy measures, the effectiveness of monetary policies differs depending on the state of the economy. At full employment, increases in the amount of money have no impact on economic activity – you cannot expand further at this point – and reductions would lead to increasing interest rates, and a decrease in investment and thereby overall economic activity. In the underemployment situations in which fiscal policy results in a partial crowding-out of private activity, monetary policy does not have that effect on private spending. Reduced interest rates make investments more attractive, private agents get more active, the increase in available funds that result from income increases in such a situation means that nobody has to be pushed out of economic activity, there is no redistribution from an existing amount as savings increase due to higher incomes. There is, however, a limit to monetary policies, namely the region where fiscal policy does not produce a crowding-out. The reason is that here, investment does not respond to interest rate reductions. Therefore, the transmission channel of money market developments into the productive sphere is severed. At this lower bound, monetary policy loses its grip. It becomes the attempt to 'push on a string'.

VII

For identifying these basic scenarios for fiscal and monetary policy and their potential to bring currently idle resources into economic activity, a closed economy sufficed for the exposition. Opening the economy means that domestic products can be exported, increasing domestic monetary income, and imports can enter the economy from abroad. By assumption, the higher the domestic income, the more will be imported in absolute terms. The domestic currency is traded for foreign currencies in order to permit paying for imports. Cross-border investments are also possible.

In this setting, the type of exchange rate regime matters for the effectiveness of fiscal as well as for that of monetary policy. The possibilities discussed are the benchmark cases of a fixed exchange rate and a freely floating exchange rate. The starting point here is the case of a small economy. A small economy serves to describe an economy that has no influence on the rest of the world. Its interest rate is given by conditions in the rest of the world.

Increases in domestic income following enhanced government spending lead to a tendency of increase in interest rate. This is expected to trigger an inflow of funds from abroad, seeking advantageous investment opportunities. This increases the demand for the domestic currency and leads to a tendency for it to appreciate.

In a fixed exchange rate regime, the central bank will have to increase the money supply in order to counter that tendency. Monetary policy cannot be independent in this scenario. The central bank has to react to changes in economic activity as these can affect the exchange rate through their impact on interest rate trends. The money supply has to be adjusted in order to move the interest rate to where the demand for domestic currency establishes the desired price for domestic currency, i.e., at the fixed exchange rate. In the current scenario, the trend for the interest rate to increase is reversed, because of the increase in domestic currency. Remember that money is seen as any other good, in that its price varies with demand and supply conditions, and that there is a given stock of it in a given situation. An expansion of the money-supply results in a further expansion of domestic economic activity.

In a flexible exchange rate regime, on the other hand, the inflow of foreign investment funds does not automatically result in actions by the central bank to arrest their effects on the exchange rate. If the central bank remains passive, inflowing foreign funds result in an appreciation of the domestic currency – it gets more expensive for foreigners to purchase a given amount of domestic currency. This reduces export potential. At the same time, foreign goods get cheaper in terms of domestic currency. Imports increase. Due to the model setup built around an equilibrium, in fact, the reaction of income from external trade is just enough to arrest the potential impact of the fiscal policy measure. Again, we only see a change in the composition of economic activity, as the, presumably, private producers lose foreign markets, at the same time that domestic government activity has expanded.

VIII

Monetary policy leads to a tendency of a decrease in the domestic interest rate, in case it is expansionary. This triggers an outflow of investment funds, and a depreciation of the domestic currency. In a fixed exchange rate regime, the depreciation of the domestic currency that would follow is arrested by the central bank by means of selling foreign currency reserves. The domestic currency thus received by the central bank is assumed to be taken off the market again, countering the initial expansion of the money supply and any possible effects it may have had. As the depreciation is not the cause for immediate action under a floating exchange rate, and thus can be allowed to occur, domestic goods get cheaper in terms of foreign currency, and exports may be expected to pick up in this case, at the same time the imports get more expensive and will therefore drop. The overall impact of the trade component is thus to increase domestic income.

Overall, thus, for government spending, the result is thus that it can be effective in a fixed exchange rate regime, but not under floating exchange rates. For monetary policy, the results are reversed.

For large economies, where domestic developments have an influence on global interest rates, the effects lie in between those of closed and those of small economies. In fixed exchange rate regimes, the effects are actually the same as in the small open economies. For floating exchange rates, the effects are the same as in closed economies, albeit not as pronouncedly as exchange rate and interest rate effects counter the impulses of fiscal and monetary policies to some degree.

IX

As stated earlier, the basic model frameworks presented here have fallen out of fashion to some degree, as modeling techniques in economics got more involved. New approaches to modeling economic situations have been introduced in order to gain a better feeling not just for the global impact of measures, but to ensure the so-called incentive compatibility of them. That is, can they be expected to work in the way hoped, against the background of agents who behave according to the microeconomic benchmark model perspective?

Individual activities shape the state at the macroeconomic level, independent of the scope for behavior that they are granted in an analytical framework. With that point in mind, for equilibrium as well as nonequilibrium formulations, the importance for measures to be compatible with individual motivations has increasingly been stressed, whether that is a basic orientation of policies on incentive compatibility in smaller exchange arenas, or that is room given to considerations of systemic effects on individual actions, for instance.

As far as additional insights gained from these perspectives are concerned, however, the results have so far proven limitedly meaningful. The overall approach to complexity reduction has remained the same, meaning that the corset that the benchmark model provides has been maintained. Given the constraints in place thereby, a more explicit consideration of movements within the corset could not offer much in terms of an enhanced understanding of economic issues.

For effects from measures, the basic assumptions of either an economy in an optimal equilibrium – and hence no scope for idle resources that are involuntarily left out of economic activities – or an economy in which, at least, prolonged states of underemployment are admitted as a possibility, shape the results attained in analyses. Additional focuses, when 'distortions' in the economic arena are permitted as a possibility that may persist for a while, broaden the modeling space, as different markets or sectors may be integrated.

The division apparent in this and the prior section – are only full-employment equilibria conceivable or does the possibility for under-employment equilibria exist? – can be carried into a number of different detailed models, of course, striving to identify the general influence of certain factors. As far as models are concerned, you may introduce any kind of intermediate or external sectors in order to produce distortions, for instance. However, the fundamental systemic character constraining relations between model components, and thus the accessible space for results, is not altered.

4.3 Unemployment and Acute Crises as Normal Aspects of Economic Activity

The view reflected in the prior models and their embedding approach make them easily commensurable to the benchmark model referred to in Chapters 2 and 3. The modeling strategy is indeed the same as well: identify individual effects in the simple model and transfer them into the complex system one to one. Analyses that address real-world problems then draw on these mechanisms to tell a story of what went wrong and what needs to be done to counter it. Appearing to be going beyond the barter system at the heart of the benchmark market model, for the macroeconomic perspective, the notion of scarcity is expanded to the monetary sector. This sector is afforded a separate place, even though money is treated like any other good. With the notion of scarcity as the foundation of the models, savings have to be available to enable lending and subsequent debt-financed spending, whether public or private. A limited pool of savings means competition for access to it, and some of the effects identified are due to this view on investment and saving. Overall, the equilibrium concept at the heart of the model constructions not only enables their derivation but shapes their results.

The underlying assumptions guide us to a specific image of an economy, namely that of a household constrained by scarcity, engaged in barter trade that is helped along a path to extending economic activity through the introduction of a means of exchange, namely money. Money permits to sell something to person A and buy something from person B, and cuts out the need to find someone to directly barter with. However, as we have already seen when considering individual action and market interactions, at the systemic level as well, other factors may play a part or may emerge that are only appreciable under different perspectives. Once such effects are permitted in the analytical framework, results are more open, as we already saw at the microeconomic level. At the macroeconomic level, we will see that employment may well fluctuate as a result of normal economic activity and in a regularly functioning economic sphere.

I

Taking systemic effects into account in a bottom-up view, the view on income, and investment and saving changes, a different perspective on economies can be developed. The focus lies on an understanding of the system without demanding constant relations between factors as part of that understanding.

For a household, the notion that its spending is shaped by its income is inherently plausible. Even if you think in terms of consumer credit or mortgages to help smoothen spending over time or as means of investment, the scope for drawing on such options typically depends on your stock maintained from past income as savings and assets, your current income flow, and some expectations about future income. The household does not, however, simply will that income into being. It receives others' spending, namely governments' and companies', as its income. For households to enjoy an income for its spending needs, someone else has to spend first. On the systemic level, we therefore let go of the analogy of the economy as a household here. On the systemic level, spending creates income. Income leads to savings – in other words, investment generates savings.

Furthermore, the same decision, say investment, can affect potential supply and potential demand at the same time. The same is true for employment decisions. Companies decide about the degree to which they use their available capacity, and the outcome of their considerations influences the demand side in economies; not just as a move along a price-quantity schedule, but regarding demand composition as well.

Further, the actual way that a modern government spends, at the national level and in control of its own currency, is not by passing on tax money received or borrowed funds to pay for its bills. Rather, the recipient's account gets credited. Money is created to do so. Tax receipts at this level, on the other hand, reduce the amount of money in an economy. Incidentally, as accounts are credited in spending, banks' assets are changed. If attempts to rebalance asset compositions include bond purchases, then government spending may be leading to lower interest rates on these (bond prices and interest rates are negatively related), in contrast to the higher interest rates identified previously, in a situation where competition for a limited pool of savings got more intense with an increase in government activity.

Private agent spending either relies on funds received earlier and retained, or borrowed funds. These borrowed funds are obtained from private banks, who typically create them in the process. Private banks undertake the majority of net money creation in modern economies. They credit the borrower's account with the sum of the loan agreed. The bank offers a promise to redeem its debt through government-issued means of payment. Thus, it borrows from the central bank at the prevailing interest rate as may be required for its operations if need be. This interest rate is set by the central bank. It is a policy variable, not one shaped by market forces; even though central bank policy is, of course, not independent of the economy surrounding it. Monetary policy is conducted through changes in the interest rate at which the central banks lend money. The private banks' decision to make loans, borrowing from the central bank as may be required, then shapes the amount of money in an economy. Decisions to lend and borrow are oriented on lending conditions, the amount of money follows from these conditions, and agents' decisions of economically relevant actions. Instead of being independently set, the amount of money is a dependent variable that reflects the mood in an economy. Money and the investment means it represents are not scarce. They respond to the mood in an economy, but can be created as long as agents wish to do so.

The focus on investment, expectation-driven as the most volatile part of activity and government spending as stabilizing demand, is stressed in this perspective as well. What we do not identify is a struggle for monetary funds. Government spending does not take funds away from private spending at the moment it is undertaken, because the act of spending creates the funds. That does not mean, however, that there could not be competition for real resources, from inputs (say, building material) to personnel (say, engineers); however, note that persistent levels of general unemployment signal a general pool of people to be brought into work is available. Nor does it mean that government spending may not be allocated to areas in which competition between private agents may generate benefits. Still, the access to the monetary funds is not an area of competition. There is no given stock of savings that has to be allocated somehow among different, mutually exclusive uses. It may be easier to wrap our mind around banking, if assuming it worked that way, but this disregard for the facts of a situation can lead people awry in analyses, diagnoses, and recommendations for solutions.

Still, government spending may eventually prove to trigger inflationary dynamics, just as it may influence the exchange rate adversely. Such effects are not simply due to an extended money supply, though, but rather respond to the prevailing economic situation, real resource availability, and institutional factors with an impact on price changes, such as the negotiating strength of the interests involved in wage negotiations. There is no constant and automatic trend from government activity linked to inflation. What outcomes may follow changes in government activity depends on the situation faced at a given point in time.

II

Therefore, here, the amount of money in an economy is endogenous. It depends on economic activity and expectations of future activity. Contrary to the concept of money laid out in relation to the aforementioned benchmark models in the quantity theory of money, here, the amount of money itself changes through economic activity. The inflation-as-a-monetary-phenomenon adage loses its claim at offering an explanation of inflation, as no general relation of causation can be drawn from amount of money to price level. At the heart of the exogenous money view lies the contention that as the amount of money is increased the price level is driven up because of the additional demand that is created. More money is available, and unless prices adjust to reflect equilibrium relations, demand goes up. But money is neutral, the values of goods are given from their usefulness and so money does not have an impact on economic structures in the long run. In an endogenous perspective, however, what we see is an increase in the amount of money in response to increased demand, not increased demand resulting from more money being available. While increases in money and increases in price level may still coincide, the causation pointing from amount of money increase to price-level increase cannot be upheld. While that does not make the previous statement wrong, when taken literally, the explanatory connotation it offers is limited, to say the least, under the different perspective offered here. It may still be peddled as a truism, but the insight it claims to offer by suggesting a specific causation has to be discarded.

Of course, said truism is phrased with the idea of an economy in equilibrium at maximum capacity in mind. Therefore, there is a whole different view behind that statement on what can be acceptable in terms of complexity reduction for increased understandings of economic issues. For price increases to be a purely monetary phenomenon in any meaningful way, a rather limited number of situations arise in which that statement might in fact be maintained. The simplifications and restrictions required for constructing a situation that justifies that statement are numerous. When they are changed, the link between amount of money and price level, or even a causal relationship between increases of money and inflationary dynamics dissolves. Demand comes first, and money is created if needed to meet that demand. Price dynamics may well follow, but looking at the monetary component only misses the actual causations.

Allowing for money creation in the course of economic activity is more easily commensurable to views that see changing structures in economies as a normal outcome of modern economic activity. Institutional factors, such as provisions in wage contracts that automatically integrate price-level increases into wage increases, introduce additional aspects to bear in mind when approaching questions of inflation and its causes.

III

Before taking up uncertainty and its effects as part of analytical frameworks, we want to address a final point regarding money. This concerns the reason that money is accepted as a means of payment in the first place. That paper, or precious metals, for that matter, should be accepted among the people in a certain territory as a means to conclude a transaction, and allow it to represent a steady monetary value, is by no means self-evident or a natural occurrence. Standard attempts at grasping the establishment of money focus here, though – self-interested individuals figured out that it makes sense to have a small and easily transportable commodity that can serve as a means of exchange in order to move beyond a cumbersome barter system, eventually extended to carrying simple representations of tangible monetary units stored away elsewhere. As everyone understood this, everyone understood the gains accessible, too, and thus decided to follow out of simple self-interest. Precious metals are the first natural commodity to turn to, as everybody understands their value and wants to get their hands on them, or so we assume. Prices would adjust to some intrinsic value of the products, as well as the transaction commodity. That intrinsic value, however, proves elusive to pinpoint, as discussed in Chapter 2. That is, for a concept of money relying on the notion of reasonableness of having a means of exchange, the value of things being traded has to be assumed, and the acceptance of whatever monetary commodity has come to be accepted has to be justified by habit and by expectations that this habit will continue. The acceptance of paper money or other substitutes for precious metals drives this requirement of general acceptance and habit even further, and still further as the link from paper to metal has been severed in a number of economies by now.

If you take the time to examine old coins, you will at some point realize that they do not have a face value. The exchange ratio between them was decided by decree, as was the precious metal content within them, and could be changed at will. And again, there is no natural reason to accept such coins as a means of payment, other than custom and habit, and the intrinsic value of the metal, in this perspective. Once some people have decided to stop accepting the legal tender, the entire monetary system – entirely built on the faith that the money you receive for something, you will be able to dump elsewhere before everything comes crashing down, in this view – is in a latent state of failure, and may unravel, and quickly, any time once a critical level of doubt in its continuation has manifested.

For a more solid foundation for monetary systems, the following assessment has been proposed: The reason that money is accepted continuously is that it is accepted by governments for meeting the obligations imposed by them. Fees and taxes set by the central authority can be met (in fact, have to be met) using the legal tender defined as the monetary standard. As long as taxes are to be paid, people have a need for the means to do so. This will also work if government has monopolist control over some resources, say water – you get your daily needs and more covered, in return you need to pay government coin. If you want to break up traditional subsistence societies, by the way, imposing a tax burden has proven a very effective way, as well. Remunerated work instead of subsistence activity becomes necessary once such requirements have been imposed.

Note that under this perspective on money, government presence as an active part of economic activity is required because it enables the private sector to undertake economically relevant activity by removing doubts about the means of reimbursement in transactions. Without government, there would not be stable money, we may surmise. The role and function of the public sector expand noticeably beyond the stabilization of transactions through setting the framework and guaranteeing adherence to contracts by means of a threat of punishment.

IV

The volatility of investment is seen to be tightly linked to one fundamental fact of life – uncertainty. Expectations inform investment decision. In a positive mood, people are more willing and prone to accept higher risk and enter into endeavors with more murky prospects. At the same time, more caution is shown when the outlook is more pessimistic and reflected in people's investment decisions and portfolios. Liquidity concerns factor more pronouncedly in times of lower expectations, as the cash flows required to meet nominal obligations become, or at least appear to be, less certain. Buyers for less liquid assets are expected to be less forthcoming. Long-term investments that can only be turned into liquid assets with difficulty, and with threatened losses, are less attractive. Such caution is doubly warranted, as investments are more likely to fail at the same time that a requirement for cash to meet payment obligations may become more pressing. Too large a share – whatever that may be, will depend – of difficult-to-liquidate investments can become a threat then, especially as the potential to turn illiquidity into insolvency will loom larger in more problematic environments as well. If there are obligations for payments, liquidity is needed. The potential interest earnings of less liquid assets may not be deemed worth the increased threat of illiquidity. Hence, the more pessimistic the outlook, the closer portfolios tend to investments that promise to be cashable on short notice. A premium (in terms of foregone interest payments of longer term projects with higher interest rates) is accepted for increased liquidity. More liquid assets are typically not those that are tied down in production processes and carry the long-run potential of economies. Furthermore, with investment waning, aggregate demand is reduced. A darkening of economic prospects, and a concurrent shift of investment means from long-term productive to short-term monetary, reduce resource employment at the same time they reduce future potential as well. Not only is current economic activity reduced, but a destruction of capacities and loss of skill, especially in case of long-term unemployment, may result which might permanently be lost, and thus reduce the potential in an economy. That means that a negative outlook, brought about by whatever cause, can trigger a process of self-fulfilling prophecy, or of a circular and cumulative causation between expectation and observed economic activity. Furthermore, it is likely to impact the future path and potential of an economy as well.

V

Having mentioned debt, another aspect that becomes apparent that is very problematic with the earlier models is the suggestion to let price levels adjust freely to absorb the impact of a shock (in the terms of those models). Debt that is incurred results in a nominal payment obligation – if you have to pay 1,000 monetary units per time period to pay off a loan you took, you have to pay 1,000 units. Some scenarios in the previous models were addressed in a manner that suggested letting the price level in the economy drop until the relative prices that prevail in the unique equilibrium are reached again. By that point, the number of items sold to meet debt obligations will have to have increased for an indebted company, the more so the more it relies on current revenue to meet its obligations. Given the fixed equilibrium in real terms that underlies the entire worldview in that approach, such an extension of production is impossible, as a sustained move beyond equilibrium production is out of the question. Now, in that model world this can be rather inconsequential. Someone else will take over as the equipment and knowledge is available and can be profitably employed at the new price level by a new investor. In the real world, however, it is highly problematic to realize this, even without the general tendency of deflation to contribute to crises by letting people hang on to their assets and postpone spending to a later date when prices have fallen even further. Assuming price level adjustments to balance economic activity is not only standing on a weak analytical foundation, it can furthermore prove very dangerous for economic activity, and hence for the individuals that have to rely on that activity for their livelihood.

Cutting wages, on a broad scale, can have similar effects as demand will be reduced. In consequence, in economies in which credit and loans play a noticeable role in the financing of investments, and even long-term consumption good purchases, resources may lie idle if expectations about future monetary earning potential are formulated with caution.

VI

Based on the shifting portfolio compositions, integrating financial markets into the analysis can cast some additional light on the functioning of the overall economic sphere and potential problems resulting in unemployment. As a starting point, risk assessments are a part of the process of re-balancing portfolios. As the environment changes, so do risk assessments and the decisions based on them. Hence, they cannot be separated from each other. Investment behavior is affected and the composition of investments and of economic activity itself, jointly with its level, change. Agents influence the environment for other agents, and shape perceptions and expectations, through their activities. We had discussed financial markets in Chapter 3, describing how over time, in stable environments, increasingly risky investment decisions are taken, or investments are sought that offer a higher interest payment but are vulnerable to pronounced revaluations should the mood of a significant number of market participants change.

As financial market calamities that result if the market mood has changed at a time of high aggregate risk exposure may affect banks, a transmission of financial market troubles into the sphere of real economic activities is possible. At that point, production structures start being affected as well, as overall demand has started to drop because of various adverse influences reducing overall spending in the economy. Hand in hand with this development, we can expect an increasing difficulty for gaining access to credit for financing or refinancing investment, as more cautious banks reduce their lending in order to protect their liquidity positions. Once the potential crisis has taken hold in the real sectors of the economy, overcoming its effects has so far proven exceedingly hard for private agents by themselves.

VII

Debts, investments, obligations, etc. are recorded in accounts. Such accounts are also formulated for economies as a whole, to record and consolidate the overall positions of all agents undertaking economic activities within an economy, following the standards of double entry. Each entry shows up in two different accounts and has a matching counterpart (good and payment, for instance). The recording of activity does not imply anything about causation, but the relations between the aggregates from the accounts can stress some interesting aspects of modern economic activity, and some considerations regarding the plausibility of some notion or other may find support here. In some ways, these accounts may be seen as constraints for overall activity insofar as they show conditions that exist and cannot be broken, as identities, simply by being derived from the basic notions that someone's income has been someone else's spending.

A starting point here is a separation of an economy into three sectors, namely private, government, and foreign. Depending on their position, the activities of economic agents are recorded in accounts that are part of one of these larger categories. The overall balance for the economy has to come out as zero, as again, someone's spending is always someone else's income, just as someone's debt is someone else's asset.

If you discount the foreign sector for a moment, the private sector can only accumulate financial wealth, if the government is in deficit. Of course, private agents can hold private debt. This has, however, a counter-position as an obligation by another private agent. For net financial wealth to exist for the private sector as a whole, someone else has to go into debt. Without a foreign sector, only the government sector remains. As a consequence, net financial wealth has to equal zero as financial assets grant rights to the cash flow that is resulting from debt in the same amount. Real assets, on the other hand, can be accumulated, so that net wealth in an economy equals the value of the real assets held by the members of that economy.

Including a foreign sector makes it possible for some country's citizens to hold financial obligations by private agents in other countries. However, globally, private net financial holdings are still zero. Only government debt can create a net financial surplus position for the private sector. Then, whether government surpluses – signaling a reduction of private sector financial assets – are desirable is a societal decision, of course. In that context remember that not only is government debt not necessarily problematic, as it does not compete for funds with private agents; the government cannot go broke as long as it can create money for its spending obligations. Inflation does not have to result, either; although, of course, eventually it may. And as far as private agents' savings are concerned, government debt may actually be welcome in order for another option for the accumulation of private wealth to be feasible. There will be no absolute, yes-or-no, statement possible for considerations of these issues.

VIII

Changes in the external accounts that jointly constitute the balance of payments – principally the current account showing income flows, from trade relations and earlier investments, and the capital account noting current investment flows – balance each other out.

The current account records the balance of trade as well as the net income from domestic investments abroad. It also includes cash transfers. Overall, it thus contains spendings and earnings of agents engaged in cross-border economic activity. The current account can be interpreted as showing the change in net foreign assets held domestically. This interpretation is related to the capital account and what it records, namely changes in the ownership of assets, by recording investment-spendings. A distinction between real and financial assets is not undertaken; a surplus in the capital account simply means a net inflow of foreign funds and a deficit a net outflow of domestic funds. Ignoring minor accounts, and especially discarding a buildup of monetary (foreign exchange) reserves, that means that a surplus in the capital account has to correspond to a deficit in the current account, or a reduction of net foreign assets, and vice versa. The accounts themselves are not tied to any specific view on economies but are utilized by all of them.

In the reference framework, a core component is the focus on the individual. All agents engage in cross-border activity voluntarily. The potential to trade just broadens their options. As transaction partners incur costs in their domestic currency that they have to cover, foreign currency involved in the transaction needs to be exchanged for domestic currency. A current account deficit is then not seen as something necessarily problematic. The willingness to exchange currency for meeting someone's import wishes above their export potential can be seen as a willingness of foreigners to invest. The willingness to invest in the deficit country can be interpreted to signal a perception of a healthy economic environment. An export surplus, in turn, can provide the funds for investing abroad, at once offering capital that may be needed in other economies, and profitable investment outlets lacking at home (otherwise the funds would stay there). The focus on productive activity, with a very passive role for financial flows, supports the rather positive point of view. However, this basic view can also lend itself to ignoring problems, as the real estate crises in some Mediterranean countries in the wake of the US subprime-triggered crises have shown – contrary to the assumptions made, not all investment is productive.

IX

Traditionally, trade was seen as driving the cross-border flows of funds. However, this interpretation is being questioned now. As financial flows take a volume that shifts the money around the globe in a few days which trade shifts in a year, the influence of these flows on currency demand and thus exchange rates has increasingly been acknowledged. Financial flows can be the driver of trade. They shape exchange rates, can influence domestic income, and have an effect on cross-border transactions involving goods and services thereby.

The potential for dangers to national economies that result from fast movements of such funds across borders has likewise eventually been recognized. Funds that leave an economy quickly can have dramatic exchange rate effects, affecting the real sector of economies. They can leave turmoil behind in domestic financial markets, especially affecting banks, which then tends to affect the credit availability for producing firms. A distinction between investment in productive structures and investment in financial markets, or speculation more in general, is then an additional aspect to take into account, when assessing countries' positions and potential vulnerabilities.

The benign view on economic systems in the aforementioned models does not allow for a consistent integration of such issues into the models that are built to understand individual shocks or policy measures. For instance, were we to allow expectations within the model, not just the story surrounding it, we would end up with a system in motion, not the equilibrium structure in which economic laws actually apply.

Another factor that has become more prominent in currency markets of late, albeit more in some countries than in others, is attempts to build up currency reserves in order to be able to stabilize one's exchange rate, or fend off speculators, should the need arise. These reserves do not lie in a vault somewhere as stacks of paper. They are typically converted into interest-bearing papers, not infrequently, but not exclusively, government bonds. A principal purpose of these, being held by the respective central banks, is to allow a quick access to liquid funds to be able to influence the exchange rate when needed, not to provide a profitable investment option for private agents. Hence, government debts for which markets have proven to stay liquid even in deep slumps are particularly attractive papers.

A current account surplus is required for realizing such options. Not every country can run a surplus – someone has to run a current account deficit and thus be indebted abroad. Resulting trends may be particularly noticeable in the economy that provides the world's reserve currency, currently the US.

X

Allowing for systemic effects from the interactions of individual agents, combined with a change in the conception of money and its creation, opens a perspective on aspects of economic systems that do not have a place in the reference framework. In consequence, the view on the functioning of the economic sphere for the individual households also changes. Potential adverse effects of government activities in economic matters take a different shape than in the models previously discussed. They cannot be pinpointed as easily, and depending on the economic environment, specific actions may bring much-needed relief or negative developments. Again, the state of the system matters.

Given the volatility of investment spending, factors that contribute to maintaining demand at a level that permits to contain and then reduce underemployment are of particular interest. Government spending can bring those resources that lie idle back into economic activity. Trying to influence private decisions and expectations can likewise contribute a noticeable impetus to economic dynamics. Stabilizing consumption allows private autonomy, also contributing to the stabilization of investment, limiting swings of activity, and reducing the economic and societal costs related to these. Stabilizing structures to support demand can be put in place that can be drawn on government finance. Particularly, the so-called automatic stabilizers are valuable for this. They are called 'automatic' because they do not need additional decision structures for implementation, but take effect as soon as the economic situation deteriorates. Unemployment benefits are a prime example of such stabilizers, and thus serve as part of the social safety net, at the same time that they help to stabilize the economic system.

In contrast to the benchmark models discussed earlier, there is no indicator here that government activity would automatically lead to an increase in interest rates or a crowding-out of private activity. There is, likewise, no indicator of inflationary tendencies resulting automatically from government spending. Note that these statements are not absolutes. There will be economic circumstances, or levels of government spending, in which increases in spending have adverse effects, possibly in the form of reducing private activity or causing inflation. There is, however, not a general tendency of this kind linked to government spending. These statements follow from the way governments spend – by creating money – combined with the assumption of idle resources. The crowding-out result in the benchmark framework relies on the assumption that government demand for savings will be treated preferentially, and that the pool of savings to draw on is the limiting factor for debt-financed spending.

What further follows is that a budget constraint is not a sensible concept to approach government accounts, because tax incomes are not necessary for spending. That higher deficits today would automatically translate into higher taxes tomorrow is not true; even discounting the fact that economies grow and thus the relative debt level is the relevant aspect to consider.

To which degree government deficits could actually sensibly be planned is another matter. Revenue results from private economic activity. The procyclical nature of matching spending to that revenue will result in fluctuations that disrupt the economic sphere further, as well as other areas of public responsibility. It will also likely result in unemployment. A full-employment objective for deciding government spending, especially given the monetary systems of modern economies, may then appear a lot more reasonable. Basically, let the private spending fall into place and adjust government activity to pick up the slack. We may also note again that if societies want private agents overall to hold financial wealth, the only way that can be made possible is through government indebtedness.

Furthermore, the supportive and enabling presence of government in the economic sector also stresses its inseparability from modern economic activity. It is not only a separate entity that offers some things that are crucial to the functioning of exchange arenas and some that limit private agents.

Note, however, that the points regarding government debt and spending rely on the notion of control over money and fiscal authority lying on the same level of authority. Lower levels of government and national governments who do not control the currency in their economy cannot realize a number of these effects – they do have to rely on generating funds, through fees, taxes, or borrowing, in order to be able to meet their obligations. Banks still create money, but borrowing has to go through them so that they are in a position of influence. A divergence between the level of authority for monetary sovereignty and fiscal authority reduces the freedom that the public agent enjoys in matters of economic activity and introduces some problems as there may be no last resort to turn to for counterbalancing crises that have been brought about by private activity. However, provisions are possible through which funds may be made available to lower administrative levels. If that happens, numerous issues may be made to run more smoothly and in line with the tasks that modern states face. For instance, in the wake of the financial crises, US states bound by balanced budget laws had to cut spending. Public health programs and education are favorite areas for implementing such reductions – stellar ideas, in both cases. Costs get passed on to communities and individuals, and an uneven playing field gets tipped even further against the already disadvantaged, and so on. Problems get worse, the budget situation won't improve, and someone somewhere down the line faces increased costs – usually a private person who is rarely in a position to find help. In the longer run, potential is reduced; and again, we do not consider the moral implications of such decisions here.

XI

Note that for this as well as for the following perspectives, the integration of actual spatial structures or connections between agents can exacerbate unfolding problems. The spaceless connection of everyone to everyone else through prices and their information in the market sphere of the reference framework abstracts from the fact that different connections exist between different agents in real economies. This may make individual agents more vulnerable to specific trends in the economic sphere for instance. Being connected to some agents, integrated into specific networks or regions, means that some agent or agents within that network running into trouble may affect the other network members noticeably. Without structure, or working with average impacts, such effects might not be determinable. Linking agents may make them become apparent, though. The links in that case are the flowing funds between agents, as goods and services, and especially the payments made and received. When such links are interrupted, they immediately affect agents who have to try and find replacements for them. That may not be easily or quickly doable without friction. The time dimension again matters, as obligations stay in place and have to be met at specific intervals. Crises can thus be more intense in some parts of an economy, or may take their starting point in some rather innocuous corner, or sector, with ripple effects building as specific agents are getting hit rather hard due to a vanishing of some of their connections, simply because in real economies, the connections between agents matter and are not necessarily easily replaced or substituted.

4.4 Unemployment as a Permanent State in Economic Systems

Heterogeneity can lead to conflict where interests are not easily compatible. Such conflict is in fact at the heart of some other approaches to economics that focus more on the functioning of the system as a whole, including its dynamics to change without imposing constraints on the system itself from the outset. Though the effects in shorter timeframes can be addressed, a long-term orientation of some of the analyses can be identified. Also, economic activity as embedded in societal activity, and serving social and political ends of agents, plays a more pronounced role here.

I

In heterogeneous societies, how individuals act upon their different interests will influence outcomes in economic system and analytical framework alike. Possible effects from different approaches and actions on the macroeconomic level are what interest us in this chapter. In the capitalist societies that concern us, the group that offers a first natural focus as an interest group is the owners of business enterprises, with financial institutions a close second; or maybe in reverse order nowadays. The perspectives discussed over the following pages recognize crises as an ongoing feature and natural part of capitalist economic activity. Crises are seen as being due to the diverse interests of the groups involved, the power of companies to push for their advantage, and emerging effects on the systemic level from their interactions that feed back to the individual agents. The view of an economic sphere operating under clearly identifiable, mostly linear, laws of cause and effect is rejected. Still, patterns exist and can be analyzed. However, developments in the economic sphere depend on the agents, their relations, and the state of the economic environment, among others.

The objective pursued by businesses is monetary profit. In capitalist societies, built around private property, whoever holds the rights of use of particular production process-components gets reimbursed for contributing them. How much, is a question of negotiating power.

The development of increasingly intricate and difficult to acquire machinery means that at some point, machinery was not broadly accessible any longer, as was arguably the case as long as it was mostly basic tools that were required for productive activity. The current difficult accessibility translates into a scarcity of certain machinery. Even though this machinery embodies and is developed with recourse to the social knowledge fund, and therefore fundamentally is a societal contribution to production processes, the scarcity of the machinery itself and views on property result in a position of strength for the owners of machines. They can set the terms under which society can participate in the products that come into being with the help of said machines.

Against this institutional background and within the value system of capitalist societies, the decision to utilize machinery in production processes is a business decision. It is not undertaken with a view on what is best for the society. For the individual businesses, it may well appear most profitable not to fully utilize the production potential of their machinery, for instance. In other words, the owner of the machine may deny society the benefits of its knowledge by restricting utilization of the machinery in question. Some degree of confluence of interests will be given, as businesses produce to sell and require labor, but more than a partial overlap cannot be expected.

The monetary value of machinery derives from their expected earning potential; on this, there is widespread agreement. However, under the current perspective, this potential is not derived one to one from productivity, the ability to convert given inputs into a certain amount of output. It depends on the business's position in a market, as well as on the wider market, or general economic, environment. Protecting the value of capital in terms of its earning capacity may require that it not be used, at least not at full capacity (think of a monopolist, or oligopolist, for instance, who restricts the scope of servicing markets in order to be able to gouge prices more effectively). Again, the degree of capacity utilization in a production process is a business decision, not an industrial one. Full employment is incidental, at best, some unemployment, in fact, is useful for companies and normal. A glut from production resulting from full employment might depress prices and pecuniary considerations dominate social or economic considerations for businesses. The negotiating position of business owners is strengthened if unemployment is a real option. In problematic times, cutting costs, reducing production, and protecting earning's potential are the guiding threads for decisions, not keeping people in work and provisioning the community with goods.

The notion of a perfectly competitive market as a legitimate benchmark has no place here. Thus the attainment of business's profit objectives and a fully socially desirable allocation of resources coincided can be assumed to be a rare and fully coincidental outcome. The aggregate effect that the pursuit of profits by business enterprises in such an environment is more likely to have is a steady state of under- and unemployment as the regular state of affairs.

Extending the degree of utilization of potential varies over time, in what has come to be called business cycles. The notion that the degree of utilization of equipment varies already includes a basic truth – namely that during a recession, production potential is unaffected. But, from a business perspective, a reduction of utilization may prove prudent for pecuniary reasons. When the economic outlook changes and agents adopt a more reluctant stance in terms of investment and consumption, protecting capital value and profit potential may be achieved by restricting output and cutting input use. To maintain profitability, you cut costs, hopefully, from that perspective, more than revenue is affected, and thereby maintain your monetary profits.

More pronounced crises punctuating a general unemployment level will likely evolve out of the intermingled production and financial sectors. The cycle itself, under this perspective, is again credit driven, akin to the prior exposition concerning credit and bad debt resulting in fluctuations of economic activity (see also Chapter 3). Similarly, the more leveraged the agents are, the more pronounced the cycle is expected to be, as the increased leverage drives nominal values up, but as also, then, original payment problems by some have more potential to affect others through a negative impact on earnings and thus a reversal toward a downward estimation of expected cash flows. This results in business decisions to cut costs, leading to a reduced revenue estimate elsewhere, which will influence banks' lending operations, and so on. With business's dominance in companies' decision-making, a degree of separation in the decision structure, seen from a perspective of societal wishes, is introduced. The community may be assumed to desire the highest possible output at the lowest possible cost to meet its material wishes. Owners, on the other hand, may be assumed to aim at realizing profit. Whether there is a more short-term orientation to this, or a long-run outlook, has depended over time, with a noticeable shift to short-term outlooks over the past decades. Either way, a perfect confluence of business and societal interests is out of reach in real-world relations, especially where industrial production is concerned.

Introducing further degrees of separation between business-related and societal interests, an enhancement of short-term over long-term decision horizons has been affected by the increased presence of financial interests in real production, from managers to stockholders to financial market agents, with different views on the revenue streams they tap into. A distinguishing feature of these is indeed the time horizon of their interest in any particular stream of revenue. Therefore, we may think that as long as productive activity has been the predominant source of profits, a long-term outlook has prevailed for businesses, the shift to short-term outlooks being due to the influence of financial sector interests on companies and corporations. An intermediate level would be constituted by a management level in companies with, in tendency, a short-term orientation in their decision-making. Managing other people's assets does not tie a person down to one specific set of assets. Changes in position are possible. At the same time, reimbursement for management activities is tied to the success shown in them. Realizing profits remains the objective, but a certain front-heaviness may be reasonably assumed to be more compatible with incentives than a long-term orientation would be. Financial capital can move even more quickly, so that an orientation on financial indicators can be expected to result in an even more pronounced focus on short-term results. Financial sector activity results in redistribution toward financial sector agents. A more volatile financial environment for productive companies is an equally likely outcome, in which shifts may well not be driven by long-term considerations and soundness of business activities, but short-term profitability. The serviceability of structures is further removed from societal needs.

The overall framework integrates an open-ended process. The technological conditions of the time open the space for production, while the institutional framework delimits the space for the distribution of the resulting product. There are no basic economic laws governing the economic sphere and activity therein; which does not mean that economic agents would not face certain constraints. There are human motivations, and the institutional framework inspiring where efforts are directed, and technological conditions shaping how they may be realized. Technological and institutional conditions, stabilizing a complex system of social interactions, influence the actual workings and scope for working of the system. Economic factors introduce constraints for the scope of activities. These conditions, and the system itself, therefore, change over time. The process of change does not respond to given and constant higher systemic constraints, its path is created as it moves along, in the interplay of technological and institutional forces and provisions and agents' dealings with them, in creative and strategic ways. For example, the development of a financial sector and the rules put in place for the interests of financial sector agents, and the other economic agents they interact with, have shaped the development of economic activity. Their impact was not only on patterns of distribution but also, for instance, on the state of production capacities and the foundation for further changes in technological capacity, whether permitting large-scale and long-term investments by making more capital available to potential investors, or shifting an outlook toward short-term activities oriented more toward immediate financial indicators.

Stabilizing the system through government activity is a definite possibility. However, the danger of government agents collaborating with influential private agents is clearly recognized here as well. The overall outlook for structuring the system is directed to inclusive political structures, therefore, and the availability of tools for individuals to make informed decisions. This is a part and outgrowth of the analytical framework here, not an add-on mirroring political preferences of the researcher.

II

Setting the financial sector aside, for a moment, the distinctive feature of capitalist production is that agents buy things that they then process, in the hopes of selling the product at a price that leaves a profit. In earlier economic systems, people produced something that they traded directly, or sold in order to buy something else they needed. Now, the production for money and profit is what drives the system, and is also what motivates changes. The profit motive embedded in a social structure awarding recognition and status on the basis of pecuniary potential, makes for a very powerful driver in fact.

As money is the objective in economic activities, how it is distributed among the different groups participating in the production process is a, at least potential, source of contention. The two principal groups under the current perspective are the workers and the owners of the machinery and equipment. As in the view discussed in the preceding section, machinery is understood to be scarce and access to it limited. The two principal areas of the resulting conflict involve the access to and the distribution of the profit that can be and is realized in production and subsequent activities. Put differently, the struggle between workers and capitalists about the distribution of the value that is created in production processes is one area of societal struggles, the struggle among capitalists when attempting to strengthen and expand their positions over time is the other one. In their effects on economic activity, and especially in their role as the factors that motivate actions which result in – ever-worsening – acute crises, they complement each other.

More precisely, not just the actual amount of profit realized is assumed to matter, but the rate of profit realized, the interest gained on your investment, is broadly interpreted. The profit rate is revenue minus cost, divided by cost. Cost consists of principal capital outlays and wages. Increasing the profit rate can thus work by increasing revenue without an overproportional increase in cost, as well as through a decrease in cost without an overproportional decrease in revenue. In turn, there are various ways open for an individual business to increase its profits by influencing components of these respective categories. Cutting labor cost is typically particularly attractive. A tendency toward the concentration of business is identified as well, as consolidation and takeovers are one way for arresting the reduction of profit rates. If, however, profit rates are too low – compared to a normal or usual rate, or compared to expectations, or some other influence factor – investments can be curtailed. The realization of profits motivates agents, and under this perspective they can earn substantial profits. If they do not, or expect that they will not, they can reduce their spending. This spending is not redirected elsewhere, however, but is, at least temporarily, withdrawn from circulation and productive structures. The shortfall in demand that results is mirrored in overproduction, and eventually a reduction in employment. The distinction between use value and exchange value again helps to understand the idea. While the workers are motivated to engage in transactions by a higher acquired use value of the goods compared to the labor power that they sell, the investing agents are motivated by increasing the exchange value they control – earning profits, where the use value of money is zero. Unless we believe that in the face of an economic crisis, the set of motivations for these investors, or capitalists, changes, so that they start spending their money on consumption goods instead of investing it, a shortfall in demand results when profit potential is deemed too low.

Over time, the intensity of acute crisis is expected to become more pronounced as the concentration in resource control and employment means that once a business is hit, the resulting impact is likely to be more noticeable. A tendency toward a concentration, or monopolization, is something we do observe. From the desire to establish an increased control over an environment, to technological attributes of production processes, and the impact of planning and other organizational issues, a number of factors combine to make a concentration of businesses a normal outcome of economic activity. Being able to inflate profits, monopoly business structures generate a continuous surplus. Aiming at maintaining rates of profits, there is limited productive investment potential, and thus an unemployment of resources, and, particularly, labor. Profits go to economically wasteful outlets, in marketing efforts, military spending, or an inflation of financial asset prices.

The combined effect of efforts by profit-driven businesses will result in sharpening the economic crises. These sharpening punctual crises will be emerging from a background of the crisis environment of persistent unemployment. In the short run, this background benefits owners of capital as a certain level of unemployment is advantageous, strengthening their negotiating position and allowing them to depress wages. Should unemployment drop to the point where workers can effectively negotiate higher income shares, the commensurate drop in the profit rate will lead to businesses folding, as their expectations are not met, releasing laborers into unemployment again, and reversing the negotiating positions the different groups hold.

The struggle to maintain a certain rate of profit is carried out on the level of the individual economic undertaking. It is the systemic effect that these result in, which triggers punctuations in an ongoing environment of crisis. In principal, the problem's manifestation is seen to lie on, or at least integrate, the demand side of the economy, inadequate to absorb the full potential production in economies. The impetus comes from the production side, though. The various routes open toward increased profit rates for businesses invariably weaken the demand side of an economy. The more business owners follow that particular route, the more likely it becomes that they will jointly produce an impact on the level of the economy as a whole. The struggle over the distribution of value created is resolved in favor of the capital owners. As a consequence, on the systemic level, the purchasing power required in the system for generating revenue drops because the demand side has been weakened. The systemic impact, brought forth by the cuts in spending on the business side that are reducing available income on the worker side, is translated into reductions in aggregate demand. Once cost has been cut enough, the impact on aggregate spending it develops will reduce revenue, and hence, profit, and the rate of profit. Consolidations of businesses and other measures to counteract the fall in profits will ensue, momentarily driving up unemployment rates and misery further than before.

The pressure on wages is further enhanced by the competition among businesses. Cost advantages and product differentiation are means to avoid having to fold in this game. Technological change is particularly attractive if it results in a reduction of employment requirements, so that the way of using technological change in order to strengthen one's profit position is likewise prone to contributing to a sharpening of the crisis environment, as the tendency toward depressing demand is strengthened. The technological changes that enable a strengthening of one's own position (or, are hoped to achieve just this) are preferably labor saving, as wages make up the largest share of cost in most businesses. Cutting wage rates and reducing labor requirements together can be expected to be exacerbating the demand side constraint potentially faced by producers.

The process takes on a dynamic that feeds on itself to some degree, as the existence of unemployed workers strengthens the negotiating position of those who seek to hire labor. In the extreme, wages can be driven down to subsistence levels because the alternative is not a better paying job elsewhere, as the benchmark labor-market view would have it, but the misery of unemployment (in its depth, dependent on possible social policies in place, of course, at least where material aspects are concerned). Again, the more threatening that perspective is made, the more advantageous the negotiating position for owners of capital. Power is a core aspect of all areas of social relations. Struggles for power in the economic realm drive technological and material changes. Power exercised in the economic realm makes the livelihood of workers more precarious and risky. The political system has been employed to counterbalance such use of private power, and for alleviating those risks effectively in some economies, especially in the post–World War II era. Currently, a back-swing toward the interests of owners and financial market agents seems to be playing out.

Reductions in domestic purchasing power can for a while be compensated by seeking access to external markets. External markets can thus serve as a temporary escape valve. However, as markets for industrial products from more powerful countries, the target countries are typically not allowed to offer direct competition to the core countries' producers. They tend to be limited to supplying raw materials and basic products, aspects of the value-added chain that are no longer profitable enough to capture the interest of producers in the core, at least not at a particularly noticeable scale. We can note that with advances in technology, production processes have changed, however, so that even though we have, for instance, an agricultural product at the end of the chain, the process of production may be industrialized. Some distinctions are blurred as a result.

Rules of international trade, including such aspects as intellectual property rights, are here interpreted as geared toward supporting the position of those producers who are already established. That countries have in general only ever embraced free trade rhetorics once their production forces established strongly competitive and leadership positions can be an indicator that this view is not without merit. Concurring with the previously discussed approach, nation states are viewed critically here as well. The rhetoric of nationalism and its handmaiden patriotism are best seen as being employed for convincing those who profit little from societal arrangements that there was a larger cause behind said arrangements that offered an advantage to them, albeit on a nonmaterial level. At the same time, the interests of owners of capital, or business, are offered a concept that helps disguise calls for measures to serve their own narrow interests, protecting them from outside influences, as serving the larger cause, i.e., the nation. Governments tend to serve capital, or business, interests over the broader interest of the population as a whole. The utilization of the political sector may have arrested and even countered such developments to some point for a while, but there is no reason to assume that process was not reversible.

With an increase of oligopoly and monopoly structures, the profits, or surpluses that companies, or capitalists, can expropriate have increased to a degree where it is difficult to find productive outlets. Product differentiation and shortened product life cycles – with replacements offering hardly if any advantage in use value – are supported by increased spendings on marketing measures. From a societal perspective, such outlays may be considered wasteful. As the embeddedness of economic activity in societal structures is part of this analytical perspective, it can easily integrate different interests regarding government presence and actions, as well. For instance, employing surplus for spendings with a societal purpose, such as education, health care, or housing, may be felt to threaten dominant interests, while an outlet in military spending may not. Not only does the military, not uncommonly, provide a large and stable spending block in economies, its utilization may also ease access to resources and new markets. Finally, private credit in order to create market segments that the general wage structure bars may be expected to be stimulated, even as it comes at the cost of an increased risk of future instability.

4.5 Change, and Turbulence, as a Normal and Ongoing Outcome of Economic Activity

I

Competition among business enterprises is the main driver of change in the following perspective as well. The owner of the business enterprise, as an entrepreneur, is the initiator of change in capitalist systems here. Social success in capitalist societies is awarded on the basis of financial success. Other, older hierarchical structures may still be discernible – such as deference to people among whose forebearers were some specimen particularly proficient at raping and pillaging and soon found themselves on the road to a hereditary title and assorted boons – but that does not change the fact that in capitalist value systems, money matters. Particularly ambitious members of society are thus drawn to business, or to making money in general, as especially financial sector activity has become increasingly promising, over the last few decades.

A trait that is uniting ambitious members of societies, across time and space, is the willingness to take risks. This willingness is important for gaining access to the potential rewards from business activities as well. The change of economies depends on the willingness of its members to take risks, with structures in place to reward such willingness as well. This is not a constant feature of societies, and may change over time. Also note that this process has to rely on the availability of inventions that can be turned to an economic utilization. The source of inventions in modern economies is very frequently government funded research, although the marketing of ideas is then usually left to private agents.

In businesses, change is undertaken under uncertainty and is thus risky to introduce. Such changes include innovations and technological changes – in the wide sense of problem-solving abilities – brought to economic use. They are a key for gaining advantages over competitors. The willingness to take the risk to try something new – untried before, by definition – will, if successful, be rewarded by profits; and in the best of circumstances by control over a market or market niche that did not exist before. Competition is seen as competition for markets, more than competition in markets. In fact, the avoidance of competition in markets, especially through prices, can be a major motivator for trying to innovate. Innovation is not limited to new product classes, it can also involve the introduction of new ways for making something known, in terms of new processes and new components (say, replacing a natural input with an artificial one), or new ways of organizing production processes (such as a just-in-time production). Additionally, the main factor for increasing the output from known production processes are so-called process innovations, tweaks in the way things are done that over time have a noticeable cumulative impact on the effectiveness of operations.

Under this perspective, the introduction of novelties, motivated by enhanced profit opportunities, improves conditions in society as the technological standard is further elevated. Unless the product was deemed desirable, there would be no customers. Customers by assumption are aware of their interests and choose accordingly. Enhanced choices mean improvements for them. Note that at the same time, demand is created. Supply comes first, and demand follows. This has sometimes been admitted to also allow for the managing of demand to some degree. However, overall, bad products are expected to be leaving markets again fairly soon. The potential for managing demand that is recognized does nevertheless point to a stronger position for the business side, and as business interests and societal interests do not fully overlap, but only partially, there is no reason to assume a generally desirable outcome to result. (As an example, think of heavy water and breeder reactors, the heavy water ones having been produced only as a prototype, originally, as the amount of waste they produce is tremendous. Faced with the threat of losing business throughout the world, these were then pushed into markets, before the much less waste-intensive breeders had been given the final touches.)

When it comes to changes in production processes, cost advantages are the indicator for success. These can also signify improvements, when resource intensities in production are reduced. Overlapping issues, such as quality improvements, for instance, can likewise be an outcome, of course, especially if they improve competitive and profit positions of companies. Overall, innovations result in more effective production processes, thus increasing productivity, and in new production processes, both of which increase the value-added in production. As increased value-added tends to be reflected in increased wages, more demand potential is created in the process as well, eventually raising all boats in a circular and cumulative dynamic of change.

On a larger time scale, some major innovation eventually finds backing and is introduced to the economic sphere. This either opens up an entirely new field, or replaces an existing production structure. Not uncommonly, in the course of the process, a combination of both is discernible. If new sectors are created, to some degree, purchasing power will be drained from older sectors. If new processes are introduced to compete with already existing ones, older processes are endangered.

Either way, a replacement of older activities by newer ones is an expression of the dynamics of capitalist systems.

Imitators are presumably attracted by the profit potential of innovations and try to follow an innovative leader. Also, eventually, related products are introduced and other new markets are thereby created. However, as more imitators flood in, the field gets crowded over time, and additional related markets may become harder to identify and define, in a process that is overall reducing profit opportunities. However, improvements in technology are still possible, making production cheaper and the product better, and can sustain existing profits to some degree. Eventually, the tweaking and shaping also runs into increasingly more effort requirements. Growth starts to dwindle until the next major innovation takes hold.

Technological changes that have more of an impact – that open many related markets and are applicable in a number of different fields – result in more pronounced upswings and longer cycles. For minor changes the impact is more reduced and the cycle shorter. Major and minor innovations overlap, and in their overlapping and their impact on other, older sectors, economic cycles are generated.

The recovery period of activity is the moment at which there is actually space for a new generation of innovators, or entrepreneurs, to enter and find financial institutions willing to put money into new and untried endeavors. Resistance by formerly dominant interests is assumed to be lowest here. The downswing will then weed out bad ideas. In a stable environment, the establishment of novelty in the economic sphere is assumed to be much harder to achieve, as existing interests can more comfortably fight back, and investors may be less willing to commit funds to innovative enterprises. For continued technological changes, the upheaval that economic downturns bring is thus seen as extremely helpful, if not necessary. Intervening in cycles may appear to be a good idea in the short run, but hinders the dynamics of the systems and thus will lead to lower standards of living in the medium and long run. It will also likely result in a petrification of social structures, as the control of existing businesses is not as fluid as under the possibilities for changes that new businesses bring.

In other words, innovation can put other businesses in a precarious position. Within markets, a cost disadvantage might result, positions of competitors in related niche markets may grow stronger, and among sectors, some products may find themselves replaced by others, with businesses losing their customer base in the process. Structural change, in the sectorial composition of economic activity, moving away from the primary sector, and within industrial and service sectors, results. Not uncommonly these development dynamics involve crises as existing businesses go under. Still, given the concept of innovations, even though crises are accompanied by hardship for those in old sectors or those employing outdated production processes, those who lose out should step aside to make room for the new. Hindering a crisis from running its course means an interference with the possible improvements at its end, as the hindrance in one way or another consists of support for those affected – the outmoded producers. If other economies are more willing to allow the 'creative destruction' of their overcome structures, additionally, a loss of position follows a loss of competitiveness vis-à-vis other economies, if there is more willingness or capacity to permit the innovations in questions to take root.

II

The result is a view on business cycles in this perspective that differs noticeably from a view proposed against the background of the benchmark models introduced first in this chapter. In the approach taken there, economies tend to form an equilibrium. Should that equilibrium be reached, no more changes in activity occur unless some parameter changes, as an external shock, which leads the system to a new equilibrium through the dynamics it triggers. As the result of a shock is a reallocation of production factors, a possible divergence from full employment can occur in its wake. Business cycles, in this regard, are a result of shocks affecting the economy. These shocks are either caused by misguided policy measures or by changes in the demand patterns of agents. They may also work through the supply side, as the result of technological changes that directly affect production structures, or lead to changes in the relative prices of inputs. Cycles are not a normal part of economic systems in this view, however. Shocks causing them lie outside the system.

One problem with this view is that uncorrelated shocks do not lead to cyclical movements but stasis. Think of someone sitting on a swing who receives a push at infrequent intervals, not at the high point of the backswing. Some pushes will counter the momentum of the moment, others will move in the same direction so that only a part of the energy will be transmitted. A continued swinging motion will not result. External shocks are therefore not appropriate explanations for a system in motion, as recorded economic activity appears to be. If business cycles are thought to exist, shocks are not suitable for explaining them. Whether the equilibrium concept is static as in the previously mentioned benchmark models, or one of an equilibrium growth path, describing the growing production potential of economies, is not particularly relevant for this point.

The following approaches in this chapter tie the financial sector into the model as a separate sector of economies. To give the concept substance, eventually, the uncertainty of agents is acknowledged and integrated into the framework as uncertainty, and not reduced to risk; even though we may refer to the underlying attitudes of agents involved in such activities to be risk-taking, in colloquial terms. Financing undertakings under uncertainty requires the formulation of expectations, including potential supply and demand conditions, as well as possible competing endeavors. Expectations and access to credit, or external funds, more generally, matter for implementing innovative measures.

Expectations change over time, along with the behavior affecting resource employment. The credit exposure of agents, as laid out earlier, can mean that some cannot meet their financial obligations and go out of business. Both aspects may trigger effects that reinforce a persisting trend. For a negative reinforcement, for instance, in terms of demand-side effects we may find agents reducing their spending on consumption and investment, which may also trigger, depending on the view adopted, supply-side effects that result from business's decisions to restrict their output, or, rather, their input employment. Mood swings, demand effects, and business decisions together result in changing levels of employment.

Expanding even further, this process plays out against the background of an economic system that is constantly changing due to the very individual actions taken within it. People's strife for social recognition, by means of economic success in capitalist societies, pits them against one another, and may introduce more egoistic motivations, to the detriment of the success of the larger group. Changes in employment are the outcome of normal economic behavior, as this behavior results in structural changes that in turn bring changing levels of employment. Another part of the general background is the persistence of an ongoing crisis that may be punctuated by more acute negative developments due to an overexposure to credit-derived risk, or to technological changes that have an impact on employment and thereby on the overall demand realized in an economy.

Complementing these views, we found an approach that focuses on innovation as the cause of structural change that drives growth. Social recognition motivates individuals to assume the risks related to innovative endeavors. That innovation, in turn, means that we do not simply observe an expansion of and within existing structures, but a change in the structure itself. The concept of technology integrated into this analytical framework is that of a combination of skill and equipment. Skill is shown in the execution of activity using equipment, and things become equipment if they are employed in acts of skill. Resource endowments, in extension, are not static but a function of technological capacity. Iron ore, for instance, is of no use until you know how to process it and then what to do with the result. Both skill and equipment are components that a financial measure of capital cannot adequately capture, much less changes in them. Learning as the process behind such advances lies outside the scope of a monetary unit of accounting as well.

Though the term business cycle is frequently employed, it suggests the movement around an equilibrium path, or trend. This is an interpretation of the economic sphere that is, as seen, a unique perspective selected from a number of possible ones. Changes in resource utilization can be observed over time, and are the direct outcome of individual action within the economic system. They are not themselves subject to regularities in their shape, form, and frequency, though. To suggest that changes in resource utilization were in fact cyclical in the true sense of the term is thus misleading, while a number of perspectives on economies still argue that different degrees of utilization of production potential over time can be expected to result from individual, business-driven decisions in economies.

III

Changes in technology take the shape of new combinations of existing skill and equipment (you put an engine into a carriage to make a car), driven by learning about new possibilities. The existing technological capacity in a group thus shapes the options for learning and development that are open at a given point in time. Compatibility to existing structures helps in introducing novelties, narrowing the corridor of potential innovations down. Expertise is acquired over time. Given the increasingly interwoven and intricate nature of knowledge that is applied in general settings, and the importance of creativity and inspiration in some leading sectors, a routinization of processes, and catching up in capacities on that foundation, is getting harder, and may in some parts of modern economic activity have become impossible; at least, in any reasonable timespan. Disadvantages can thus persist and deepen, if the distance to currently advanced technologies has become too pronounced. An easy integration into existing structures, and the capacities to do so gainfully, may simply cease to exist at some point because of a lack of ability to achieve the compatibility required.

Within an economy, institutional provisions that permit experimentation and the communication of results support changes. Innovation capacity is therefore not a static feature of a society, but can be expected to change over time, responding to changes in the institutional framework. Depending on the viewpoint adopted, the economic advantage that successful innovations enjoy can be seen as generally positive, reflecting the values of the agents involved in the process of creation and acceptance. It may also be viewed more skeptically, acknowledging different effects over different time horizons and an ability of one-side business interests, to steer the process according to its interests without a general working of the economic sphere that would force these interests to be pursued in a way that serves the overall economy's interest in the best possible way.

Economic growth typically involves a process of change, around new processes and new products, and the concurrent evolution of social structure. Circular and cumulative causation, by its nature outside the scope of equilibrium-analyses, is a main force in these economic processes. We can also see that path dependence can not only be utilized for making sense of the establishment of specific standards, but can also be drawn on for assessing processes of change and development here.

Technological progress is an endogenous process within economies. A natural rate of growth, described by an equilibrium growth path, does not exist. In consequence, in this view, macroeconomic theory cannot afford to abstract from real time and existing conditions when approaching a number of questions. Policies that shape aggregate demand, distribution of cost and benefits, and innovation potential, among others, can change the potential in an economy. Given constraints from economic factors, in this process, a sole focus on either a driving supply side or demand side can be misleading in analyses as well. Novelties have to be introduced, but also to find acceptance. Capacities to signal that acceptance in economic terms – namely the means to acquire resulting products – are as important as the ability to actually introduce novelties, and the existence of a pool of inventions to draw on before an economic rationale becomes involved in their assessment.

4.6 Different Perspectives on Crises in Economies

We understand crisis, here, as the under- and unemployment of resources in an economy, and particularly of labor. What this chapter has shown is that there are different interpretations concerning the causes of such crises, ranging from external shocks to normal behavior in economic matters. Among the causes for crises that result from normal economic behavior, shortfalls in demand, in consumption or more likely on the investment spending, are one area of factors that can trigger crises. Developments in the financial market that negatively affect productive activity are the other large area of normal causes for economic crises. These interpretations are formed and informed by the respective perspectives on the economic system. Appropriate ways for addressing and mending crises, correspondingly, differ. The more real-world complexity is integrated into an analytical perspective, and dynamics emerge from bottom-up considerations, the more diverse the causes of crises that can be identified and analyzed become. In turn, dealing with crises, and potentially preventing the system to enter crises states, becomes a more involved, and less technocratic, task.

I

The two reference points for equilibrium analyses that we saw focus on economic activity and price level, and economic activity and its relation to interest rates, respectively. Both assume that overall economic activity is bound by one equilibrium at a given moment in time. The price-level focus permits only full-employment equilibria. The second reference approach is formulated with a view on potentially persistent crises, i.e., it permits equilibria in which involuntary unemployment exists.

There are some similarities in the results offered. Most notably, monetary policy does not crowd out private activity, whereas government spending does (when expansive); by assumption. However, whereas all changes in policies, as well as technological change, affect the price level in the first reference frame and can only change the composition of economic activity, in an underemployment equilibrium, expansionary measures can increase employment levels. While government spending will still affect private activity negatively, overall employment can increase. Monetary policy does not affect private activity negatively, there is no crowding-out, but its potential depends on the willingness of agents to invest. Depending on the state of an economy, and expectations regarding its nearer future, that willingness might be very limited. While we may discern a general preference for monetary measures, thus, we need to amend this statement by permitting room for fiscal measures under specific circumstances. This preference is underlined when open economies are considered.

At the heart of both aspects of an equilibrium perspective on economies, we find the representation of an economy as a larger household. Scarcity of means and resources dominates the problem structure, and their allocation is their central concern. Technology is given. Savings are what enable investment by making the funds for investing available in the first place. The amount of money is given. The value of goods is given, representing their use value, and represented in the relative price structure. And so on.

Where a full-employment equilibrium forms the foundation of a perspective, a crisis has to be introduced from outside the economic sphere. Some shocks or unwarranted interferences in the economic sphere, limiting the competitiveness of markets, limit the system's ability to guarantee the most beneficial resource allocation possible at the moment. Adopting this perspective, the search for causes is thus naturally directed to potential influences with the ability to impact the economy and misallocate resources. Typically, this is the public sector, possibly by proxy, as in its support for unions. Where underinvestment triggers crises, strengthening demand and improving supply conditions to make investments more attractive come into view. Lately, the emphasis has often been on the supply side, based on the assumption that demand would follow, with investment leading the way if profit conditions are only made attractive enough.

Changes in analyses in economics under this perspective have largely been driven by changes in modeling technique and the integration of computers, permitting large scale simulations. The focus has been on integrating more disaggregate structures at the outset, as microfoundations. However, results obtained differ marginally, at best, from the basic effects the benchmark models serve to illustrate, because the overall framework has not changed. Individuals are integrated into the same system as before. 'Normal' demand and supply curves continue to be employed, and unique and stable equilibria result from the interplay of these. Scarcity of resources is the principal factor of interest. Economic activity is bound by the equilibrium market-system in which it is located. Even when imperfectly competitive markets are integrated, the equilibrium results attained are evaluated as distortions from the perfect setting, whose validity as a reference point is thus assumed to persist. Outcomes are seen in terms of distorted allocation patterns in an economy. Shocks may increase the degree of misallocation or may help reducing it, depending on their nature. Still, more distortions can be modeled, of course, in a more disaggregate model structure.

II

Relinquishing the equilibrium toward which an economy was drawn can lead to markedly different perspectives and results in analyses. Without an equilibrium, we view economies as ongoing processes, emerging from individual interactions. There are, generally, no clearly identifiable cause–effect relations that remain stable over the entire range of a system. There are no generally valid economic laws. How the economic process plays out depends on the state the economic system is in. The economic environment influences behavior, and this behavior in turn shapes a changing economic environment. The objectives pursued in analyses focus, in tendency, on gaining an understanding of specific processes, or characteristics of the system to be analyzed, which are not given by assumption, but become part of the analytical frame itself.

III

In the more open analytical perspectives, different aspects of economic processes can be stressed, including the role and nature of money, the role of business interests, or the role of technological change, among others. Processes result naturally once the system is not constrained and constraining by assumptions.

Once we let go of the idea that there was a given stock of money, and see how money is introduced into the economic system, it becomes endogenous. Money is created in the course of economic activity. Savings no longer limit the investment funds available, investment creates the income from which savings are fueled.

Businesses that strive for monetary profits do not automatically also contribute to larger societal objectives. Their more individualistic, if we may use that term in relation to businesses, motivations in tendency may in fact be expected to harm the overall stability of the system, and bring about crises. More subdued crises, in fact, may be expected to serve business interests, more than harming them, strengthening their negotiating positions facing workers as well as political actors.

Once the process perspective is adopted, we see that there is no reason to assume that an economy would naturally follow a path that is characterized by full employment, absent artificial constraints. Crises no longer appear as the outcome of shocks from outside the economic system (although at times they still can, of course), but may very well be due to the unfolding process itself. They are generally due to reductions of the demand for goods, especially investment goods, or developments in the financial sector that have repercussions on productive activity as well. Furthermore, ongoing change means structures and sectors may become obsolete, and interests in them will be harmed. Macroeconomic reality emerges from individual decisions, and those decisions shape the system and the way it changes. Different areas in the overall economic system that contribute to crises, or perpetuate an ongoing crisis, come into view.

IV

Business interests focus on the profits of one particular business. But even there we have seen earlier that different interests may be involved. Differences in goals may include different attitudes toward a social sphere that can be drawn on for reducing business's own costs, different time-horizons pursued, such as between owners, managers, and financial sector when evaluating a company's future course, or differences in attitude concerning a willingness to act for mutual future gain over immediate personal gain. What is successful is evaluated by monetary measures over a given period of time. (Hence the attractiveness to try to socialize risks and costs of private activity.) Especially where external funding is involved, rather short-term interests are not uncommon. Again, the institutional framework, shaping what is permissible or at least acceptable to achieve what is desirable, plays an influential role here. Furthermore, interests may differ between workers and management, and employers and owners, concerning the distribution of the revenue obtained. Conditions outside any particular business will influence emerging patterns, as negotiating positions shift over time, depending on social values and the state of the economic environment, for instance. However, beyond the short term, a too profound influence of one side of negotiations may harm the overall prospects of businesses, as conditions may develop that negatively affect the viability of the business sphere, and thus the individual units comprising it. A short-fall of demand is one example for such a development.

Unemployment can be a very helpful component for further strengthening the negotiating position of specific groups. Changes in the economic sphere – general technological progress brought to use in economic matters as innovation – may be assumed to be chosen with a view on furthering negotiating strength and distributional gain, as opposite to other interests in a business venture, such as the workers employed, or with regard to external influences, such as competitors.

Defining economic crises as a state in which people cannot gain access to the means of participating in economic life as full-fledged members of society means that crises are perpetual states for modern economies, as an outcome and normal part of their functioning. Acute crises can punctuate the general crisis if employment levels drop as businesses try to protect their position by reducing cost in more difficult times, to make up for losses of revenue. In one way or another, such acute crises are likewise a normal part of a capitalist system in this reading, as the motivations on the individual level lead to actions that build up to a situation which eventually proves unsustainable.

V

The role of the public sector, in its position as a main creator of demand in an economy, provider of structures for private agents to draw on, stabilizer of the economic system, provider of reliable money, counterweight to private power, and guarantor of conditions that permit private agents to undergo economic endeavors without facing too costly risk calculations, is often neglected or at other times misunderstood, and against that background, frequently criticized. Constraints on private action of some agents weigh more heavily in some views than in others, in which the concurrent enabling effects of government presence are given a more pronounced role (without denying the constraints). That being said, a weariness of public actions is shared by practically all approaches. Where the equilibrium framework lends itself to a technocratic justification of measures in order to conform with a specific analytical framework, proper democratic controls of government action, in order to guarantee the fulfilling of an overall mandate to better the conditions of the population in a territory, are seen to be a key ingredient for the proper realization of its potential role in most other perspectives.

In the analyses themselves, different positions are embedded. The potential for actions in the economic sphere changes with the characteristics the economic system is assumed to have. What democratically controlled and empowered public action can actually achieve is thus evaluated differently. What values may matter for formulations, focuses, and implementations of policies is another area in which emphases in different perspectives differ, ranging from static resource allocation to dynamic allocation and change, and the use of economic means for strengthening positions of influence. Acknowledging the complex nature of economic systems emphasizes the complementary and cooperative aspects of private and public agents' actions over a purely antagonistic role. The fact that public agents can often provide the only counterbalance to private power stresses the need for the proper embedding of public structures in a democratic process, but also hints at reasons for outspoken opposition to public sector presence and activity by specific private interests. We may at the very least note that we may be hard pressed to find a shared logical foundation for an assumption that pressing for the support of business interests may lead to generally beneficial developments, while pressing for the support of workers' interests is generally detrimental to economic interests.

The overview of economic analyses of macroeconomic issues hardly merits a pronounced opposition to an active role for public agents, if we put brackets around the extreme benchmark view that removes all real complexity in the formulation of its perspective on economic issues. How to conceive and deal with this role becomes a more pressing concern then. While this is not the text to dive into matters of political organization, the outline of policy frameworks and what they can involve very much is, and will be taken up in the following Chapter 5.

References

For the full list of references, see the bibliography at the end of the text.

Ayres, Clarence E (1944) The Theory of Economic Progress: A Study of the Fundamentals of Economic Development and Cultural Change. Chapel Hill, University of North Carolina Press

The author analyzes processes of change in economies and the influence that the formal and especially also informal rules and norms in a society have on the shape of the process.

Bhagwati, Jagdish (2002) Free Trade Today. Princeton University Press, Princeton and Oxford.

The author presents an overview of arguments for free trade policies.

Eichengreen, Barry (2003) Capital Flows and Crises. The MIT Press, Cambridge and London

The author addresses the issue of capital flows, and their potential for positive as well as negative effects on economies, from a number of vantage points.

Friedman, Milton (1962) Capitalism and Freedom. University of Chicago Press, Chicago

The author argues that uninterfered economic activity is a necessary building block for political freedom.

Galbraith, John K (1967) The New Industrial State. Houghton Mifflin Co., Boston

The author analyzes the influence of large corporations in the economic sphere, and in society more in general.

Harvey, David (2010) A Companion to Marx's Capital. Verso, London and New York

The author offers a, post-crises, overview, guide, and interpretation of the first volume of Marx's Capital.

Heilbroner, Robert (1953) The Worldly Philosophers: The Lives, Times, and Ideas of the Great Economic Thinkers. Simon and Schuster, New York

The author presents and analyzes economic thought and ideas, embedded in the times and circumstances of those who articulated them.

Kalecki, Michal (1971) Selected Essays on the Dynamics of the Capitalist Economy. Cambridge University Press, Cambridge et al.

The collection of essays analyzes aspects of economic systems from a vantage point of economic activity as an ongoing process.

Kapp, Karl W. (2011) The Foundations of Institutional Economics (eds. Sebastian Berger and Rolf Steppacher). Routledge, London and New York

The author analyzes the role of institutions in economic systems.

Keynes, John Maynard (1936) General Theory of Employment, Interest, and Money. Macmillan and Co, London

The author develops a framework for understanding an economy, which may not return to full employment out of its own dynamics.

Kindleberger, Charles P. (1978) Manias, Panics, and Crashes: A History of Financial Crises. Basic Books, New York

The author presents and analyzes financial crises over the centuries.

Metcalfe, J Stanley (1998) Evolutionary Economics and Creative Destruction. Routledge, London and New York

The author discusses competition as leading to an ongoing process of change.

Minsky, Hyman (1975) John Maynard Keynes. Columbia University Press, New York

The author offers an interpretation of Keynes' work that integrates a number of aspects of that work which are frequently neglected.

Minsky, Hyman (1986) Stabilizing an Unstable Economy. Yale University Press, New Haven

The author analyzes how dynamics in the financial sector can lead to instability in these, and how that can spill over to productive economic activity.

Nell, Edward (1998) The General Theory of Transformational Growth: Keynes After Sraffa. Cambridge University Press, Cmabridge et al.

The author analyzes how ongoing innovations in markets change the functioning of the economic system.

Nitzan, Jonathan, Shimshon Bichler (2009) Capital as Power: A Study of Order and Creorder. Routledge, London and New York

The authors analyze frequently used notions of the concept of capital, and offer a new definition to overcome flaws in existing concepts.

Ormerod, Paul (1994) The Death of Economics. St. Martin's Press, New York

The author assesses the state of economic theory and analyzes what a theory will have to include to successfully address current economic problems.

Robinson, Joan (1956) The Accumulation of Capital. Macmillan, London

The author develops an analytical framework for addressing questions concerning developing economies.

Schumpeter, Joseph A (1934; first English edition) The Theory of Economic Development: An Inquiry into Profits, Capital, Credit, Interest, and the Business Cycle. Harvard University Press, Cambridge

The author analyzes how the drive for profit leads to ongoing changes in economic systems.

Schumpeter, Joseph A (1954) History of Economic Analysis. Oxford University Press, New York

The author provides overview, interpretation, and analyses of a few millenia of economic thought.

Sraffa, Piero (1960) Production of Commodities by Means of Commodities – Prelude to a Critique of Economic Theory. Cambridge University Press, Cambridge et al.

Relying on classical economists' view of economic activity leading to flows of commodities through economies, the author provides an alternative approach to determining the exchange value of goods and profit rates in their production.

Sweezy, Paul M (1942) The Theory of Capitalist Development – Principles of Marxian Political Economy. Oxford University Press, Oxford et al.

The author examines Marxist theory, and analyzes how far it can help to understanding the dynamics of capitalist systems.

Sweezy, Paul M, and Paul A Baran (1966) Monopoly Capital: An Essay on the American Economic and Social Order. Monthly Review Press, New York

The authors analyze the effects that the monopolization of markets in modern economies have.

Veblen, Thorstein B (1904) The Theory of Business Enterprise. Charles Scribner's Sons, New York

The author analyzes the role of companies in modern economies.

Wray, L. Randall (2012) Modern Money Theory: A Primer on Macroeconomics for Sovereign Monetary Systems. Palgrave Macmillan, Basingstoke and New York

The author lays out how money is created in modern monetary systems, and what follows for our understanding of macroeconomic problems.

5

Frameworks for Economic Policy

All perspectives on analyzing economies that we have seen share the objective of supporting individual emancipation. Assumptions about the economic system shape the avenues that come into view to that end, and the policies that are proposed vary with them. Regarding general policy frameworks, for the top-down perspectives, we see frameworks that aim at supporting the regular functioning of the economic sphere, and addressing obstacles to that functioning where that approach is less costly than the original distortion. For the bottom-up perspectives, we see frameworks that aim at an ongoing support for economic processes, in interaction with and as part of the possibly ongoing change of the economic system.

Economists working with top-down frameworks in their analyses typically favor rule-bound, technocratic government, to outsource political decisions to 'the market'. Individual competition improves conditions, and plays out toward societally advantageous ends when linked to the economic arena. Where we cannot identify 'economic laws' because the complexity of the analytical framework prevents them from coming into being, more detailed considerations of specific situations and objectives may become necessary. Policies have to be approached with a view on the state of the system at the

H. Schwardt, *The Path to a Modern Economics*,
DOI 10.1007/978-3-319-52785-7_5

time and objectives have to be made clear, as there is no price mechanism to automatically align all interests involved in a matter in the best possible way.

We will look at policy perspectives in this chapter, on the one hand, to see the alternative possibilities that develop, and how they may relate to one another, on the other hand, to be better able to identify upon which analytical frameworks different policy proposals may rely when we encounter them.

I

Independent of one's perspective, regarding policy approaches in very generic terms, we look for factors that may interfere with the objectives we have set and try to remove them, or find measures that can counter their impact. Alternatively, we find factors that may merit further strengthening or enhancement. Where to look for, and what supportive or distorting factors may be, is informed by our analytical frame. What we may be able to do is suggested by the analytical frame as well, regarding the focus as well as the scope of action. This may be a focus on individual factors to counter on a one-to-one base, just as a systemic view integrating different influence factors and their relations. The choice and applicability of an analytical framework to a situation is important. When economic policies go awry, the negative impact can be rather pronounced.

Whichever avenue may appear most promising for enhancing the functioning of the economic system, actually steering the economic process in that direction is likely not going to be too easy, or at least unambiguous, in practice. None of the aforementioned frameworks necessarily offer a readymade set of solutions for approaching economic affairs; this emphatically includes the top-down formulations. If assumed to have an impact on economic activity, addressing the various potential sources of market failures in a constructive manner may be a rather involved affair, for instance, even as the general approach is rather straightforward. Put differently, the complexity of the economic system, no matter how it is introduced in the formulation and application of an analytical framework, has to be taken into account in policy formulations, even if only in the determination of the choice of a particular model over others.

At the point of policy formulations, the openness of the economic system is likewise something to give consideration to. Even if we can garner a good understanding of economic relations in isolation, at the time of implementing policies other areas of life are also affected by them. Societal arenas outside the economic sphere, say related to health, education, or the political system, affect the capacity of individuals to develop their potential and thus fill a theoretically possible freedom with actual meaning. How to assess the impact of measures on different areas of life has to be debated, in order to stand on an agreed value foundation. Furthermore, the thinking brought to bear on different societal arenas influences agents' behavior, the structures in place, and their evolution, just as the ability of individuals to actually participate freely in economic exchanges is affected by the outcomes achieved in those other areas of life.

II

Broadly speaking, we can distinguish two basic fields for policies to engage in, namely the economic system itself and the consequences outside the economic sphere that follow from economic activity. Regarding the latter, disputes about policy-related matters include whether an attempt at restricting the economic system itself, or addressing consequences emanating from it, seems more advisable.

The first area broadly consists of attempts to support economic activity, protect individual agents, and reduce their vulnerability, and generally continue to foster individual emancipation by reducing economic constraints on their decision-making. The second area broadly focuses on actions in areas that accept vulnerability as a part of modern economic activity and on reducing individual insecurity as well as economic activities' adverse impacts in other societal spheres, including nature. Obviously, the two focuses are not mutually exclusive, but are generally pursued in parallel, even if under different emphases and to different degrees. Whichever detailed approach may eventually be put forth, for decisions to be reached, a clear value basis has to be in place in order to assess objectives and priorities given to different objectives. In addition to other things, this will bring trade-offs among different areas and objectives into sharper relief, including those that are by their nature not, or at least not easily, converted into a single dimensional metric such as monetary units.

The considerations over the following pages will follow the structure of the preceding chapters to a good degree. However, we also need to remember that where policy issues are concerned, a macroeconomic policy that does not take into account the fact that it addresses issues that have emerged from the interplay of individuals at the microeconomic level, and in its implementation influences those lower level interactions, faces an increased danger of failing. A macro-level analysis for an overview over potential problem areas can still be a good and suitable starting point, but may also bar the view on certain aspects of developments. An average may at times obscure as much as it may reveal. Where policy implementations are concerned, we will need to draw on results from different levels of analyses to advance suitable measures.

For policy decisions, the fact that an economic sphere is not isolated from the rest of societal structures, likewise becomes more important. For modeling economic effects, this has often been ignored and for keeping an analytical framework manageable, it may well have to be. For making decisions shaping people's ability to go through their lives and develop their potential, however, such relations will have to be considered as well, which we will address beyond the micro-, market-, and macro-level for directing policies. But for starters, we will consider the fact that policies, or at least policy makers, need support, and that, therefore, the communication around policies matters, and given the complex nature of their subject, as much and more as the analyses behind them.

5.1 Communicating Policy Proposals

Once theoretical frameworks have been consolidated, they provide the foundation for explanations of economic phenomena, identifications of interfering factors, predictions about what effects may follow policy measures, or developments elsewhere in the world for that matter, as well as suggestions and advice regarding policies to impact economic activity and the structure embedding it. They form and inform people's thinking about economies and economic issues. They shape people's views on situations and on which issues are, in fact, identified as problems, as well as recommendations given for addressing and possibly overcoming these problems. Top-down and bottom-up analyses invariably lead to the emergence of different pictures of economies, partly to different problems focused on and different suggestions forwarded for addressing presumably problematic situations.

How the analytical structure is set up also influences how the stories to communicate findings are formulated. This communication reflects the interpretation of framework and analytical results, and also influences perception and perspectives of people as well as their approaches to finding solutions, or accepting suggestions.

Especially, but not exclusively, where the model structures themselves tend to be mathematical constructs that are then translated into a verbal context, you need a story to communicate your results, whether the audience are academic peers or a broader public. The general vocabulary for the standard stories is settled within each perspective. Note that beyond simply providing technical terms, vocabulary may be specialized in a way that uses terms very differently from their common usage. Some examples for such differences in use taken from the currently dominant discourse include terms such as competition or trust, whose reference-perspective meanings have nothing to do with their common use, but stand as surrogates.

The 'perfect competition', or competition, for short, of the reference framework, for instance, depicts a system structure in which competition in the sense that noneconomists (including business) understand it is virtually absent. By assumption, there is no scope for strategic behavior of anybody involved. All information is immediately available to everyone, and there is therefore no incentive for anyone to try to find new information, or even to innovate, for an economic advantage. In effect, it describes a situation in which all real-world aspects of competition have been overcome in a static state.

However, the results of such perfectly competitive structures, defined as the optimal utilization of existing resources, are an important rhetorical tool in arguments concerning the superiority of competitive structures in real-world economic settings, including their fostering of innovations and ongoing change. What the concept of competition is actually supposed to encompass in the translation of the model framework to real-world structures remains unclear.

In the framing of the stories to communicate the results of related modeling approaches, the process character of competition is frequently stressed. Companies act and react, technological change is fostered by competition, and individual ambition is checked by what a competitive environment with strategically acting counter-parties will allow. On the other hand, the model-setting abstracts from anything process-related or strategy-oriented. In fact, it takes many things out of the equation by assuming they do not matter in the state that is analyzed, or at least provided as the reference point for analyses. The interest lies in identifying allocation patterns, and identifying possible improvements in those patterns. If processes, strategies, and change were integrated, such identification would be impossible, at least in the way it is desired under an equilibrium perspective, as we have seen earlier in Chapters 2 and 3. As a side note, once we integrate those aspects, from the societal perspective, we find tremendous levels of waste associated with economic activity, from overlapping R&D spending, marketing efforts to attract customers and increase control of market niches, and others.

The structure required for fostering successful competitive markets from an equilibrium perspective is unclear as well. The theoretical model is defined by its outcome, the reflection of goods' fixed values in their equilibrium-relative prices. However, how that can be brought about cannot be defined from the framework. The outcomes reflect the proper equilibrium valuations of resources and goods, but, in an environment in which the necessity for structure, through property rights etc., is recognized, how to set up a structure that permits proper valuations is left open. Unfortunately, the economists following this route cannot measure true values, or determine proper prices. Hence, estimates and guesstimates have to provide the foundation for policy suggestions, and the belief in the market reference point is often transferred onto real-world structures as a simplifying rule of thumb of withdrawing public agents as a fix to problems. That is not necessarily a reflection of the considerations of the reference framework, where market failures play a noticeable role, but a simplification of that framework to a belief that the reference point will approximately work for capturing economic situations.

The static foundation of the perspective, among other aspects, matters because processes and movement do introduce additional effects into a situation. Perfect competition that promises harmony and effectiveness encounters real competition that brings upheaval and waste. Statements that are true in a static environment are not necessarily true in a world that is changing – try going through the motions of taking a turn on a bicycle that is not moving. The comparison of two static outcomes may offer a perspective that neglects fundamental aspects of a situation that is characterized by ongoing changes, in consequence. If something is moving and that movement is part of its inherent character, then the comparison of two snippets, as glimpses of a system in motion, may fail to identify fundamental factors of interest and of consequence. Especially if, for the sake of simplicity, cause-and-effect relations are assumed not to be changing over time, depending on the state of the system, or reacting to technological changes. The functioning of the system itself may, however, develop over time as an outcome of its ongoing transformation.

So, which place actual competition has within the reference system is unclear, once we try to find out what it is supposed to entail – the model formulation of competition depicts a system that has moved beyond current competition. Whether to focus on process or outcome, on competition between individuals or groups, on constraints to stabilize a competitive environment, an advice of fostering more competitive environments does not really offer any clues for its realization. The resulting necessities for more detailed considerations may, however, easily be lost in the belief that competition is an easy enough concept to grasp.

'Trust', as a second example, in the reference framework means that agents believe that their counterparts understand a situation well enough to be able to choose a mutually beneficial course of action. It does not mean that they are putting themselves in a position in which another person can take advantage of them and benefit from doing so, as trust in its core meaning implies. The use of the term trust may colloquially involve the notion focused on in the reference framework, but the notion of vulnerability is at the heart of its actual meaning. We might say trusting behavior in the reference world leads to mutually beneficial coordination, where everyone would be worse off if coordination failed. Trusting behavior in the real world means that at least along some measure, someone involved is worse off than they could have been.

That real-world trust matters is widely recognized by economists. However, as it is not commensurable to the reference assumptions of self-interested individuals, it stands outside the reference perspective, if taken seriously. So, it is integrated as something different, allowing the use of standard methods, but diluting or distorting the insights that it might bring as a concept.

Under a policy perspective, trust matters because it enables a number of interactions among agents that go beyond competition. Such interactions do not have to aim at collusion, but can foster innovative potential, for instance. In general, costs related to transaction will be reduced in more trusting environments, as formal protections will be less necessary.

Overall, we may note that the vocabulary employed for communicating the results of mathematical models can obscure as much as it can clarify. The purported advantage of clarity that mathematical formulations hold over verbal formulations is not a given. It can be, but does not have to, and where the distance between simplified mathematical structure and complex object of study is too pronounced, a noticeable degree of freedom is reintroduced in the translation of mathematical results into verbal statements anyway. The fact that analysts, in that case, still have to pick what they consider the appropriate model moves the level of analysis outside the actual analytical framework, furthermore. Gaining an idea of how analyses are structured, and what questions are meant to be answered by the researchers employing a particular framework, can then help sensitizing us against potential pitfalls.

5.2 Microeconomic Policy Perspectives

I

Microeconomic perspectives analyze interactions of individuals, and the exchange arenas in which they meet, to understand the potential from interactions, and pinpointing possible problems and distortions. Depending on the perspective, the focus ranges from markets only, to interactions of more widely socially embedded individuals. Views on behavioral options and behaviors tend to change, in nontrivial ways, under different perspectives.

The main area for individual interactions in economies is the market. Independent of the focus of analyses, the function of markets, as seen in Chapter 3, is to foster a number of purposes, including an efficient resource allocation and the reduction of waste in production, enhancing innovation, as well as an increase in the availability of information for individuals. Other exchange arenas complement markets. Where the market outcome serves as the reference for evaluating results in the top-down formulations, under the bottom-up perspectives, no way of coordinating activity is inherently good or bad, and monetary competition is the default option that offers the best possible results. Environment, objectives, and constraints influence how coordination can be best achieved in a specific setting.

Policies aim at incentivizing activities that result in the desired effects or outcomes. Depending on the framework and its suggestions, policy orientations differ.

In policy formulations, considerations regarding trade-offs among different objectives have to be weighed. For instance, control over markets and wastefulness of resource utilization may be affected in opposite ways by measures, while both are found to be undesirable in and of themselves. In another area, innovations may clash with a desire for stability and the prevention of turbulence. Distributional issues by nature entail trade-offs. Technological change has to be compatible to existing structures, requiring knowledge about existing structures. Making such knowledge accessible is likely to interfere with the interests of existing companies. If the advantage granted is what motivates innovation, then a medium ground has to be found permitting scope for novelties to be brought to the economic sphere, and permitting companies who do advance such novelties to exploit their position. The position taken in considering such trade-offs depends on the overall view on the economic sphere, and the possibilities and risks it holds, for instance with a view on tendencies toward monopolization, or differences in the functioning of markets for different goods, and the information that prices therefore entail. Which measures may be deemed more appropriate will again depend on the view of the economic system itself, the agents in it, and their relations.

A first check, at the point of involving the public agent, will try to estimate whether the problem that will be fixed may merit the efforts that will be undertaken to fix it; depending on our perspective, how measures may contribute to changing the dynamics in an economy becomes a more natural component of such analyses, or remains an addition in uncomfortable relation to the analysis itself. Also to be looked into, is who bears the respective costs in different scenarios. Furthermore, effects in other areas may have to be considered as well, and weighed against the potential improvements that are to be achieved. Notable focus areas for economic policies concern the structure of interaction arenas, the strengthening of innovative potential, and other supportive measures, as well as securing involved and uninvolved parties from avoidable risks and costs they might otherwise face. A number of these measures and impacts may be very difficult, at best, to capture in monetary terms, and thus may not be adequately represented in market prices.

How costs and benefits are conceived and calculated, of course, has a potentially significant impact on the results of estimates. Furthermore, such calculations are frequently undertaken with a view on a specific status quo, and the changes to it, and thus the weighing of potential gains against often more tangible losses, or at least potential losses that seem more threatening than potential gains may seem rewarding. As losses are more likely to be realized in the present, or close to it, while gains are realized in the future, there is ample scope for weighing gains more optimistically or more pessimistically, depending on whether there is a preference for change, or for a conservation of the existing situation. While numbers may give an impression of precision, for their assessment, we always need to know how they have been constructed.

Other areas of societies may be affected by policy changes in economic matters where effects may not necessarily be tangible. If you think in terms of health-care access, for instance, the potential for economic gains for a healthier population is not typically included, as it is impossible to put a number on it. This will include aspects such as a temporary absence from the labor force that can be remedied in a well-functioning health-care environment, but may be permanent where such an environment is not given; skills may be permanently lost, thereby, just as with long-term unemployment. Not to mention gains in quality of life for healthier people. If only headline numbers, not unlikely in our sound bite culture, are included, they paint a distorted view. In more general terms, we can say that dynamic developments, whether positive or negative, from policy changes cannot properly be addressed, so that studies focusing on tangible aspects of change will only understate likely outcomes. A result for policy approaches will be a focus on accompanying economic processes and an ongoing attempt to improve its working, in reaction to unfolding developments.

II

The top-down reference framework, for the individual relation to the economic environment and the market-model that results, suggests that the allocation question for societal resources could best be solved through free market exchanges, where, again, 'free' is defined by its result, not any particular structure in place. If a proper structure can be found and established for transactions, then everything, including labor, would be utilized according to its collective valuation, reflected in its respective prices, and potential trade-offs would be resolved by these prices. No allocation patterns that would improve the outcome for the group could be found for the given environment.

What is traded specifically is not of particular concern here, the general market mechanisms of the reference perspective are assumed to hold independently of any specific market. Any individual market can be approached from the same assumptions about its functioning as a guideline. A reference point is established, and interferences hindering the realization of the reference result may then be identified. Subsequently, try to devise ways to address these issues, if that appears to be doable at a reasonable cost.

III

As you will recall, a number of issues can interfere with the allocation mechanism in markets under an equilibrium perspective. The three prominent aspects were differences in information about a good, with incomplete information for some agents resulting, the possibility that agents who are not party to a transaction are affected by its outcomes, as well as the possibility that once a good has been provided, its consumption could not be controlled and restricted by the provider. An additional aspect in which market results may differ from the reference outcome was given in the form of a situation where market participants find themselves in a position in which they can take control over market outcomes. Resource allocation patterns will in these cases not be socially and economically optimal.

Regarding measures to address suboptimal outcomes, an important result of analyses in the reference perspective stresses the fact that once some optimality conditions are broken, there is no clear way for bringing about the next-best attainable result. Typically, a number of interferences in exchange arenas are required for realizing a good outcome once the first-best outcome is not attainable for one reason or another. What is more, you cannot gradually move toward the best conceivable outcome once distortions are in place. To address causes of distortions gradually, or only partially, may lead to an improvement of the situation just as it may lead to a worsening of a situation. For an example of the concept, think of a market where a few employers face a union. Distortions are present on both sides of the transaction over labor. However, disbanding the union will not necessarily, or even likely, improve the results in the market from a social perspective, as that simply shifts the power in wage negotiations more firmly to the employers. So, a market is perfect, or it is not. If it is not, numerous interventions will typically be required for bringing about a second-best, or third-best, etc., outcome. The direction of measures for improvements can be counterintuitive, from a foundation in the reference framework; e.g., support unions if employers can be expected to enjoy positions of influence, or limit capital flows if short-term investment flows lead to negative external effects through their impact on exchange rates.

The theoretical structure of the reference outcome can therefore not be a guide for the direction to move into in terms of the policy environment, unless you make all changes required for a perfect market outcome to result in one leap. If you knew how that leap was supposed to look like, that is, which may be doubtful as well, given the opaque relation of some of the concepts employed to a real-world counterpart. That providing economically for a group is best undertaken by simply reducing government presence or more generally deleting rules that regulate interactions is not a result coming out of the reference framework. This notwithstanding, it is frequently employed to argue in that direction.

Effects that result in disturbances of the assumed proper market functioning arise either due to institutional structures in place, characteristics of goods, or characteristics of production processes. Now, influence on others, information advantages, or impacts on other arenas are a rather common feature of economic activity. Various ways are open to address such sources of market failures, such as the creation of new markets, changes that aim at enhancing the functioning of existing markets, changes in incentives that aim at inducing behavior patterns more in line with the reference point behavior, or limiting the scope for individual behavior. Regulating sectors in which powerful agents exist is another option to consider. Where potential results have been identified as desirable, but unattainable due to malfunctioning markets, the public agent has the option to step in more directly as a producer, as well. The notion of removing something from the economic sphere is only infrequently entertained as an option in suggestions relying on the reference perspective, though.

Against such a background, policies can get rather involved even when the reference point of market exchanges is accepted to be viable. When addressing possible cures for market failures, an estimate of the reference point result will provide the foundation, to see, where results are supposed to be moved. Other estimates will then see what costs may be related to measures, and quantify whether they are worthwhile at all. Given the loose connection of theoretical framework to reality, the researchers offering such estimates enjoy a noticeable degree of freedom in the derivation of their results, which seems to be a point worth stressing, as the ability to produce numbers that suggest precision is most pronounced when relying on this analytical framework.

IV

Supportive structures for market exchanges have to be in place, including property rights, monetary system, and a number of other aspects of modern economies. These supportive structures mean that there is always some influence on the exchange arena, including influence factors on prices and costs. In turn, there are always trade-offs between the interests of the different parties involved in transactions, as the supportive structures have an influence on the distribution of risks and costs incurred through transactions. What is more, withdrawing the public agent entirely will result in informal rules and norms, and customs governing transactions; or at least, this has historically been the case. Even without an official regulation, there is no exchange arena that is free of external structure. As a consequence, there is no neutral reference point to draw on for evaluations of observations, in terms of assessing structures. Now, as costs and risks are shifted between different agents and markets continue to function as exchange arenas over a range of these possible distributions, there are many different possible detailed forms of market exchanges. These cannot be separated from the result obtained, and identification of one proper and truly optimal potential outcome reflecting goods' given values is therefore not possible either. That means there is no neutral reference point for the evaluation of outcomes in markets either. The neutral reference point at the heart of free market thought-exercises can therefore not be a meaningful guide to thinking about market structures in terms of policy proposals. That is not to say that some of the aspects stressed within that framework, such as the desirability to check public and private power, would not have merit. However, these are introduced as observations and assumptions at the outset.

V

The reference outcome and the importance of supportive structures for economic activity also serves as the foundation for some policy approaches that consider human behavior patterns that are not economically rational. The goal is to use the biases in human decision-making which are directing attention and action away from economically rational behavior, and set up a structure in which they can be used to move decisions into that direction. That is to say, the validity of the reference framework and outcome is accepted, as is its evaluation. Recognizing that human agents, however, do not behave as they would have to, to actually bring that result about, policies are sought which nudge them in the right direction.

For instance, regarding different decisions depending on how specific information is presented, when offered the choice of private savings accounts, we find two very different outcomes regarding the use of a private retirement savings option or not. If people are automatically enrolled, being free to opt out at any time, most people use such accounts. On the other hand, if they are told that the option is available, all they have to do is enroll, most do not bother.

Of course, private companies have long taken advantage of their increasing understanding of decision-making patterns. There is no neutral reference point, only a confluence of influences and behavior patterns. This confluence occurs within the defined limits that time and space set. You have to arrange the food in a school cafeteria in a certain way. How you do that influences kids' choices of lunches. You have to make use of supermarket shelving in a certain way, and again, how you do that influences choices. You can direct people's attention onto certain items you'd like to sell, for instance by making them seem more appealing to people through the provision of a comparable but clearly inferior option. How far we acknowledge this, can influence our stance on policies, as we may set limits to the influences we permit. Note that this does not interfere with individual decision-making, it interferes with the degree that other private agents can exert an influence on our decisions. This is not a decision to be taken lightly, but in some areas, such as school lunches, it may just make good sense.

VI

Considerations regarding the complexity of the economic system lead to a focus on competition and markets as problem-solving devices under an alternative top-down formulation. Competition includes a competition for markets in an ever-changing economic environment. The complexity of the system is interpreted to mean that targeted policy measures cannot be expected to achieve what they aim to. Rather, proactive policies, most likely open the doors for undue influence to be exercised on behalf of private interests. Still, the supposed ineffectiveness of policies provides an important aspect informing the position on economic policies as well. That a general framework has to be provided for economic activity, to establish property rights and contract enforcement, is not disputed, and the same categories of effects leading to market failures are acknowledged.

The arguments made to support this system of thought rely on individuals acting purposely and markets providing the information for purposeful action in a neutral manner. Individual signals are aggregated through their impact on prices. These prices carry the information required for making good decisions. Markets are more effective devices for gathering information regarding the social valuations of goods than any other conceivable ones. The collective market outcome sets effective constraints for undesirable outcomes, and undesirable behavior, by extension. People who ignore market input into their decisions will find themselves in a worse position than they otherwise would be, with customers losing purchasing power and companies losing market shares. As self-interested individuals, they will correct their behavior accordingly. Though by themselves, agents cannot be expected to be capable of much where information gathering, aggregation, and processing is concerned, the system can accomplish these feats and provide the proper foundation for decisions. More in general, the system corrects irrational behavior, and points to outlets for promising endeavors. Where markets may not produce particularly good results, because of external effects, for instance, a clearer allocation of property rights can help. This serves to bring negatively affected areas of societies into the market sphere, where clear signals regarding the trade-offs involved in addressing external effects can be sent. Monopolies, where these are technologically rooted, are another area of concern. However, the belief that market competition and technological progress are the best bets for breaking monopoly positions up, leads to the general consideration that private monopolies will be the lesser evil, when compared to public monopolies or regulation, as the private structures lack the additional political protection that public structures are assumed to have.

Thus, the impersonal aggregation of information that markets permit and the constraints that competition sets for self-interested individuals are believed to structure resource allocation in societies, for current needs and the development of future potential, in the best possible way. Again, a plethora of information is aggregated into market prices to guide individual action. At the same time, profits realized signal promising areas to concentrate efforts for producers, so that market activity also signals the direction that change should take among the available options. Hence, allowing individuals' scope to follow their self-interest has to be the center of policy formulations.

Basic tenants of this perspective hold that competition for profits means that dominant agents will eventually be losing their position to others, because of new technologies, for instance. This might take a while to come about, but private activity is seen as better at allowing this to happen than publicly coordinated activity could. Any interference will only lead to delays in the process of technological progress, reducing future benefits, and potentially misdirecting change, as public agents respond to different signals than private ones. Competing individuals mean that many alleyways toward improvement may be explored simultaneously, offering much more variety and creativity than a centrally structured process could. While this is certainly a valid point, it misses the fact that basic research is generally undertaken in publicly financed structures, not privately, whereas private efforts focus much more on tweaking and refining ideas for marketability. It also assumes that general improvements, economic success, and foundations would be naturally aligned. As private agents are assumed to understand their self-interest, any change that can sustain itself in a market environment has to signify an improvement of conditions. Whether a profit motive alone can direct energies into desirable directions, as a general rule, may be disputed, though. In fact, see Chapters 2, 3, and 4, for examples to the contrary. On a side note, the system here forces behavior onto individuals, as every action is measured against its impact on profits. The only choice open is to participate in the system or not.

This does not mean that other organizational structures would automatically fare better. However, the reasoning for abstaining from policy interventions that lies behind this particular perspective is therefore not necessarily particularly strong. Regarding a policy stance, more narrowly, the lines drawn limiting government actions are impossible to lay down clearly. This does not necessarily have to be a drawback, though, as it may keep the system open to debate.

Still, for guiding policies, this perspective is limitedly useful if we acknowledge that there may be more to society than a focus on economic success and that human beings are not adequately captured by forcing them to consider economic success, above all else, corresponding with monetary units as the only measures for aggregating individual voices.

As a side note, among other things, societal values may be expected to shift to the detriment of overall life in such an environment. For instance, if all is subject to economic consideration, why would anyone expect that laws would be respected and not simply provide the framework for cost–benefit calculations. Treating satisfaction from consumption as equivalent to the freedom to make informed choices, or from there even to happiness, is quite a stretch. Seeing the support of freedom as the attempt to put people into a position where choices become options, we find that such a situation relies on other areas of life to open choices up in the first place, resting on adequate access to education and health, among others. These are not areas where market-based activity can be expected to produce adequate outcomes, for societies, or most individuals.

Even in the market sphere, the results that emerge may not be unambiguous. Among other things, as soon as individual decisions are not taken independently, but influenced by others, valuations will be biased and subject to ongoing changes in the course of economic processes. Price signals are not unambiguous with regard to the information they actually contain in such circumstances. Then, there are different levels of competition, and depending on which one is the most important in a given situation, say individual or group, the development of processes takes different directions. Long-term consequences of the dynamics thusly triggered can be expected to differ. That a money-metric would set a group onto a decent long-run path while maintaining acceptable short-run results, is not a given, especially if assessed under 'one-person-one-vote' instead of 'one-dollar-one-vote'. Also, human decision-making patterns can be used by companies for establishing a position of strength, and this and other mechanisms combine to allow control of markets or market niches. Such control can be maintained for longer periods of time. Where change eventually takes shape, the foundation is not unusually based in research that is undertaken in public structures. Aspects such as these, developed from considering emergent effects and uncertainty, are left out of analyses, or addressed in a way that maintains the private competition was the best way for dealing with them.

While the restriction of governmental power is a well-warranted objective, this is given as an assumption from the outset, and is nothing we learn about in analyses. The system that is being proposed for achieving limited government power would, however, mean that the vacated areas are most likely filled by private influence and power. The only line of defense against such a dynamic is the belief in a particular functioning of the economic system, with an ability to aggregate signals and information in a manner that allows to undermine private power. What we have learned about complex systems suggests that such a specific way of functioning is highly unlikely to result as a general rule.

VII

The bottom-up perspectives on economic problems tend to offer analytical frameworks that introduce components which make situations less easily accessible. Markets may have more than one area, or price-quantity combination, where they might come to a rest. Resting here implies that both sides of the market are willing to continue their activity at the given price level, where the resulting price ranges and relations have been born from and reintegrated into customs and habits, without denying an impact of supply and demand conditions on price formation. With more than one area in which activity may settle, market interactions cannot distinguish among the different possible outcomes. This means that, without interfering with individual decision-making, policies can shift the framework for interactions so as to enhance the likelihood of advantageous results.

The behavior of agents in a market arena might change, depending on the state of a larger environment. This does not only refer to decisions of buying more or less at a given price, but may include such changes as increased demand in the face of increasing prices. Different characteristics of goods may be expected to lead to different particular behavior patterns. Markets themselves may be changing over time as they emerge from individual behavior patterns, without systemic characteristics that would automatically bind individuals to particular positions or actions. In different markets, different sets of rules are likely to be required, even if the stated objective behind their implementation, say fostering an effective resource utilization, was the same.

Market outcomes may be better grasped as a continuous process in a number of cases, and a process-based perspective can offer insights that an equilibrium view is not equipped to grasp. Understanding market activity as a process, especially including the possibility of changes in the functioning of market arenas, will likely require adaptations of policies for structuring and supporting market activity. A single set of rules is unlikely, to say the least, to be able to help bring about consistently good, or at least decent, results. Especially, as in such a process agents can act and react with regard to their environment, adapt to rules in place, and shape their environment to take advantage of rules, etc. This cannot be prevented from the outset, and will have to be met in said ongoing process.

Accompanying processes and keeping them on a path that is characterized by acceptable conditions at the moment, while moving in a direction that promises improvements in the future, is the way for approaching economic policy under these perspectives. Systemic effects, uncertainty, different interests and related actions, and human limitations are factors to contend with when deciding about a policy framework, when the system does not automatically correct misguided or harmful actions and directions. For a general approach to policies and the structures carrying them, it further merits bearing in mind that in changing societies, the conditions within which policies are enacted may change, or interests in maintaining existing structures may develop over time. In short, policies are accompanying the economic process and are, in fact, a part of that process, not separate from it.

VIII

Taking up a general aspect that runs through a number of general considerations regarding the structure of economic arenas, the concept and place of competition should be briefly addressed here as well. Competition between different entities has been an instrumental force for change, without a doubt, on natural, social, technological, and other levels. Its increased integration into modern societies is certainly one of their distinguishing features. Calls for policies to foster competition to make more use of this tool, however, need to be specific at what level and for what should be competed. A generic reference to the benefits of competitive forces is not particularly instructive, nor helpful for laying out policy frameworks.

We saw that individualistic behavior can lead to noticeably worse outcomes for individuals and groups in some examples for interdependent situations in Chapter 2, for instance. Put differently, behavior aimed at competitive success at one level may lead to harm at another. This seems more noteworthy for success at lower levels with negative effects on more aggregate levels. And not only individuals compete, groups can also compete. Assemblies of groups, as large as modern nation states, can compete. Depending on the level at which particular competitive pressure is felt, processes differ. Different traits can prove advantageous at different levels of competition, hence directions and developments can diverge depending on the state of an environment and the particular competitive pressure brought to bear. Fitness is not a fixed value and state. It is a condition that is defined with respect to the environment.

In a situation in which improvements are sought, the process of competition has to be embedded in an appropriate structure in order to harvest its beneficial potential. The means for competing are restricted by custom and law, of course. How they are embedded impacts how they can work. Again, processes are not automatic occurrences. Without supportive environments and structure, they cannot play out. Discarding considerations concerning the need to structure an environment by appealing to some generic concept of automatic order to bring about desired outcomes cannot satisfy more than ideological desires. Concrete rules and structure are needed, and will differ in different environments.

5.3 Policies for Specific Markets – The Labor Market

The first market to consider will be the labor market, as in Chapter 3. Wages and salaries are the principal source of income for most people in modern economies. In order to participate in society, a job is required.

Labor market policies are aimed at protecting workers in their workplace, and setting frameworks for wages and wage negotiations. The range of more specific measures can be somewhat wider.

Opting out of labor participation is not a choice most people have. The vulnerability individuals face in economic matters is rooted in the fact that they may lose employment and employment opportunities due to effects outside their control. How much insecurity results for individuals depends on measures taken for stabilizing economic activity and on measures put in place to afford them an alternative income when they are, or if they are, out of work.

The integration of systemic effects and the openness to process-based views instead of static ones, in bottom-up versus top-down perspectives, influence the positions taken on issues of work, wage formation, the motivation to work, and on a higher level, the impact of measures to reduce economic insecurity and vulnerability, among others. But not only systemic and economic effects matter, where the labor market is concerned. Work, and the structure and sense of accomplishment it offers, are a major part for fulfillment in life for many people. Discarding this as unimportant may have adverse impacts on the structures of and around workplaces, and may come back to affect the labor market in general as well.

I

In the reference framework, allocation patterns are of interest. Faced with involuntary unemployment, the existing economic potential of a group is not exhausted, and activity lower than it would and should be. This reflects a misallocation of labor from a societal perspective. Hence, measures that may be expected to produce distorted outcomes should not be taken, nor supported. They harm individuals who find themselves out of work, and squander resources from a societal point of view.

For the labor market, willingness to provide labor and to employ labor are the two aspects that have to be coordinated, in the best of cases, in a way that everybody willing to work (for a certain wage rate) and everybody willing to hire (at that wage rate) can implement their plans. Then, the labor market, or its individual segments if that is a preferable perspective for the question at hand, is in equilibrium.

If people are unemployed who would be willing to work at the market clearing wage rate, this will be due to distortions in the labor market that prevent the equilibrium wage rate to be realized. Addressing these distortions, the principal question to answer is whether market power, for employers or employees, is playing a role in shaping observed outcomes, or not. Of course, rules and norms, as labor laws, safety standards, and other 'cost factors' will also be under scrutiny.

In a functioning market environment under this perspective, any interference with market prices for labor, i.e., wage rates, will leave people unemployed who would work at the equilibrium price. Such influence can be exerted from demand as well as supply side, directly, or indirectly from the political sector influencing the factors that shape demand and supply decisions. For instance, offering an alternative income in case of unemployment may lead to people deciding not to work, even if employment was available. On the market side, minimum wages may have the same effect by reducing the willingness to hire workers. What the undistorted market outcome is, however, remains unclear.

For the labor market itself, unions can allow workers to reach a position constituting market power, increasing their wages over the equilibrium wage. This reduces employers' demand for labor and leaves some potential workers unemployed. Under this perspective, unions are thus good for those who can get a job or have one already, but lead to shutting others out of the labor market. In fact, in a somewhat astonishing reversal to simplistic explanations and views, a number of economists by now appear to believe that unemployment in the Great Depression was primarily due to wages being too high. To mention a few key issues, this is astonishing insofar as it has difficulties accounting for the fact that, in fact, falling wages were observable, and unemployment still increased. Further, it neglects the fact that wages provide the income needed to maintain demand. Also, debt obligations exist in nominal terms, so that any combination of factors reducing revenue, especially including a generally falling price level, will harm debtors, such as investors who have resorted to external capital, because they will need to see volume increases to maintain a revenue stream to service their nominal obligations. In a problematic economic environment, that increase is typically not forthcoming.

Employers, when they find themselves in a position of influence facing their workers or in the product market they service, can be expected to restrict their employment below the market equilibrium levels. Their influence in product markets manifests in their ability to reduce production volumes to increase prices. Fewer personnel are required. Note that, depending on how unemployment is assessed, this may however mean that officially, unemployment may be seen as low, if people are not willing to work at the prevailing wage rate. If employers dominate their labor market segments, they can negotiate wages from a stronger position. While it may appear as an equilibrium, if labor supply at the going wage rate is reduced so that there is no involuntary unemployment, nevertheless this represents a suboptimal state as people willing to work at the actual equilibrium wage cannot. In this case, as laid out in Chapter 3, minimum wage requirements can actually increase employment. (As you will recall, such legislation changes the marginal calculus of employers, as the marginal cost of additional labor units is now fixed, and not increasing as more workers are hired.) An analysis of the situation is required in order to gain an impression of the conditions, and of which specific model structure may come close to capturing the situation at hand.

Other points termed as causes distorting wages include the assumption that employers cannot fully observe employees' efforts, in which case it may be beneficial for them to pay above equilibrium wages to induce higher efforts. Workers have more to lose if they are caught shirking in that case. Wages above the equilibrium wage, even if voluntarily paid, mean that employment will be lower than it would otherwise be. Given that the problem here is one of information, which cannot really be remedied – valorous attempts at timesheet hour-accounting and other rather heavy-handed and distrusting control measures notwithstanding – there will only be workarounds to limit the impact of such asymmetric information about real effort.

Note that in a functioning market environment in a top-down analytical structure, the possibility for employers to take advantage of the necessity of people to participate in the labor market and press wages down is kept in check by the fact that those who undercut standards in work conditions and wages find themselves wanting for willing workers.

Employment can be found elsewhere, at prevailing standards and remuneration. As the employers' willingness to hire people is taken to signal a profitable production process, they will not be able to realize otherwise accessible profits if they do not adhere to those standards. Again, this presumes that the labor market under observation can be grasped by recourse to the perfectly competitive market model.

How standards may have come about without outside influence, or how improvements may have been realized, is left open; and in all reality cannot be addressed within this analytical perspective. In any situation, they cannot come about from within the functioning market sphere. A unilateral introduction would result in a disadvantage for a producer that nothing could make up for within this framework. The company would have to leave the market arena. However, introduced from the outside, they are usually seen as cost factors for companies that should be avoided in order to make the employment of people attractive to employers. Even the standards that do exist may frequently be called into question, as burdens to companies and distortions to competitiveness, and thus a drag on potential employment in general; especially attractive to employers is the referral to conditions outside the borders of the employment site in question.

Note that shifts of standards then affect the individual workers, whose economic insecurity increases in case of reductions. Depending on our conception of labor markets and their embeddedness in overall economic and wider societal spheres, their economic vulnerability may increase as well, if adverse labor market relations affect the overall macroeconomic sphere; as discussed in Chapter 4, and to be taken up later, they are very likely to do. Either way, if societies decide to provide at least basic measures of protection to their members, then reduced labor standards, beyond the shift of risk and cost to the individual workers and their families, will also mean a socialization of risks and costs from private economic activity, while shifting direct and indirect benefits to companies.

Let us stress the obvious fact that over time, standards have shifted toward improvements for workers, not uncommonly against the resistance of employers who see their negotiating position weakened, and therefore their share of revenue threatened. Raising the minimum working age in the UK from 8 to 9 years already provoked outcries of government overreach and interference with private markets. The fact that it did not spell the end of the capitalist system, or even UK economic supremacy at that time, may be taken as a hint that economic activity can continue under numerous constellations of negotiating strength and risk and cost distribution.

Off-loading risks to workers does not make for a more solid economic performance. At the same time, it is not to discard the fact that at some point, employers may feel it is not worth to continue their operations any longer as larger shares of revenue bypass them. Here, again, an influence of the environment, domestically and internationally, and expectations, for instance concerning acceptable profit rates, will play a role for developments after policies have been introduced. Values and attitudes will have an impact as well. One example can include the time horizon adopted by the different interests involved. We had pointed out in Chapter 2 that the same situation may be approached differently where the time horizons differs, shifting a perspective from a short-term zero-sum struggle of revenue shares to long-term considerations with regard to the stability and expansion of the economic environment. Trying to establish structures that foster long-term thinking and goal-setting can then have numerous positive effects for labor, and societal, relations. The changes in production structures moving away from integrated toward networks of nominally autonomous units in cross-border production that we have increasingly observed over the last few decades may make a common long-term perspective more difficult to realize, as aligned interests may be more difficult to perceive. Resulting changes in negotiating power and concurrent possible changes in willingness to compromise under a long-term perspective have made the position for workers more difficult again, relative to the immediate post World War II decades.

II

Overall, from the reference perspective, we can find good cause for noninterference with labor markets, if we believe them to work approximately like the perfect benchmark market, in conjunction with well-functioning markets in the rest of the economy, and think that the valuation that perspective includes is acceptable for structuring labor relations. We can as well find a solid justification for an involvement, for instance in the shape of minimum wage-legislation, if we believe there to be cause for assuming an influence on the employer-side when determining wages. Other measures can be seen as sensible and advantageous, as well, depending on where negative influences of employment relations have been detected, as some areas – such as health and safety standards – cannot be expected to be addressed from within the market sphere. As such measures are captured as costs for employers, and thus privately accounted, they may come under fire elsewhere when employers do not have to contend with the same level of protection for employees, leading to the persistently resurfacing calls for a socialization of those costs, or a shift to the individual employer, depending.

Something to bear in mind is that for many practical purposes, there hardly is such a thing as a national labor market. An unemployment statistic is without much doubt a good indicator for an overview over the situation in an economy. Even though, for labor market statistics as one example, in the US, if you consider the vast numbers of people that would make the statistics look bad who are excluded from being reported for one flimsy reason or another, how much of an overview is really gained can at times be debatable. For considerations about labor market policies, as well, a less aggregate view may at times be fruitful. More information about sources of unemployment may become accessible; e.g., do changes affect all sectors or are they concentrated in specific ones. Also, in a regional labor market, an employer may exercise more of an influence than would appear discernible from a more aggregate perspective. Finally, for individual households, their principal asset is typically their house. From the perspective of the individual agent, then, moving away to another job may not be as simple as that, and, from an economic perspective, may not be without losses either. For instance, the moment when you have to move may not be the best to sell your single biggest asset. This does not even take into account another factor that is very important for individual well-being and quality of life, namely social structures that people have grown up in and grown into; their life outside of work.

III

Note that the reference equilibrium outcome says nothing about the ability of market participants to actually sustain a living or a full participation in society. Questions that arise involve whether a job that cannot offer the means to make a living actually should be maintained or not, even if profits in the business exist? How far are private businesses subsidized, through an earned income tax credit for workers, for instance, that supports their livelihood and aggregate demand levels? On the other hand, societies may decide to put measures in place that guarantee everyone with a job to actually be able to live of it, say through minimum wage provisions. That may, however, mean that some areas that were profitably integrated into the economic sphere before that decision was taken will not be so any longer. Profits alone would no longer be seen as a justification for undergoing some activities then, especially if based on the ability to take advantage of workers in a weak negotiating position. Also, as we had noted in our discussion of labor markets in Chapter 3 that labor is the main means for securing material necessities for making a living and participating in society. Labor market conditions have a vast impact on human lives in general.

IV

A key to the benchmark perspective's view on the labor market, as on all markets, is the single equilibrium toward which the system is presumably drawn. Potential states of the environment can play no part, as the value of resources and goods, and of labor converting one into the other, is given and guides people's decision. All consumption and production decisions are compatible at that point. This proves tricky even if only assuming more than one possible equilibrium. If we permit the economic environment to have an influence, expectations to have an influence, or spatial structure, among others, to have an influence, we cannot rely on the reference perspective. The benchmark result is invalid, and the disturbances identified, while possibly interesting aspects per se, may fall well short of grasping a number of relevant aspects of situations.

A principal component to the single equilibrium is the decision to supply labor. In the aggregate, the higher the wages, the more labor offered. As we saw in Chapter 3, this is not necessarily the only approach to conceptualizing the amount of labor offered at every wage rate. As wages increase, consumption potential increases and eventually the options to fill leisure time expand. There is more scope for permitting oneself to enjoy leisure. Hence, it can be surmised that eventually, a point may be reached at which the labor supply is reduced when wages increase further. At the same time, when wages fall from our original level, people may eventually want to work more to maintain, at least minimum, living standards. This line of reasoning still works with assumptions in the benchmark framework. However, the single equilibrium no longer exists. Now, there are options for equilibria in which people work a lot and earn relatively little, just as there are equilibria in which people work less and earn more.

The interplay of supply and demand, that is assumed to take the system to a resting state, cannot distinguish between those different possibilities. The structure of the system moves labor-market results to one equilibrium or another. You move the system to the basin of attraction of one attractor or other, i.e., through the rules you influence activities in the system. Then, decisions on how to regulate a labor market can be supporting specific outcomes, without mandating them. There is not an interference with individual decisions. Rather, because it is acknowledged that decisions depend on the environment that agents face at a point in time, we see the notion of structure enabling interactions reflected, without space for a recourse to a neutral reference structure. Which areas of labor relations seem more attractive from a societal position can be determined, the system moved into that general area, and people's best decision in the unfolding environment establishes the overall outcome. No superior market outcome is interfered with; and the outcome realized is, in fact, a reflection of free decisions given a certain labor market structure. This does, however, by no means imply that any kind of regulation and policy proposal would always improve conditions.

V

If we assume a perspective that is process-based, then employment partly depends on the overall state of the economy, the mood in a particular moment, and its changes over time, and thus depends on issues outside the labor market structures themselves. If the mood is cautious enough, there may be times when hiring seizes and lay-offs increase, just as investment may slacken. If the mood is optimistic, hiring may pick up. The mood reflects the beliefs about future demand conditions, which in turn are a function of income received. As income for the household largely determines its spending, letting people drop out of the labor market without much support can have further negative consequences elsewhere in the economy, where demand is reduced and production thus scaled back in response. As pointed out in Chapter 4, the production potential of a production process does not change in a recession or in a depression. The valuation of likely future profits does. This monetary element determines business decisions. A brighter outlook, on the other hand, can increase the willingness to hire people.

With business interests determining employment decisions, safeguarding profits may mean a reduction of employment in order to cut costs. As pointed out in Chapter 4 as well, the confluence of interests of businesses and society is coincidental, even as some degree of overlap exists because of the need to find work and the necessity to employ people for realizing production. But businesses not only prefer to have the costs they produce to be borne by the general public, directly or indirectly, they also do not make production and employment decisions with a view on the greater good, so to say. How far we are able to structure rules that lead individualistic interests to activities which are in line with societal interests is a principal issue to consistently address and assess. Some competitive environment can enhance the confluence of interests, some other can lessen it. Structuring the competitive process to try and enhance a confluence of interests thus is one principal task for regulatory measures. Our more detailed understanding of competition, as laid out previously, will have to be carefully formulated. Not interfering with free private decisions, in the space of acceptable behaviors, means that there is unlikely to be a full confluence, though, as some conflict between individual and group level is likely to crop up at some point or other eventually. However, as the dynamics of change that may emerge from separate individual decisions can be utilized for finding improvements to situations, better than a singularly planned processed can ever hope to achieve, this is not all bad either. A counterweight to private power in business decisions is required, though, directly or indirectly, by attempting to level the playing field between different interests. Also helpful is the offer of alternative employment options for those who find themselves at the bad end of business decisions. Given the importance of income, leaving individuals at the whims of balance sheet procedures, and even more so of resulting systemic effects with swings in overall employment levels, appears somewhat cruel. In a complex system, without the validity of the reference point of the unique equilibrium to guide the thinking about economic structures, it is also unnecessary even from an already purely economic perspective.

VI

Making use of the fact that the public sector is a part of economic activities, not a separate entity, also makes sense when we acknowledge issues of spatial structures and networks. As seen in Chapter 4, connections between agents mean that vulnerability to single events will differ between them. An immediate switch to other connections when some partner in a network runs into trouble may not be that easy, for specialization, spatial constraints, or compatibility issues, for instance. The troubles of one or a few partners do not necessarily have much to say about the viability of all companies in a network. Some support, for the general structure, or some members may well be merited in order to allow the viable ones to reintegrate, or become part of new networks. Now, this is certainly easier said than done, and may open a number of avenues for abuses of power in some form or another, but that is not the same thing as saying that there were solid economic reasons for letting everyone fail. There are not, and alternatives should at least be considered. There may then be good reasons for discarding these, but there are no a priori reasons to not even try. However, whether that means to let more companies go bust in order to maintain dynamic and changes in the business environment, or saving more companies in order to establish more stable economic environments will still have to be answered by societies. Option one in combination with schemes for alternative employment opportunities provided by the public sector, as an employer of last resort, may be a decent compromise, for instance, complemented by focused job-placement and training programs to not just manage unemployment. This way, the ongoing turbulence that has proven necessary for preventing a petrification, or ceremonialization, of structures, may be maintained.

VII

So, in addressing labor market issues, the interpretation where root causes for unemployment lie will matter, as a generally depressed mood halting hiring is not likely to be successfully tackled by forcing wages down, for instance. Sectoral and structural changes may likewise play a noticeable part in employment changes. Creating demand, on the other hand, may alleviate a situation easily. Labor market policies are thus not only microeconomic policies concerned with conditions in a specific market, but are also part of the macroeconomic policies in an economy. We will take this back up further down in this chapter, among others when we address the so-called automatic stabilizers, as measures put in place that kick-in in crisis situations to put a floor under overall demand in an economy, from the macro-perspective, and allow to maintain a certain level of living standards for people at the individual level.

When we let go of the equilibrium concepts and consider economies as continuously changing systems, the general laws governing the benchmark system do not apply. That means, there is no automatic correction if well-intended measures overshoot. The task for policies here is to keep a situation in an acceptable range, preferably with a view on some medium-term and long-term milestones to reach (just as in companies' planning processes), to be corrected and updated regularly. It is in such systems, that individuals become vulnerable to systemic risks, things outside their control, and therefore outside their direct responsibility. How far is individual exposure to such risks supposed to reach? This is not a question that economic theory can answer; it has to be addressed by societies through their social and political systems. As soon as that is acknowledged, however, note that the theoretical foundation for arguments that are based on an equilibrium view of the system are no longer commensurable to the framework in which the problem is posed, as that framework entails systemic effects and processes, not fixed equilibria that force specific behavior of the system's components. If we take the question and problem seriously, we will have to draw on other perspectives on economic systems to address them, at least if we want to do so consistently.

VIII

A final point to consider is that there are costs around labor that are not accounted for in many economic approaches. Labor cannot be separated from the person providing it. That person is more than a worker. Numerous aspects of a life are touched by the conditions in the labor market that people encounter. As people are not automatons, these aspects of their lives matter, and can also have a noticeable impact on the performance in the workplace. Depending on how much scope is given for people to integrate noneconomic aspects of living into their lives, workplace relations change. If noneconomic aspects are deemed to be of little importance relative to economic and business matters, the negotiating power for employers is strengthened, and working conditions tend to be worse for the individual worker who is more quickly replaced, if observation is any guide here. Such aspects, as for instance the ability to enjoy family and leisure time, may well be considered worthy of playing a part in considerations regarding the structuring of labor standards. To argue that some people will want to work more and should be allowed to do so is certainly merited. However, we may have to qualify a binary position because negative external effects caused by workplace attendance decisions may be expected and may have to be addressed. Some people may be working longer voluntarily. However, thereby they may well be reducing the liberty of others to only do what they have actually been hired to do, instead of, for instance, also covering the slack created by positions being left understaffed. From here, habits and expectations may take hold that compound the situation, through promotion decisions, hiring decisions, or feelings of obligations toward coworkers, for instance. The young and hungry may well be the inexperienced and gullible, working a lot more than they get paid for, and permitting increases in profits, or simply the sustenance of business models that are not viable under the standards societies have chosen to establish.

Legislation to limit the time spent at a job might prevent such a negative spiral from happening, to some degree, at least. Similar arguments have been made around and for mandatory retirement ages. The negative external effects, in the reference view, of individual decisions may merit such involvement. The recognition that people who are better rested and have some counterbalances to workday requirements in their lives tend to be more agile mentally, more concentrated, and more productive in the hours that they do work, should not be discarded either.

5.4 Policies for Specific Markets – Financial Markets

Lending and borrowing, and trading rights to future cash flows, including insurances against undesirable developments, however undertaken and labeled in detail, are at the heart of financial market activities. The possibilities this may open up can help to significantly expand the scope of activity in an economy. Funds can be made available for large-scale investments. For investors, there is the possibility to reduce their risk exposure by hedging between investments. Trading papers with third parties has become the rather voluminous central issue of financial market activity.

On the other hand, most crises in modern economies have had their origin in financial market developments. How far financial market operations are permitted to reach is a question of rules and regulations in place. These rules and regulations, in turn, are informed by the framework used for analyzing financial markets.

Even though there are activities in financial markets that relate to real, productive economic activity, in general, it is a derived activity. Money is earning money. Monetary investment promises compound interest, and can in principle be moved among different options relatively quickly - until it cannot, which is one of the problems that we will have to bear in mind here. It has the potential to grow quicker than real activity for a while. Monetary capital then has to eventually be reduced again relative to the productive potential in an economy. Developments that destroy monetary capital are a normal aspect of modern economic activity in that case. Even though some financial activities can fuel productive activity, there is a potential for disrupting it as well.

Broadly speaking, thus, two focuses of financial market regulation can be identified, one referring to the stabilization of the financial sector itself, the other being concerned with links between financial sector and the rest of an economy.

As in all markets, structures for financial markets are supposed to permit ongoing activity, and try to establish an acceptable distribution of not only gains, but risks and costs related to activities among the parties involved. Addressing effects on noninvolved parties, and the economic system, also has to be taken seriously, given the effects that financial market developments can have on productive activity, and thus the livelihood of people. This will have to include foreign investors' involvement and cross-border flows of financial capital as well.

I

Top-down perspectives' recommendations for financial market regulation are rather clear; namely pursue a hands off approach while trying to establish equal footings for all participants (e.g., in most countries, insider trading is prohibited). Financial funds should be expected to be allocated to where they can earn the highest returns. These returns are assumed to accurately reflect earnings and earnings potential in real, that is, productive, economic activity. Policy suggestions are based on assumptions made about markets and their functioning. There will be one market structure that allows the true value of financial products to be reflected in their relative prices. However, as pointed out before, acknowledging the need for some structure through rules and norms, the model framework has to stay silent about the actual setting in which such market outcomes might be achieved. And 'hands-off' is an interpretation that is only one of a number of possible ones. How external effects of financial market activity, and thus the potential for market failures, are assumed to weigh, will further influence the position taken to more specific rules in top-down approaches.

Only if we assume that market failures may be a rather prevalent factor in financial markets, do more active policy outlines become important. If external effects resulting from financial market activity matter, then a policy structure may be worthwhile that influences private activity in a way so as to internalize the social costs of private actions. Taxes are, of course, a rather straightforward measure to take – whether the impact may introduce more distortions than are fixed will still have to be assessed.

The bottom-up perspectives do not lend themselves to a detached approach to financial market regulation. The integration of the complexity of financial markets into analytical frameworks, and the emergence of financial market characteristics which may lead them to function differently from other markets matter here. Uncertainty, the specific, forward-looking nature of financial papers, and the manner of the embeddedness of financial markets in economies are principal aspects to consider, as is, related to uncertainty, real time as reflected in ongoing processes. When these aspects are integrated into an analytical framework, we find financial market activity that can be subject to sudden reversals of trends as part of normal market functioning. Financial market activities and developments influence activity in the real sector of economies, and sudden changes in levels of activity and prices can be transmitted to the real sector through the impact on behaviors and decisions of agents in real economic activity. For policy measures, a differentiation between measures that are aimed at financial markets directly, and measures that focus on an insulation of real activity from financial market disturbances, provides a useful distinction.

II

Different agents in the financial sector can play different roles. Recently, the distinction has become rather blurred, however, as regulations preventing activities in multiple financial arenas have been noticeably loosened. General areas of functions are still identifiable though. Banks making funds for productive investment available fulfill a different role than agents trading rights to cash flows. Most stocks, for instance, are traded in a secondary market; which does make the primary one more attractive, for sure. Further, bundles of papers can be combined into one more complicated paper to tap into the underlying cash flows in the hopes of reducing the risk exposure of agents. Such financial products do not influence resource allocation patterns in production directly as they do not make funds available to companies. Still, interpretations of the signals that price movements for stocks are supposed to entail, lead companies to try and manage their stock prices. Thus an indirect influence of financial market activity can be noticeable, as companies' funds are dedicated to managing financial indicators, and not their future earnings' potential. And the ability to presumably permit a more pronounced spread of risks should make investment projects more attractive, fostering real-world investment. We will come back to this point.

Productive investment is frequently financed by resorting to external capital. Financial market actors that are participating in activity related to real economic structures as well as in activity focusing on financial investments are a main conduit for transmitting financial market developments to real economic activity. Banks are the foremost examples, of course. Though they do not directly act in real markets, activity therein nevertheless relies on them for an access to credit for financing investments.

The position of financial sector agents to make the funds for productive investments available results in the possibility of spillovers of adverse developments in the financial sector, when agents engage in investments in financial market products at the same time that they serve as financiers for real sector investors. Once they run into trouble, they will have to restrict the scope of their operations. The directions into which funds would be taken are not a primary factor in decisions at that point.

The general upswing of the relative weight of financial investments has had an impact as well, of course, but is not connected to any specific role of particular agents for a possible impact on real investment. Between those two fields, it is a question of the relative attractiveness of financial over real activity, or vice versa, that shapes allocation patterns.

Separating the areas in which entities and agents can be active by dividing support for real activities and financial investments would likely result in an increase in the stability of the production side in an economy and can enhance the stability of the entire economic system then, as principal transmission channels are severed, or at least substantially narrowed. A limitation of scope for agents, through the known separation of commercial and investment banking, is a way forward here. Banking would be limited to the role of supporting the real economy. Investment banking would not require the pronounced guarantees it can force through the threat of disrupting the entire economy. Whether under such circumstances, and in parallel, size limitations for, especially banks, should be considered for reasons of eliminating possibly destabilizing dynamics – that is, beyond concerns about undue market power – may be deliberated as well.

Financial market developments may still impact the real sector, for instance as price movements trigger changes in demand patterns, or as interest rate changes affect real-sector investment. However, the connection would be less tight, and it should usually be easier to contain adverse developments in the real sector as the link to investment in production should be weakened.

III

The so-called innovation in financial markets consists of new ways to trade and distribute risk, and increase possibilities for leverage in investments. The hope, assumption, or rhetoric, depending on the standpoint, is that repackaging risk allows to spread it more widely, reducing the exposure of any individual agent involved in trading-related papers, and thereby enhance the stability of the financial sector as a whole. For independently taken decisions, faced with events that are happening independent of each other, this approach may work. However, systemic effects in the financial sector mean that the risk evaluation of investments that forms the foundation for the reference perspective may be more involved than is assumed there. The risk of an investment vehicle may depend on the economic environment if systemic effects can play a part in shaping it, i.e., risk positions may develop with market movements. Such effects may be the result of emerging developments based in individual actions, positive feedback mechanisms among decisions, or among events. Then, risk components that relate to the connections of agents change with changing moods and economic environments, and the reduction of risk is not due to a broader spreading of risk, but momentary advantageous environments. That will, or at least may, then reverse in adverse environments, showing a pro-cyclical systemic risk component. Suggesting that a pronounced share of financial market activity in an economy's investment activity could be seen as a sign of a strong economy – in the sense that structures are in place to provide for its members without subjecting them to too pronounced a risk for maintaining their material positions – may be rather misleading.

A distinction of investment flows toward real or financial sector can therefore help establish a clearer picture of an economy, and its potential, whether those funds originate domestically or externally.

Past patterns that have been drawn on for structuring a portfolio may change in response to changes in the economic environment, and third-party problems may affect agents that do not have direct links to them because of the linkages of cash flows between agents. If agents are aware of these possibilities and react accordingly once trouble has started to brew, or is even only thought to become more likely, they can trigger the trend they sensed, or at least contribute to its unfolding. This view strengthens the focus on systemic risk exposure, and especially the connection between the agents involved.

For bottom-up perspectives, risk is not a given characteristic of individual investment vehicles. Considering the possibility that the risk connected to investments changes during economic processes, as economic environment and attitudes are not static, points to the fact that the overall risk in the financial sector may change as well. Times of higher risk exposure are times during which a quick price drop becomes more likely, due to the interwoven cash flows and balance sheets of agents that may trigger a chain reaction of actions, which in turn may lead to pronounced distress sales by agents. Preventing an overexposure to risk would likely provide a stabilizing effect. However, that risk is a risk potential during good economic times, and thus is not necessarily immediately apparent. Stressing financial market function and the dynamics from the relations of agents becomes a key point for approaches to regulation.

During times of stable economic activity, we expect a tendency of agents to accept more potential risk in their investments by relying more heavily on borrowed funds and enable a more pronounced leveraging of investments. Such funds for leveraging in turn strengthen the transmission channels between agents, adding the balance sheet connections to the general problems that falling prices can mean for other leveraged investors. If a positive trend is discontinued, a self-reinforcing wave of financial troubles for agents becomes increasingly likely. Once financial institutions are in trouble, financial sector activity will be reduced. Depending on connections and risk exposure, this can cast a wider net, or a narrower one. This, in turn, depends on the rules and measures in place that shape the connections between financial sector and real sector in an economy. Keeping the financial system outside such potentially instable regimes may then be one objective of economic policy. Again, preventing the phase transition to instable areas may be achieved by limiting the leverage permitted, for instance. This can be done, for instance, by requiring increasing capital buffers for increasing credit exposure of lenders, and may be further tied to changes in specific indicators, for instance, those showing real estate price developments. The goal is to make a credit expansion more unattractive as the exposure to credit risks, in case of adverse price developments, increases.

The fact that the risk attached to individual investments may depend on the financial market environment, the relevant economic environment, and the general economic mood and environment has, however, so far eluded full integration into formal models. In fact, for a number of analytical approaches to financial markets, this aspect is excluded by assumption, and all risk taken to be understandable, calculable, and given, for a certain investment. Furthermore, the distribution of individual risks is assumed to be describable by a bell curve; something that empirical data calls into question. Under different assumptions, the mathematical foundation these models rely on could not be formulated, however. Risk that is influenced by environmental factors and the state of an ever-changing system, itself changes over time, and depending on other economic factors. Previously uncorrelated investments, may well have to face reassessments under changing economic conditions, because prices that were thought to be independent of each other turn out not to be in times of crises, and show correlations, or because overall economic behavior affects financial markets in an unforeseen way.

Depending on the perspective adopted for analyses, the assessment of potential and problems arising from financial activity will differ. For instance, a perspective on financial markets that excludes possibilities for emerging changes in risk, may well miss core aspects of the functioning of financial markets, and therefore focuses for stabilizing or other supportive structures to be put in place. A reduction of the scope of action permitted to agents with different functions in the financial sector can be fairly easy to implement, if truly desired, and would reduce the possibilities for financial sector trouble to spill over into the real economy, and wreak havoc among those who are strongly dependent on regular employment for making a living. Spreading of and hedging against risk can thus already spell trouble for the stability of financial market operations and, depending on the connections to real activity, the productive sphere of the economy. Speculative activity may further increase the likelihood and enhance the impact of adverse developments in financial markets.

IV

Prices in financial markets tend to move continuously, so other motivations for transactions besides reducing risk and adverse effects of uncertain conditions through hedging can play a part; namely speculation about price movements. As laid out in Chapter 3, arbitrage options exist if the same product is priced differently in different markets and you can buy at a lower price in one market and then sell the same product at a higher price in another market without delay. Options for speculation result from expectations about future price developments; this does not have to be a distant future. In markets in which participants can influence prices, through large sums they move or momentum they can generate by timing transactions, speculators may run relatively little risk, especially if their original capital buffer is large enough. Speculation can produce price movements that can cause harm, so limiting the scope for speculation is a worthwhile objective for policies to pursue. Additionally, speculation is not uncommonly undertaken with the help of leveraged investments. Not only can a single investor have more of an impact on market prices, but the connection to other entities, namely those who provide the funds for the lever, introduces risks for agents who are not directly involved in the speculative transactions themselves. Still, we had seen in Chapter 3 that different views on options for and scope of speculation exist, depending on the framework applied for grasping aspects of financial markets. Again, different views on regulations and structures follow.

Speculative activities in the financial sector are the first focus for critics very often, and prove contentious in the discussions about financial markets. Depending on the perspective, speculation is supposed to be impossible in well-functioning markets, may only be possible to a very limited degree by taking advantage of a slight temporal advantage regarding newly available information, or is stabilizing markets, as good speculators buy when the market is low and sell when it is high, while bad speculators are forced to leave markets because they lose money. Finally, some perspectives assess speculation as entirely possible, and common, as well as potentially destabilizing.

The first positions are developed from a view on financial markets that mixes the static equilibrium view, as the outcome toward which market dynamics are automatically drawn, and a nod in the direction of people who point out that information is a special kind of animal. Once it is known, it is not worth paying for, but before you know it, you do not know what it may be worth. Still, all relevant information is supposedly priced into markets immediately. The conundrum is that nobody should have a reason to gather information and analyze it for its impact on earning potential of companies, for instance, while someone has to do it in order for the information to become part of the proper pricing. Thus, the analytical structure is modified to allow that someone may gain a short temporal advantage and make money by forecasting price movements reflecting newly available information. In connection to this, temporarily, price movements may result as agents adjust to new information and price movements, possibly even causing an overshooting of the price correction. This may also open the chance for speculation, if confusion abounds about the degree to which prices have temporarily diverged from their proper level. Knowing this, and knowing to which level prices will eventually return, may permit some additional scope for speculation. The assumption behind the idea of good speculators is, of course, that some agents know better than others about where the true, fundamental value of assets lies. Recognizing the trend moving away from such fundamental values, they also know that at some point in the future the trend will reverse, and can enter deals to make money of that insight. Note that speculation may well be stabilizing in this case, as speculators will be taking actions that will eventually support the return to proper prices.

Regarding a stabilizing role of speculators, it is hard to justify as a regular attribute even from within a framework endowing the market environment with extraordinary structuring and constraining capacities.

While successful speculators may well stabilize markets from time to time by betting against an unfolding trend, if the market cannot be beaten systematically, who is successful and who is unsuccessful will change over time. Weeding out the bad speculators is nothing more than weeding out those who suffered from bad luck or circumstances, and not only systematically unsound decisions at a particular point in time. It does not translate into an environment where the able speculators will stay standing, fulfilling their tasks of stabilizing financial sector activity by countering mistaken trends. That those who remain will be solid pillars of stability because of a natural proneness to successful speculation is not a possible outcome against the market view adopted, so that the weeding out of incapable wannabe speculators only changes the composition of the group, leaving the overall situation intact – some will find themselves above the average market return in a given period of time, some below.

What is more, depending on when agents run out of funds, they may worsen the situation because they may have to sell into a falling market, for instance. The constraint that liquidity introduces is at times not acknowledged, but can increase destabilizing tendencies easily, as liquidity is not boundless for individual agents. We also saw that the idea of a fundamental value of financial products, and goods in general, stands on a dubious foundation. Where that is not given, there can be no divergence from it.

A successful speculator needs to understand moods and changes in expectations, to form an idea of where other agents may drive a price. For a while, speculative activity will support a building price dynamic, and at some point, it will support a countering trend. A productive role for speculators is very much limited to a world of true values, in which some extremely insightful agents can counter the movements in prices brought about by the less informed mass of people who are active in financial markets. That is not necessarily a world which resembles ours particularly closely. In the latter, fluctuations in markets are at least as likely to be enhanced by speculative activity as to be dampened. Overall levels of risk and the systemic risk component are likely to be enhanced as well.

Finally, as a large volume and strong liquidity in market, restricting individual influences, is by no means guaranteed, and in fact not given for many market segments of financial sector activity, moving markets is a definite possibility for some agents. They can also make their speculative position pay off by inducing behavior in others who make the result they need come about. As expectations are an important factor in driving market prices, this is always a possibility, though it may be easier at some times than at others. Under uncertainty, speculation is possible, and given the money that can be made from it, and the possibility to trigger market movements, can be very worthwhile. It can be unsuccessful, as well, and can produce pronounced instability in financial markets. If successful for the speculating actors, it can still produce noticeable instability, depending on its target, say an exchange rate, and its impact on real economic structures, say through their effects on trade flows, and thereby on productive structures.

The motivation for speculation is different from motivations underlying contracts that aim at reducing risk and effects of uncertain events for the parties involved. Regulating transactions following one motivation – speculation – without limiting options for the second kind – hedging – may be possible, even if there may be a gray area in which the distinction is not easy, and where some unproblematic transactions would not come to be. Whether that seems a price worth paying for reducing volatility in financial markets is up for societies to decide.

Curtailing speculation therefore appears to be a legitimate objective. Rules may differ in detail, but making certain operations costlier, or potential gains smaller, will be the way forward. This may refer to fees to be paid that are reduced with the time a financial paper is held, restrictions to capital flows, taxes on certain transactions, or transactions with certain characteristics, rather, reductions of leverage that is permitted, other measures in a similar vain, or even a simple ban of certain operations. This will likely make some selected helpful transactions more costly as well, but the overall reduction of turbulence and thus of economic insecurity for individual agents may well be seen to be worth it. Limiting leverage will additionally have the potential positive effect of keeping financial systems in general out of the areas of their functioning in which systemic risks increases noticeably due to the balance sheet connections between the different agents involved.

Whether the costs of speculative activity are severe enough to set up regulations trying to prevent speculative activity, and whether such measures can be expected to result in more good than harm, is, in fact, a matter of the perspective on the economic sphere, to a good degree. The evaluation of this question will partly depend on the ability of financial market changes to affect real activity in an economy, as well as on the attitude of people with regard to financial market operations. How far financial markets can influence real economic activity depends on the regulations structuring connections between financial market agents and production in an economy. An evaluation of individual measures without regarding the overall environment may then only offer limited insights.

However, all this may well be seen as too much of an interference with people's right to gamble. If the principal motivator, as may well be assumed, is the protection of real economic activity from financial market-triggered distress, then the transmission channels from financial sector to real economy may be a more promising focus for policies. The stranglehold that financial market agents currently enjoy, namely to force protection payments when things go south, would be loosened, at least. On the other hand, we may note that societies rely on financial markets for other things than quick money for people who are lucky in their gambling (and fees for those shifting portfolios compositions around). Long-term investments, such as retirement funds, are a part of financial market activity, for instance. Sudden losses of portfolio values can then hurt people who have nothing to do with triggering the dynamics behind sudden reversals of price developments. Limiting the attractiveness of speculation can then be seen as a legitimate objective, protecting people from the negative external effects and distortions of a relatively few financial market actors.

V

A specific area of financial markets is the trading of currencies. As seen in Chapter 3, the exchange rate is supposed to reflect assessments of short-term and long-term potential of economies, relative to other economies. Markets in the reference perspective aggregate the assessments of these issues by numerous independent agents and thereby provide the best possible valuation of currencies. The thought of a proper price for a currency indicates the assumption that the potential of economies was fixed and knowable at a given moment, balancing the different interests involved with its formation better than any other mechanism could. New information and changes in potential are presumably priced into the exchange rate as they become available. There may be some adjustment time required, but currency trading in markets is the best option to get a proper price. Setting an exchange rate might seem to alleviate problems in the short-term, but if it is necessary to get involved, then imbalances will continue to persist that will eventually lead to a pronounced correction, with substantial cost for the agents in an economy. So far, so familiar!

If we assume that different time horizons may be difficult to reconcile in an exchange rate market, we can capture the resulting imbalances as a form of external effects. Short-term flows of financial capital may have effects that are damaging to long-term capacity developments, for instance. We had also mentioned the Dutch disease in Chapter 3. Fees for transactions, or outright limits to certain kinds of capital flows, may then be a worthwhile policy focus.

We already saw that the utilization of available potential is a business decision, employing available machinery based on monetary considerations. These monetary considerations become potentially more volatile once cross-border movements are included as an additional component that has nothing to do with technological potential, and activities with a view particularly on short-term profits enter the fray; in this case, most likely oriented on the financial sector and thus even further removed from production potential and technological considerations. Basing assessments on a bottom-up framework, the volatility of exchange rates is a monetary phenomenon, not so much the result of decisions evaluating production potential and its possibility for changes, as well as fiscal policy, monetary policy, social policy, etc.

There may then be cause for some interventions aiming at stabilizing exchange rates. This is not that easy, of course, as a target range for exchange rate for a traded currency has to be stabilized by central bank interventions; namely the acquisition or sale of currency in order to maintain the rate. Mandating a range of acceptable exchange rates does not remove expectations and potential for financial gain. For maintaining the rate within the desired range, foreign currency may be required, which has to be acquired somehow in the first place. The trade surpluses that we have seen in developing countries in the wake of the Asian crises, and up until today, are certainly owed at least in part to considerations about capacities to stabilize exchange rates to protect production in the economy, and the technological capacity that goes with it, by maintaining rates that allow producers relying on imports to continue their operations, and prevent domestic debtors to foreign lenders from facing solely exchange rate-based problems. The prevention of the short-term costs and instability that disruptions and ensuing crises have caused likewise offers a motivation to prevent quick exchange rate changes.

Targeting an exchange rate is thus one option, but requires, possibly substantial, currency reserves. Especially where these are known, determined speculators may undermine an exchange rate by harnessing superior funds. This has nothing to do with the suitability of an exchange rate for production structures, and everything with the potential to make money by forcing its change.

Another option for isolating against, at least some, turbulences from international money flows, are restrictions on cross-border financial capital flows. One possibility there would be to impose a tax on sales proceeds in financial markets that decreases the longer papers have been held to discourage short-term financial market movements. Currency trading itself can be subject to similar rules. Of course, a simple focus on time-frames may punish some transactions that are undertaken for purposes of risk reductions, but the notion may at least offer a starting point for considerations. Still, it will not prevent the potential rush out of a currency following shifts in the general mood. As always, some trade-off will surface once rules are contemplated. Capital controls, i.e., limits to how much foreign capital can leave an economy how quickly, can help address this latter aspect. Overall, while some potentially beneficial transactions may be negatively affected, it seems fair to state that under this perspective, as a rule of thumb, financial activity that is deterred by such buffering measure is not the most likely to actually contribute to generating value in an economy.

Still, such measures do not solve problems of accessing goods and technology available in and from other economies. For entering trade relations, something has to be available for trading. The development of internal capacities is a prerequisite for enhanced gains from economic activity and increasing living standards that may follow.

5.5 Policies for Specific Markets – Cross-Border Relations: Trade and Development

The overall objective of trade is to increase productivity, through enhanced competition, increased output, more advantageous resource allocation, in combination with the fact that you can specialize in production and then exchange across borders. Access to other goods may also mean access to information about production techniques that have not been acquired in an economy yet. That access may also be a part of larger agreements for cross-border contact or access to markets. Overall, as specialization in trade will offer differing potential for technological development in an economy, trade policies may be seen as part of a larger development policy direction.

I

In the top-down perspectives, stepping back and permitting trade and investment flows is the way to go. We had seen in Chapter 3 that resource allocation patterns to production processes will change to allow increased production. As an economy has access to limited resources, specialization from trade allows a more focused concentration of these resources. They can be employed where they are most productive when comparing the trade partners involved. Trading economies can increase the overall output available and exchange their respective products to at least match a (hypothetical) pre-trade situation. Subsequent exchanges lead to every economy involved having access to a higher volume of goods. Trade should not be hindered. For defining the impact of specific aspects of trade, individual mechanisms are focused on, thus not permitting people and technology to move between countries.

A similar logic is applied to investment, especially when scarcity of monetary means for investing is assumed. If there are attractive investment options that domestic investors cannot take up, then funds from investors in other countries should be allowed in. These funds would not enter, if expectations about returns for other investment opportunities were higher, so that a free flow of funds also allows the best possible allocation of investment funds globally. As returns on investments and physical product are equated, here, conveniently, that means that global output will be maximized.

It is acknowledged that an opening of an economy to trade flows can hurt sectors. However, two issues are usually raised in that regard. The first is that the economy as a whole is better off, and that distributional issues are not part of the area of interest here. The second is that consumers will be better off regardless, as goods get more abundant and more affordable. The potential overlap between workers and consumers and its implications are not explored further. As the representative individual is owner, producer, worker, and consumer in one, it does not have to be; and, in fact, cannot be within the logic of the reference perspective.

II

Once the static outlook focusing on allocating given resources to given production processes is expanded to allow a dynamic perspective, other issues may start playing a part. Especially, if it is taken into account that technology is not automatically usable everywhere once it has come to be mastered somewhere (see Chapter 3), complementary issues such as the development of production capacities come into the picture.

A production focus and specialization based on static conditions would cement existing structures. If an advance in technological capacities is desired, policies concerning trade will have to address issues supporting the ability of economic agents to integrate newer and more productive technologies. Such concerns will have to focus on sustaining and developing skills, access to knowledge, and capabilities of working with that knowledge in order to adapt technologies to local conditions, and enjoy a solid foundation for further technological advances. What incentives agents respond to when deciding whether to try and innovate, or not, will have to be a core aspect of related considerations. All experience suggests that the notion that free trade was conducive to technological upgrading cannot be upheld. While it may not hinder the development of further capacities in the economies that benefit most at a given moment, it makes it very hard for those who are not in that group. At least, none of those has managed to close the gap to more technologically advanced structures without concerted efforts by public and private agents to advance such technological upgrading. Even in the more technologically advanced economies, a lot of the actual novelty to turn into innovation is developed with government backing; the US military-industrial complex being just one, albeit very noticeable, example. A more careful approach to trade-related questions focusing on objectives and possible means to achieve these will be required.

This observation has also been part of a perspective that focuses more strongly on relations of power between agents and economies. While technological change happens on the terms of the most advanced economies, and in a manner compatible to their internal structures and interests, weaker countries, not uncommonly ruled by narrowly self-interested cliques and elites, provide markets for advanced countries' production, and offer the resources to produce them, as well as the less sophisticated products for which the premium that can be commanded – the value-added in production – is no longer sufficient for meeting the objectives of the controlling, more advanced producers.

III

Economic growth is the outcome of developing and integrating technological capacities in and into economic processes, besides the more short-run impact of drawing new societal areas into the realm of transactions. Improved technological capacities can translate into more effective resource-transformation and higher value-added in production processes. They also expand the economic sphere by making more goods available. Long-run economic growth is substantially the result of an ongoing process of structural changes in economies. Technology itself is a combination of skill and machines, its application in economic processes refers to production processes and the support of these. Its change is the outgrowth of an increase in knowledge and understanding. The skills employed in production processes are learned, and then honed and improved while exercising them. Skills do not only relate to the actual production of a good but to the surrounding structures, organizing the access to inputs, marketing the proceeds, organizing the production process itself, and so on. Skills are acquired over time, and improved over time when they are utilized. Now, whether an activity can continue is subject to constraints that an economic evaluation of the processes sets – is it profitable to continue. But, whether a process can be undertaken depends on whether necessary machinery can be acquired and staff can be found to man it. Whether it can continue, then, depends on whether the expenditures related to setting it up and running it can be covered by the proceeds gained.

Concerning trade that means that in a position in which an already established company is faced, unsupported newcomers generally find themselves at a disadvantage, in skill and experience. The original disadvantage may be counterweighted to some degree by cheaper inputs, most notably labor, but on the other hand a number of issues around production processes and their organization, as well as quality concerns can stand against that. Infrastructural and other considerations can play a part as well. Also important is the fact that in industrial production, increased production volumes typically translate into lower unit costs, so that a newcomer faces a potential cost disadvantage due to lower initial production volumes and lack of experience in the management of related production processes. More importantly, a quality and knowledge gap is likely, and may extend even to well-established production processes. As companies bringing parts of their value-added chain abroad have also increasingly realized, for instance in moving from Western and Central Europe further east, labor cost advantages are not everything when it comes to production. Hence, a number of them have started moving back. Organizational capacities, surrounding structures, as physical and institutional infrastructure, for instance, and other aspects are typically significant contributors to the success of industrial undertakings.

Establishing new production structures against existing competitors can be difficult, therefore. Experience takes time to build. Costs related to volume require such volume to grow. This likewise takes time, as increased volumes need customers, and a number of issues concerning increased throughput of resources and pre-products require learning and experience as well. When industries face established competition from the get-go, they are likely not to have the time to develop what they need. Given the short-term economic constraints in place that have to be overcome, developing skills and gaining experience may require to shelter companies for a while. Larger internal markets offer an advantage here, as when those are not as easily accessible to established companies, newly established domestic producers can gain volume and related experience at home. Protection for domestic producers may make sense, to allow the establishment of volume and quality levels; as do trade agreements, or free-trade areas, between neighboring countries at similar levels of technological capacity. Bearing the argument of capture by public agents for individual private interests in mind, such trade areas may be preferable, as capture may be more difficult to establish where larger territories and different representatives are concerned, although it certainly does not have to be. In any case, political structures are a rather important component, obviously, as the relations between existing interests need organization and outlets.

Arguments against such approaches tend to center on the static allocation viewpoint and a temporary reduction of accessibility of, at that point, better goods from abroad with concurrent disadvantages for today's consumers; or on a political angle. On the other hand, if you do not even try, future potential faces much steeper odds to overcome in its development. All industrialized economies have massively supported the development of technological capacity in their territory, to lay the groundwork for an industrial sector, and have thereby been able to help establish companies that could eventually orient their activities beyond their own borders as well. From the British competition with the United Provinces to the competition the UK faced from other European economies and the replacement of the UK by the US as the preeminent economy in the world, and the rapid development of technological capacity in East Asia following World War II, a structured integration of private and public agents into the economic process and sphere has always been a key to upgrading production structures. That a public sector presence would hinder the process is bogus, how to structure the coordination and cooperation between different agents and interests is the interesting, and challenging, aspect of the process.

Referring to the process character likewise allows to point to a couple of further related points, namely that structures that have worked at some point during the process are not necessarily suitable for later stages, and that structures that help overcome short-term challenges may contribute to the buildup of potential problems in a more distant future. Neither aspect signifies that a different structure would have been better, much less that there could be a fixed set of policy organization and structure that would be well suited for the entire process of economic development that economies have undergone. As technological change is a process, leading to changes in conditions and environments, on the contrary, that an adaptation of rules would be required to continue changing along an advantageous trajectory only seems to be expectable.

IV

Trade serves a dual function for upgrading structures. Access to knowledge and others' experiences is the first and fundamental part of cross-border contact, and allows to gain knowledge without having to experiment and incur research costs for activities that were already undertaken elsewhere. You need the knowledge and experience to recognize things and integrate them into your operations; issues of compatibility with existing structure likewise play a role here. The most fantastic new car that, however, runs on an engine for which the necessary energy infrastructure is not in place cannot be a sales winner. Hence, technological upgrading also takes place on an established foundation. For being able to upgrade, and stay compatible, what is done elsewhere and how it is being done needs to be known. The second role trade fulfills is to permit access to larger potential demand volumes, which can further foster specialization and thus support productivity increases in production.

Policies addressing access to economies and terms for such access have included numerous different provisions for gaining access to knowledge. Squeamishness about intellectual property and patented products and processes has always taken a backseat until a certain, relative, level of technological competency had been reached. It is very much a luxury that only the most advanced economies have allowed themselves, and propagated to others, with varied degrees of success in enforcement. Balancing these different aspects, and acknowledging that people outside one's influence are involved as well, is not an easy task, and will have to be continuously reassessed with structures redrawn. In any case, much more important for technological advances than financial funds is knowledge.

An issue that is frequently raised in support of a free-trade stance is the possibility that domestic companies focus more on maintaining their protection to stay in business, and less on improving their products and production conditions to actually become competitive. This is certainly a valid point. However, rules and structures allow the improvements sought, just as they may permit sheltering businesses. Structuring political and administrative spheres and the interaction of agents in different functions and arenas appears more important, and a fruitful point to consider than a black or white picture on separate public and private sectors. That policy support indeed results in significant and long-term technological upgrading depends on how the political sector is interpreted, used, and controlled in a society. On the other hand, where the political sector is abused for private gain, one might wonder how a withdrawal of public agents might lead to a constraint on private power and its exercise. Integrating vested interests in a suitable manner to permit dynamics of development and change to unfold has always been a critical component of the process of technological upgrading. Of course, the same problem areas persist in circumstances in which modern economies face structural change.

An important issue to consider, furthermore, for the development of technological capacities is the disruption that financial market activities can cause. While financial capital is of lesser importance for the development process, financial market developments still affect the stability of economies. Hence, rules governing cross-border financial flows, to prevent sudden swings in exchange rates, and rules governing relations between financial markets and productive economy, internally, may be expected to foster an environment in which the actual development of technological capacities is facilitated.

5.6 Other Societal Arenas and Economic Activity

I

One aspect that we have not gone into much in the overview of concepts is the issues of permitting economic activity to draw on inputs from other sectors of societies. As far as the overarching objective of emancipating individual agents is concerned, noneconomic areas of life play as much of a role in the process as economic ones, and mutual influences can be detected between all of them, from health, to education, and environment, for instance. These should be considered in economic policy formulations, as economic activity is not separated from the rest of the human existence. Economic activity is part of life as a whole, and though for some questions we can ignore this fact, every once in a while we may do well to remember it, and consider the overall consequences of our choices. As effects in other areas of life are difficult to impossible to quantify, they are, however, frequently not included in the estimates for the impacts of measures. The same is true for what we may call dynamic effects – policy measures can lead to developments that change the foundation of economic activity, for instance by expanding technological competence, improving the health situation, or deteriorating the natural environment, and therefore can have effects for which we may be able to designate a general evaluation as desirable or not, but may not be able to put reliable numbers on. Where the guesstimation of numbers is attempted, there is quite a bit of freedom in shaping them. The outcomes are distorted assessments of policies and their effects, possibly with an ever stronger bias toward a preservation of existing interest and influence structures.

Defining the role of the economic sphere has to be a part of policy considerations. The interrelation of economic issues and society at large requires an understanding of what economic activity can help achieve, and what side effects may come with it. It then requires a discussion of what may be an acceptable impact on life that is not quantifiable in terms of money. Decisions affecting these issues mean that there will have to be considerations of trade-offs, as robust economic activity provides the material means of life, whereas other areas of life provide the means to actually living that life beyond the fulfillment from work itself.

Environmental issues, for instance, often serve as examples for external effects, which result in distortions of allocation patterns, when seen from the reference perspective. These distortions typically result from the provision of, at least approximately, free inputs to production processes. Standards of environmental protection put in place include restricting the rights to an individual use of certain inputs by the group, potentially providing intangible gains to the group over tangible costs for producers. An analysis informed by the reference framework would stress a solution in terms of a willingness to pay, for the conservation of a specific area, a park, for instance, or the purchase of pollution rights from the group by producers, in forms of carbon taxes or permits for instance. Again, once the reference framework is drawn on, one-dollar-one-vote becomes the accepted means for decision-making over one-man-one-vote.

Prices for using free inputs may be established, either directly or indirectly, by establishing threshold values that signal a certain degree of permissiveness. Such indirect approaches may, for instance, come in the shape of maximum permissible emission levels in industrial production sites. Existing interests and their scope for negotiations will shape the decisions that are made in these areas. There is no market to fall back on, at the moment and independent of the perspective adopted, by definition of the problem structure; due to a lack of existing price patterns, as well as the limited number of agents who are actually directly involved in negotiations and decision-making. How far economic activities are permitted to influence other areas of life depends on the perception of what can be achieved by allowing them to do so, and the ability of affected groups to be involved in shaping the decision-making process. Labor regulations, to take up an example from the social sphere, may be an area in which regulations applying to economic issues are set up with a view on protecting other areas of life, through work-safety rules, restrictions on the length of the workday, maternity and paternity leaves, sick days, prevention of children's participation in labor markets, etc. Note that the absence of such restrictions would significantly shift negotiating strength to employers.

An attempt to focus on economic issues alone is not a problem in and of itself, as the economic interest is one aspect of relations. Elevating it above other interests and focusing on a one-dollar-one-vote rule for allocation decisions without proper discussion may be, on the other hand. Furthermore, the separation of economic aspects from others is not necessarily easy. Our decision-making faculties may provide a bias toward decision structures that are easier to grasp – comparing two numbers, for instance, even if (economic) effects that cannot easily be quantified have been ignored when estimating those numbers. That there is more to activities than their immediate economic impact introduces a level of arbitrariness into cost and benefit calculations that are often hidden from view, behind the suggestion of precision that numbers afford us.

We might take this moment to stress again that absent the neutral reference point, there will only be shifts of risks and costs between different constituents and groups. Some regulations may result in patterns of distributions that make participating in a certain market unattractive, but that outcome may well be acceptable, or even desirable, from a societal point of view for some sectors and activities. Also, absent formal regulations of activities, private regulations have to fall in place to provide the necessary structure for transactions. Private power can play a more pronounced role, depending on the values and general institutions embedding the exchange arena, of course.

II

A different kind of interaction between general societal structures and economic sphere lies in the influence of thinking in terms of economic and business constraints on thoughts and ideas about other societal issues. Which areas of societal life are drawn into the economic sphere, toward one-dollar-one-vote, is a political decision. The more aspects of life are coordinated by economic considerations, the larger the economic sphere. For economic growth, this trend is thus good; at least for as there may be effects down the line that counter an initial up-tick in measured transactions. How much of an impact such countering trends can have depends on the way in which aspects which are subject to economic considerations may change over time, and how they are managed then.

Changes in social structures and arenas that have not been previously touched by an economic logic may be a part of potential costs, which should in that case be acknowledged (if foreseeable), or integrated to proceed with caution, as any structural change will bring new interests who happen to profit, economically or in other ways, and thus may provide concentrated resistance to later changes.

Education and health-care sectors have been treated according to considerations that were not strongly based on an economic rationale by a number of societies over the past decades. Alternatively, a consensus may emerge to restrict access to education or health on an 'ability-to-pay' basis again and thus moves extended areas of societal relations into the economic sphere, even as that removes those areas from the reach of a number of potential beneficiaries, and thus conceivably weakens a group, society, and economy in the longer run. Such a removal may be evaluated in terms of general human development or, more narrowly, in terms of a reduction of as-of-then unquantifiable future economic advantages from a healthier and more educated workforce. Also, access to specific services is more limitedly available for individuals as a consequence, and individual insecurity increases as individuals face a number of risks alone that have often been shared through specifically regulated markets or in communities. Negotiating power on behalf of individuals, with a view on the means for leading a good life is, on the other hand, reduced as a consequence. However, a rather pronounced potential for monetary profits for a relatively few agents may be expected to open up.

When education is primarily made available on the basis of an ability to pay, risks would include those emanating from the individual financing of education that brings an obligation in economic terms arising from the financing of a personal development that may, at least temporarily, not be easily marketable. Education in such settings might be expected to shift away from actually offering a foundation for educating people to providing skill-sets that may be hoped to prove marketable more easily, as the marketability of skills may be more easily appreciated from the outset. That way a student may at least avoid problems of a general matching of skills in markets, as business cycle–related trouble in finding a job can never be prevented by an individual. This trend can be expected from the side of the students, or parents as stand-ins, demanding more marketable content and training in their education, as well as with the education providers, orienting their offer on the demand that their, by then, customers signal. A school that promises good job placement after attending it is more attractive than the school that does not, independent of the course work required. Contacts and networks count. Over time, we may see the effects of path-dependent developments at work in establishing schools' reputations. In terms of shifting costs and risks, risks are borne increasingly by individual agents and the cost for skill provisioning is shifted from companies to private agents and the public education system. We may see a similar trend in matters of research as well.

An 'ability-to-pay' approach in health care may have similar effects. Human development, and in fact freedom, is reduced for those who are unable to afford certain measures, even if they lack funds only on a temporary basis. Long-term consequences may constantly deprive them of options of participating in society though, and thereby produce costs that are unaccounted, if the perspective is to be limited to economic matters. Shifting risks to individuals may thereby also deprive society of long-term economic potential; not to mention the wider social, political, cultural, moral, and ethical implications beyond the narrow economic consequences of making education and health subject to constraints based on an ability to muster the monetary funds required to partake. (That single-payer system can be expected to produce better results in terms of a population's health for a lot less money than private health-care systems has already been discussed in Chapter 2, and can in fact be witnessed throughout the world.)

For companies, besides the obvious monetary benefits available from setting up shop in education or health care, a shift in perception and evaluation criteria toward market-based terms may also mean that they may be able to increasingly draw on public structures for their research. Partnering may be beneficial if results were freely available. That is no longer the case once these can be patented, as it may restrict future research and thus limit the foundation for further advances of knowledge. A valuation in monetary terms will become increasingly normal in such environments. This signifies a notable shift from the idea of universities as places to foster knowledge that is available to the public, even if in a capitalist system, the notion of using public knowledge for private gain has always been a driving force behind emerging economic structures. Universities are redefined as entities that serve private companies' interests in training, cost coverage, and risk coverage; or at least, they more obviously function in these roles. In return, education budgets are supposedly more manageable for the public. As a side note, this may be one of the very obvious areas, where a budgeting structure set up around the annual agricultural cycle may not be the best way to go.

What we may perceive, and what a process-based view is likely to sensitize us for, is the fact that values and thus institutions change over time, and change in an interplay with the structure in place. So, which mindset is brought to bear – or used as ideological justification – shapes not only an initial reorganization, it triggers changes in interests, but it also triggers changes in the interpretation of issues, and mindsets, with additional ramifications that follow. Societies are not static entities, they can shift and change over time, in reaction to what is perceived within and observed without, and people's learning and forming of ideas.

5.7 Policies Concerning Resource Utilization in Economies

Policies at the macroeconomic level are approached from a view on indicators that describe certain aspects of an entire economy, such as inflation, unemployment, or growth rate. If these are off some acceptable range, measures to counter underlying trends may be taken. What appear to be promising measures frequently depends on the perspective on macroeconomic relations.

This bird's eye perspective on an economy in the first step does not distinguish between different sectors, population subsections, regional concerns, and other more specific matters. Once an overview has been established, breaking up aggregates can, and most likely will, help generate a clearer picture of a situation. Changes in unemployment may be occurring at the same rate throughout the economy, or concentrated in particular sectors, for instance. For a generally positive development, average income may increase, however, the gains may be over-proportionally concentrated among the highest incomes. Different potential sources for developments are more likely to show in different cases even as average indicators may show the same changes. The additional information offered by a disaggregate consideration may make it easier to implement measures which can achieve stated objectives; increase activity in general, target certain sectors, or help workers transition into other sectors, as three very general options for actions in the first example. The same disaggregation of general information can offer more insights into other general issues, such as aspects concerning economic well-being and work. For instance, people do not get older equally throughout the population. Increasing life expectancy is concentrated outside manual labor, and among the better-to-do. Raising the retirement age and reducing benefits hits those the hardest who may need it the most.

Still for a first impression of where an economy may be headed, an overview of the larger situation will certainly be helpful, without too many details that may distract if drawn into the picture before the general assessment of the situation has been possible. The general measures proposed will then be fine-tuned depending on what a more detailed analysis of problem areas may suggest.

I

Under the top-down perspectives, a reference state for an economy can be formulated in which all resources are employed to their best possible use from a societal perspective. Changes in the policy status quo tend to have undesirable effects in the economic sphere, with the exception of reductions of government spending, which open scope for more private activity, although it may come at the cost of a period of deflation. An expansion of government activity will reduce the private presence in an economy, on the other hand, as, by assumption, preference is given to government in lending and in spending when vendors decide whose demand to serve. Under full employment, monetary policy eventually results in a proportional change in the price-level, without the displacement of private spending that accompanies fiscal measures.

The underlying theme is the potential of market arenas to offer an environment in which individual agents find everything they need for themselves in the best possible way within the relevant group. Any kind of interference in markets could at best hope to duplicate the results private agents manage to produce for and by themselves. The interference would have to be organized and informed, however, and structures for doing so would have to be maintained, taking resources away elsewhere.

In the static perspective, the equilibrium assumption ties the whole system, and any change in one component of overall activity affects others in a clearly defined and easily identifiable manner. Now, for developing the analytical framework and its policy relevance, it is recognized in the next step that economies grow. The equilibrium of the economy thus shifts, still binding the system, but reflecting the higher level of economic activity that is growth along its equilibrium growth path. The assumptions to accommodate growth developed resting on this static approach, where the treatment of money and public sector presence are concerned, are shared by top-down approaches that argue ongoing innovation is a key feature of a well-functioning economic sphere.

If the money-supply was not adjusted as an economy grew, then price-level distortions, during a period of falling prices to accommodate the relatively scarcer means of exchange, would arise. However, as the actual growth-rate in a given time-period cannot be known in advance, a growth in the money supply to exactly match the increased demand of money to facilitate smooth transactions is impossible. An automatic growth of the money supply has been advocated here, in an effort to avoid surprises to the economic agents and costs of adjustment to an unexpected change of relevant parameters that come with these.

When following the policy suggestions offered, we find that this position is also motivated by a general wariness of active policy engagements. For fiscal policy, a limitation of activity by public agents to the bare necessities for stabilizing an economy and its functioning is preferred, in order to allow private agents to utilize as many resources as possible for their private use. In a complementary strand of argument, the room for discretionary action by the government is advocated to be removed as far as possible, in order to limit the possibilities for populist policies under a short-term time horizon as much as possible. The belief that monetary policies can result in short-term distortions of the perception of the true values of economic indicators results in advocating rule-bound monetary policies. Similarly considered is a tendency of administrative structures to grow over time, hence trying to prevent such a dynamic before it could take root is equally advised in order to avoid economic waste and political limitations to individual freedom that would result – the grown administrative staff needs something to do, after all. This is combined with the recognition that shifting a situation in one's favor will always have an allure, and an influence on public agents by powerful private agents is one way to achieve this. In order to avoid the otherwise unavoidable corruption of the public administration by private partisan interests, a reduction of the influence of the public agents is seen to be merited. We have to assume that this means that a corruption of weaker structures cannot have as much of a negative impact, and apparently, the willingness to corrupt structures will have less of an impact if private agents are directly left to act on their own devices. The point is that a competitive market sphere is supposed to provide the best possible guard against abuses of power, and the best possible way out of situations in which power is abused. However, we have to remember that such a market sphere cannot come into being without support and structure provided by the public sector. The overall notion, while very understandable when focused on extremes, loses its power for providing policy guidelines once the larger gray area in the middle comes into view – which is where real-world economic and political structures are rather firmly situated. There is no actual ability to draw a firm line regarding what is merited public presence, and what may lead down the presumed slippery slope of state-controlled public spaces. A lot will depend on the relations between agents, as these grow out of the social structures in place.

Overall, we thus find a combination of economic analyses with considerations reflecting the authors' take on political structures and their experiences with and expectations regarding these. Some authors have actually advocated that economists maintain more radical stances concerning economic policies, in order to keep the door for discretionary interventions shut, even as their own research underlined the potential for improvements through active policies. The danger they perceived from public knowledge of potentially helpful more active economic policies, to result in an overextension of interventions, has guided their public stance there. It has, however, nothing to do with their economic analyses, and everything to do with their political perception. Faith in a specific kind of market system is in fact the single antidote to influence-peddling and distortions of the economic system for private gain. By assumption, competition at the individual level offers the simplest and best solutions.

II

Considering the possibility of unemployment as an equilibrium state for economies, policy proposals can take on different shapes. Nominally distinguishing productive and monetary sectors allows equilibrium interest rates at which investment is too high for full employment. Importantly, the economic system may come to a rest in a state of unemployment that persists, without competition and market forces at the microeconomic level bringing it back to the full employment equilibrium. Resource employment can be increased here through policy measures.

Government spending can bring idle resources into the economic sphere, as might a stimulus to private spending, for instance, through tax decreases. The former option may still result in a partial crowding-out, though, as to maintain government spending, its borrowing may have to be increased, reducing available investment funds under this perspective. Monetary policy that leads to changes, notably drops, in the interest rate may stimulate investment spending. A preference for monetary policy here derives from the fact that it does not displace private activity, as fiscal policy measures do, but rather works through changing incentives for private activity.

The demand for money depends on the overall economic activity here, and an increase in activity increases the interest rate for a given money supply. That means that investment spending is reduced. As government spending is a discretionary component of spending, the interest rate's impact on overall economic activity must be realized in the private sector. Monetary policy stimulates private activity through its direct impact on the interest rate. However, if the situation is so depressed that investment spending is not reacting to policy measures at all, monetary policy does not have an impact, and fiscal policy does not have a negative effect on investment. It is in fact the only available means for kick-starting economic activity again. Whether a situation merits this approach can, of course, be argued at length. The preference for monetary policy extends to open economies, where it is rather effective in economies that operate with a floating exchange rate, not interfering with and fixing it to a certain level.

Not strictly within the model itself, but as one of the parameters that can shift overall activity, investment is recognized to depend on expectations. The brighter the future appears to be, the more agents will be willing to invest at any given interest rate. The overall investment activity at one interest rate therefore depends on the environment. The interest rate at which full employment is achieved varies over time. On a side note, against this background and already under this perspective, speaking of tight money when interest rates are high and loose money when they are low is wrong. If things look like activity will pick up, and profit opportunities thus increase, more investment will be undertaken at any given rate as the amortization of investments will seem more likely. If, on the other hand, the outlook is rather glum, investment activity at the very same real interest rate will be much more subdued, as the overall difficult trajectory that appears the likely course will make it more difficult to earn the required return on said investment. As central banks increase rates when activity picks up, and lowers them to boost faltering spending, we may even say that an expression like tight money has it backward.

Regarding the importance of expectations, the point is, of course, that the creation of a positive atmosphere may be able to nudge some agents into investing again, in the best of cases supporting an upward spiral of increased investment, increased overall economic opportunity, an upswing in the general mood, and more eagerness to increase economic activity by private agents. In the most advantageous of circumstances, a self-fulfilling prophecy is triggered without much more than encouragement for private agents; which, in truly difficult times is admittedly rather unlikely. But even then, proactive behavior and proactive rhetoric combined can do some good by reinforcing each other's effects.

Nevertheless, treading the line between a perception of overboarding optimism that would not be taken seriously, and too glum an outlook that would threaten to prolong a slump is not necessarily easy; and a dire enough situation will not be corrected by rhetoric alone.

Now, we may note here already that an integration of expectations into investment behavior means that credit in a dynamic environment is pro-cyclical. It expands when expectations are positive and spending increases, and contracts when they reverse. Here, because brighter expectations mean more spending, creating more income, savings, and with those more means for investment that are drawn on as credit.

In the views we introduced subsequently, acknowledging that private banks create money, credit becomes a driver of spending. This adds further potential for instability. Increased credit in fact drives periods of growth, and its drop signals a reversal of dynamics. Furthermore, this situation introduces the response of banks to changing conditions and expectations as an additional impact on the fluctuation of activities in an economy. Not only the willingness to borrow money for investments matters, but the willingness to make money available also does. We will take this point up momentarily.

As the economy is not at its full capacity for the interesting bits of this equilibrium perspective, shortfalls can be addressed through policies. Still, the equilibrium-view is very noticeable, and the focus for introducing changes lies on improving supply conditions to induce investment (though the model has to admit the interpretation that a strengthened demand side can only be helpful). The antagonism between private and public spending is likewise still a pronounced feature of this perspective.

III

As a first of the bottom-up perspectives, we can refer to one that is based on the understanding that on the level of the whole economy, spending creates income and employment; just as investment leads to savings. The self-reinforcing notion of expectations and trends is an important aspect of an economic system. Changes in these are reflected in changes in investment behavior, leading to changes in consumption spending. A continuous process of economic activity is more suitable as a framework, when influence patterns can fluctuate, for instance, depending on the employment share or the current trend in an economy. Activity also shapes the future path for an economy, as more investment increases the chances to improve production potential and technological capabilities, reinforced by increased employment and therefore the potential for skill acquisition. The state of an economy influences the states it can reach, in path-dependent processes.

Investment is the most volatile part of economic activity and the driving factor for changes of employment. The willingness to invest depends on perceptions about the returns to investments at a certain point in time. As said, the productivity of a machine does not change, the potential demand for its products may. That demand has to be a focus for measures that aim at maintaining employment levels.

Among others, government spending plays a key role in maintaining overall demand. The process perspective adopted here leads to different assessments of the effects of measures, however, as compared to top-down perspectives. The measures mentioned earlier regarding a stabilization of private spending apply here as well. To prevent pronounced instability, a reduction of the relative weight of private investment and an increase of the relative weight of the public sector is a possibility. As private activity relies on public infrastructure in its broadest sense, and the input from public research and development facilities, as well as the demand from public agents in the provision of general services, a relatively higher share of public investment over private investment does not translate into a stifling of private activity.

Stabilizing activity, based on stable demand, is a central issue. The immediate negative impact on economic agents that instability brings is to be avoided, and beyond the immediate impact, a solid demand side can also be recognized as the foundation for further expansions and changes in the future.

An often elaborated problem with government spending in times of crises is the notion of its timing. Where automatic stabilizers are, well, automatically kicking in, other spending has to be decided, planned, and implemented; once it has become clear that there has in fact been a slowdown or reduction of activity. Normal recessions may well have passed already by the time measures are implemented. In that case, they add momentum to a recovery, but at the same time may also add competition for resources that private activity has to contend with, or inflationary pressure. They may push against private activity at times when this is undesirable. In order to counter that danger, Germany, for instance, instated a law, originally in 1967, demanding that plans for public projects, such as in infrastructure development, had to be kept ready and updated, to be executed in order of priority. This way, the planning process did not have to be started at the point of economic duress, but existing plans could be implemented as soon as slacking private activity was noted (Gesetz zur Förderung der Stabilität und des Wachstums der Wirtschaft). Other measures mandated therein have included, for instance, savings during times of booming economic activity. Compliance was not necessarily always high though. More importantly, the staff necessary to maintain competencies and capacities was reduced as public private partnerships and privatization dynamics took root, resulting in a loss of knowledge and experience. This has, possibly, weakened future capabilities of the public sector, not only because quick reactions to dropping demand have become more difficult to implement, but also because the stripping of public administrations of competencies will weaken their ability to serve the public in general.

Indirect routes to stimulating spending can be pursued as well. By changing the interest rate, credit conditions for banks can be altered. Whether these decide to pass improved conditions on to their customers in new loans is not in the hands of the policy authority though. And whether agents are willing to take out loans is outside the hands of banks. So, as mentioned before, transmission channels may well be severed and measures lose traction precisely when traction is needed most when indirect routes are chosen. Complementing them with more active involvements at the least will likely be a necessary component of stabilizing economic activity.

As a first instance of an issue to exemplify the larger differences that result from the separate perspectives emerging, overlaps in policy measures notwithstanding, we can briefly point to the effects that government spending may have. One point raised in top-down frameworks was the tendency of public activity to crowd out private activity. Under the current perspective, the direct link from government spending to the interest rate does not exist, and competition for limited savings is not an issue. A competition for specific resources is entirely possible. However, there is no need to suspect a general negative impact of increased government activity on an economy and its potential and path. There will be thresholds beyond which such an impact may become noticeable; however, not as a generally valid rule. This can also be expected to differ by sector, as different types of resources will be relatively more or less prevalent, and competition for them thus more or less pronounced.

The interpretation of government debt also differs. This debt is often seen as a future burden as service payments have to be made. Now, we had seen that if government spending and monetary authority lie at the same level of authority, then government debt is not necessarily problematic. A number of issues thought of, future taxes, future burden, future deadweight, and so on, that are thrown into the ring, are not based on sensible or generally valid arguments, but draw on extremely simplistic perspectives on economic systems. This is not to say that, in more detail, there may not well be undesirable distortions in specific areas. But that is an entirely different matter from the general assessment and law-like statements regarding negative consequences of proactive policies. Money is created in the act of spending, while it vanishes through taxation. Taxes and fees are still important sources of income for lower levels of government, and on the economy-level they can serve as tools for achieving other policy objectives, such as keeping a check on inequality. They are also necessary to guarantee that government coin continues to be accepted in economic transactions. They are not necessary to make payments on debt obligations when fiscal and monetary authority lie on the same level of government.

Especially against this background, one might reconsider the role of government in macroeconomic relations to firmly focus on employment. Private spending and private investment are undertaken by private agents. The same is true for cross-border transactions. All of these private transactions generate tax revenue. Planning for a specific revenue is not possible. Of course, experience allows estimates. But it cannot be known in advance. Scrambling to adjust spending levels to revenue introduces instability and a lack of planning security. Given the fact that a balanced budget is not a necessity for protecting future maneuverability, for instance, it does not make much sense. Tasking government with full employment, and establishing contingencies that can automatically pick up any slack from lackluster private activity, akin to automatic stabilizers, but tied to providing work might offer much more beneficial economic structures and outcomes. As a side-effect overall demand would be more stable, and as public work projects would be a constant feature in an economy, infrastructure, public spaces, and public administration would presumably be more stable and kept up. For lower level governments, support structures to stabilize their activities and presence from higher up make sense then. Otherwise, we can expect costs to be passed from higher to lower levels as spending decisions vary with activity. For instance, where public health spending is reduced at a state level, county and city may well see increased demands toward their coffers; directly, if a need to increase policing presence is felt, for instance, or indirectly, due, for instance, to hospital closures.

Assessing economic activity not on the basis of individual behavior and aggregate systemic outcomes, such as unique equilibria, but on the basis of recorded activity, in an economy's accounts, helps shed light on some additional aspects of macroeconomic relations. Particularly interesting may be the fact that for net private sector holdings of financial assets to be possible, a public sector deficit is required. Depending on how objectives for private sector savings are formulated, a public deficit may thus be a necessity for achieving societal objectives. These issues, including sensible limits to public-sector activities, have to be discussed publicly, in order to come to an informed decision.

IV

Where economic activity is considered as an ongoing process in the analytical framework itself, financial markets play a more important role in the understanding of potential, as well as potential disruptions of and pitfalls in, economic activity. They are assumed to be more than a market for money and government bonds in static savings decisions under this perspective, and there are connections that link the financial sector to the real sector in more involved ways than chosen to focus on in the reference frame. As a result, where investment is concerned, a firm distinction between real investment and financial investment is in order. Financial market expansions are not necessarily a sign of healthy underlying real structures. They may well expand in response to monetary reasons that drive financial markets; the feedback they threaten to real production and employment in case of disadvantageous turns, may merit, again, a more reserved approach to them from the outset.

As laid out earlier, in Chapters 3 and 4, agents are assumed to restructure their portfolios in reaction to changing expectations about future levels of economic activity. The more cautious agents get, the more they value liquidity. The general dynamic in shifting assets is thus toward more liquid assets, all the way to cash, as the economic outlook is perceived to worsen. More liquid implies shorter term, which usually signals a move out of productive investments, and into financial papers and money, in savings and cash. This introduces a double impact on real activity, both reinforcing the assumptions behind them that have shaped individual decisions. A reduction of real investment reduces demand and reduces employment directly, as well as indirectly as a consequence of that same reduction in demand. It may also reduce the availability of willing creditors for other potential investors so that it is reasonable to assume that those still willing to make long-term commitments will have a harder time to actually be able to realize them, if they require external financing. And to repeat, future potential may be adversely affected, if knowledge and skills in production processes are lost as a consequence of not being applied in a slump of activity.

The structure and linkages in modern economies mean that companies that go down during a recession were not necessarily out of touch with customer desires. Think of service companies who see their revenue drop as other businesses get more cautious in their spending decisions in expectation of a downturn, or the trouble a supplier network may run into if demand for the final product is temporarily constrained. Trouble may also simply constitute a reflection of their current financial position, and their creditors' disposition to stick with them, i.e., to renew loans to help them tide over difficult times. Now, for the creditor the decision not to renew may well make sense, as a company can absolutely run into trouble in difficult economic times, and a business model may have run its course. However, the decision not to extend a loan does not necessarily have to reflect a proper assessment of the long-run viability of the creation of value-added in a company, but may be due to a host of factors which have nothing to do with the longer run viability of a particular business. To lump all business failures under a creative destruction heading will fall short of a reasonable analyses. However, it may not be practical, nor in most cases feasible, to try and assess the general health of companies at different stages of their business models and product cycles, and offer assistance to those who face liquidity shortages that have nothing to do with their business and business model, but rather with unfortunate financing decisions, or generalized drops in demand. How to go about this, given the interconnectedness of modern economic activity, would be fiendishly difficult to figure out anyway, even if large blocks of data were available for every single agent. More stable demand structures, upheld by stable income and spending levels and the effects those entail, will thus have to provide an overall core focus of policies. There are other effects to consider, as well, however, that we will address momentarily, as change has generally, historically required instability, so that short-term and long-term considerations will have to be balanced.

A noticeable relative weight of government spending can contribute to such more stable environments. Automatic stabilizers and other measures supporting demand may help prevent recessions from getting worse once they have manifested. Distributions of revenue to maintain aggregate demand levels based on workers' consumption spending will contribute as well. This can easily be achieved by private parties willing to take a long-term perspective on their mutual dependence. However, the changes in the organization of production structures into cross-border networks that we had referred to may challenge achieving such a joint outlook. A more carefully regulated financial sector with a view on leverage and systemic risk potential may cause fewer disruptions, as may a division of labor in the financial sector, keeping non-investment entities out of trouble. This should lead to less of a reduction of credit availabilities when the imbalances and risks, that financial investment results in, come to a head. As far as the protection of skill and knowledge is concerned, therefore, stabilizing economic activity has a number of merits. However, remembering the trade-offs referred to earlier, a certain degree of fluctuation will be supportive of structural change. Where to draw the line can likely not be set out in advance. And the aspects focused on will include individual's vulnerability as well as insecurity, so that measures taken to stabilize economic activity and measures taken to shelter individuals from systemic developments will have to be considered jointly.

V

The focus in the aforementioned models lies on stabilizing activity. In a transition to objectives of growth, driven by technological change, stabilizing demand in order to make investments to expand capacities and innovate worthwhile is part of the necessary overall structure as well. Though the changes are introduced on the production side, and demand for novelties is only then stimulated – invention is the mother of necessity in modern economies – the decision for venturing into such risky endeavors depends on the expectation of making the move worthwhile. Innovations in existing processes are actually more easily attempted in the face of solid demand as well. How to tap into a perceived spending potential is for the modern company to figure out.

Producers, or potential producers, need reasons and possibilities for innovating. Competition and potential competition play an important role here, as their maintenance becomes a key issue for policies to support. This includes barriers to collusion by incumbents, accessible financing options, as well as a supportive social environment for people willing to take the risks connected to competing for new markets, or replacing old market niches. The willingness to let the space for newcomers become available has to exist, which means that existing structures cannot be overly protected either. Stabilizing activity and fostering change may be at odds at times. At least the production side cannot be too stable; how far a somewhat volatile production side impacts income received and demand realized depends on the overall policy framework.

Furthermore, the odds for introducing innovations successfully may fluctuate over time. A number of economists believe that only recessions can clear the economic sphere enough to make room for novelties to gain a foothold once the following upswing unfolds. A trade-off between stability, reduced vulnerability, reduced insecurity, and protection of knowledge and skill on the one hand, and increased scope for introducing novelties in a more volatile environment on the other hand may have to be accepted. Permitting vulnerability and dealing with insecurity are political decisions, to reflect societal values and structures.

Questions to ponder will be how the market signals that supposedly direct innovators to promising endeavors can play out if these innovators have to create the market niches and market they will then service in the first place. Or how it is that market signals work better in a slump than in an upswing. Now, for the first question, we will have to concede that indeed, there are no market signals at first but that activity is rewarded, and that draws in competitors. The initial step is taken into the blue. For the second question, we will have to consider that part of our focus is structural change so that we can lay the groundwork for a new business in an upswing, but that the market signals reducing older activities' scope will only show their full impact when overall spending is reduced. We thus have to remember that, even though in a top-down perspective and in a system populated with self-interested rational agents, change is a normal aspect of economic activities. There are no economic laws to derive here, even as we assume some identities that for instance establish a relation between amount of money and price level; even as that directly contradicts the notion of a system in motion, because said identity only holds under a known and understood full employment of resources.

From each perspective on an economic sphere, different aspects appear to gain in importance. For an economic policy that has to weigh different objectives, trade-offs between such different objectives will be unavoidable. In the case of development and growth, for instance, there will be no generally valid answer evaluating the merits of protection and stability versus destruction and renewal, as these are likely to change over time. We can stress, yet again, that turbulences on the productive side of an economy do not have to be fully borne by individual agents, but that we can shelter these agents to some degree without a disruption or loss of overall economic dynamics.

VI

Change means that time is a component in considerations, and where real time is concerned, so is uncertainty. The lack of an inclusion of time and possibilities for processes in the reference model can lead to problems in policy proposals. Deference to the changes in interpretations that different perspectives lead to can be a good thing at times, especially if combined with an open forum for discussing related issues. In an open system that is dynamic and complex, adjustments and changes can improve the relative results obtained. An openness of decision structures that sets the framework for policies can support this. A rule-bound execution of measures only, on the other hand, is likely to produce undesirable side effects and relative underperformance over time. A disregard for current conditions in a focus that is predominantly on the development of future capacities, on the other hand, may lead to an acceptance of conditions that are less than desirable for the current population. This designates another area of trade-offs for policy makers to consider.

Business decisions in an uncertain environment may result in an unwillingness to keep production processes up and running. Skills that are being lost as a consequence have to count as additional costs of such decisions. On the other hand, too tight a rein can stifle technological change, if it limits the foundation for the introduction of such changes, and thus, over time, may lead to a reduction in the foundation for advancing knowledge that exists relative to one that would have been possible. That the limited selection criteria that market exchanges impose could give very good, or maybe even only acceptable, answers once different issues, over space, time, and different societal interaction arenas are considered, is not a given. That political processes were naturally given to providing better answers, is equally dubious. Both political and economic sphere can be used for exercising power over others. The structure of the political sector and a conscious decision regarding the selection criteria employed for economic policy decisions then gains importance. Awareness that such criteria will in all likelihood always entail trade-offs may help setting up structures that prevent a backlash. Pretending one set of selection tools was superior to the rest may be understandable but cannot be assumed to be accepted for long, even if it meets one's personal criteria and satisfies one's ideological leanings.

VII

A blanket approach to economic policies cannot take account of the fact that it is possible that in changing environments, relations between influence factors change, either because of changes in the environment, be they economic, political, or social, domestic or foreign, or because of the impact that the production technology itself has on the functioning of the economic sphere, for instance. Acknowledging different and changing environments makes it easier to focus on different approaches that economies have followed for growing. In the development of industrial capacities, for instance, export-led and internal demand-heavy periods have tended to alternate in a number of countries, with internal demand laying the groundwork for developing capabilities for exporters, who then go on to face international competition and reap the benefits from servicing larger markets. This can be a repeating pattern, as technologies change and with them the economic structures. Different phases profit from different emphases of policies.

Different economies come with different sets of problems, or potential problems; and these problems can compound over time. What is certain is that up to some degree, vulnerabilities differ, as external and internal factors play different roles for different economic structures and depending on the larger economic environment. Stabilizing the general trend in economies requires different emphases as well. As measures can only be directed where the respective public and private agents actually have an influence, they rely on domestic measures or concerted international ones. Strengthening domestic demand is always a key for stabilizing activity, mutual access to other markets can further strengthen this foundation. At the same time, for the public actor, we had seen that governments in control of currency emissions in their respective territory will not face liquidity problems, whereas governments that do not have that control (say, in the Euro area) actually rely on an access to money for paying their bills. The room to maneuver is designed differently in these cases; the shape is to a good degree determined by the choice of social technology in the monetary sector.

For a different example for changes in social technology, we can refer to the use and understanding of the interest rate in central bank policies. For a while, the interest rate was used to rein in inflationary tendencies. If the threat of inflation was perceived, or starting to manifest, interest rates were increased, attempting to trigger a recession in order to take pressure off prices. Once the recession took hold and price increases ceased, the interest rate was lowered again. That is to say, the interest rate was used to trigger crises and changes in the interest rate were interpreted under that approach. Nowadays, the interest rate is lowered before a crisis becomes apparent, and the decline therefore becomes a signal of a potentially problematic situation, not one of a successful achievement and room for recovering activity, whereas increases signal faith in robust economic activity development. Note also that inflationary dynamics appear to have changed. Overall inflation rates in Western countries have seen a reduction, although they have continuously stayed positive after WWII even when economic activity was reduced for a period. Whether that is improved monetary policy or may have to do with overall structural changes in the economy is debated. Pressure on wages because of the outsourcing of jobs and the loss of automatic wage adjustment clauses to match price level increases in general employment contracts since the 1970s will certainly have played a noticeable part in the US, for instance, as that severed one of the main lines in the wage–price spirals behind sustained inflationary periods. In Europe, a willingness by unions to accept wage increases below official inflation rates to protect domestic employment will have played a similar part.

The earlier influence on economic activity through interest rate changes worked, among others, because of a close link between interest rate and construction. Reduced construction activity following interest rate increases, in turn, spread to other sectors due to the demand effects that played out. Concretely, for the US, that means the Federal Reserve's influence on construction was rather tight. Now, with the changes in other economies' approaches to currency stocks, among others, this has changed. As other countries seek to build up dollar reserves, they do not just hold cash. They hold interest-bearing dollar-denominated debt, such as US government bonds for sure. With the large trade deficits of the US economy, equally large quantities of dollars abounded looking for some interest-bearing place to be kept. Large mortgage providers, for instance, did not have to seek the funds they passed on as mortgages at home any longer. They could acquire dollar-denominated loans abroad, from agents whose motives were influenced by maintaining access to dollars and finding some interest-bearing way to store them, and not only a desire to drive up profits. This has broken the tight domestic link from internal credit conditions to domestic construction activity existent earlier in the US. For the countries holding dollar reserves, while maybe not reference-frame economically rational, in a world of uncertainty in which future adverse exchange-rate developments are possible and can, as seen during the 1990s up front and close, cause tremendous economic and subsequent political upheaval, it may well be seen as real-world rational.

These are but a few select examples. They mainly serve to illustrate that it is not likely that a given set of policies can always be successfully employed. They can likewise serve to stress that the common interpretation of influence factors can have an influence on their impact and effectiveness as well. Continuous adjustments, and of course the capacity to recognize that need and implement the change, will be required in an economic system that is open and changing. That makes it more difficult to pinpoint specific guidelines for policy formulations. The environment in which they will be enacted influences the impact they may be expected to have and their chances of success.

5.8 Contrasting Frameworks for Achieving Economic Objectives

I

As the conceptions of the economic sphere itself differ, so do the policy frameworks that are rooted in these different conceptions and resulting perspectives. How to best support the individual agents in an economy is, hence, contested as we have seen. This refers to the support structures for economic activity, as well as the effects of developments in the economic sphere on the individual agent and measures put in place to address adverse outcomes.

Specialization and increasing division of labor over the course of the industrialization process and beyond have helped to continuously expand the economic sphere and allowed tremendous productivity increases. For the individuals in a society, participation in those gains has allowed to reduce the constraints they have been facing in economic matters. How far those achievements spread through a population depends on social policies, but also, among others, health-care and education provisions. The wealth to engage in these provisions is there in many countries. Whether the willingness is as well, that depends.

The same developments basically require individuals to participate in the economic sphere. In relative terms, risks individuals face have shifted from natural to social and economic spheres due to these developments. Where dire situations followed wars and natural disasters, and resulted in shortages, today's economic disaster is hailed by overproduction that will eventually lead to layoffs. These systemic developments result in the economic insecurity individuals face. How this insecurity translates into actual economic vulnerability, depends on policy measures in place to address insecurity and reduce vulnerability.

A core aspect of all perspectives, in general terms, is competition between individual agents. How that is approached in more detail differs. Even though competition as a generic concept has played an elevated role in modern economies, and societies more in general, how it is in fact integrated, and how it is reflected in different analytical structures, differs. The approach is very much influenced by the perspective on the economic sphere into which it is respectively embedded. Hence, among others we find competition among individuals for profit within markets, competition for markets, or competition for social status through economic activity, but also competition between different interest groups, in economic analyses, with potentially very different consequences for the outcomes that result. Beyond competition, other forms of relating, such as coordination and cooperation, also matter for economic activities. These do not have to mean collusion to the disadvantage of the many, but can also reflect aspects of human sociality that may be required for a functioning economic sphere, contribute to reducing waste, strengthening R&D collaboration and fostering technological advancements and competitiveness, strengthening a regional economy, or a plethora of other effects. Resulting relations and developments cannot be replaced or reproduced by trying to force individuals into exclusively competitive relations.

How relations are organized, and in which structure they play out, matters greatly for economic activity. Concerning competition, for instance, do we, or our policy makers, focus on competition between individual units, such as workers, consumers, producers, and companies, or collections of such units, such as sectors, regions, or whole economies. Competition at some level of aggregation, say between individuals, does not have to produce in any way desirable effects at a higher level of aggregation, say for the group these individuals are part of. Not recognizing that competition at different levels can favor different traits and outcomes is a significant flaw in frameworks that mainly put their faith and hope in competitive structures to foster socially desirable results. Assuming that all forms of relations that cannot readily be identified as competitive would aim at colluding to harm the public unnecessarily limits the range of possibilities we find for supporting individuals in modern economies.

II

That some structure is required for economic activities is undisputed among the different perspectives. The rules in place do not only define obligations, but shape the distribution of risks and costs, as well as benefits, of course, of economic activities. A simple withdrawal of supporting structures and regulations does not automatically increase individual freedom, as the capacity to act freely. At times, restrictions for individual actions are required in order to expand the space available for all members of a group. Each individual can benefit from such a dynamic, where absolute developments are concerned, even though the relative advantage that some enjoy to exercise power over others may well be reduced.

Without rules and support for competitive processes, the energy of the competing agents involved may not be, or may be unlikely to be, steered in a direction that is desirable for the group. In fact, if we look at economic competition, the utilization of a single measure of evaluation of success, such as monetary units, means that developments in other areas that have to be accounted for are unlikely to be fostered by individual activity. Market competition may offer incentives for agents to find new and better ways for reaching certain objectives. Unless we structure those objectives, however – say tightening pollution standards, or energy efficiency requirements – these objectives will not be primary concerns for competitors, and, in fact, a race to the bottom, in terms of standards and societies' bearing of costs of private activity, may well be expected. Even where a competitive mechanism can help to align individual and social interests better than any other tool at our disposal, a structure to support a competitive process is required.

A world where everybody fends for themselves, mistaking this as the ultimate manifestation of freedom, can be a lot sadder in a number of ways than one in which limits are imposed to each individual in order to expand social capabilities. Whether this refers to a legal system that supports and upholds contracts, and a stable monetary system, or moves beyond this to include more aspects of structure, differ. That is to say, the definitions of institutions that economists work with differ. For most economists, the term applies to the rules and norms structuring transaction arenas, and their purpose should be to bring the outcomes in those arenas as closely as possible to the best possible market outcome. Where agents do not or cannot act like they should, say because of market failures, these rules and norms thus should aim at inducing behaviors as if the reference framework applied, in support of the top-down visions of functioning economic spheres. (At times, it is unclear, though, why agents aiming only at profits should follow rules even if cost–benefit calculations suggest they will individualistically be better off not following them. Say, where environmental regulations and costs to comply versus fees for non-compliance are concerned.)

Other conceptions of institutions focus on their social nature, their emergence, and change over time, and possible reflection in formal rules and norms, which gives them a wider scope of application and impact. They structure individual interactions in social contexts, and find reflection in economic structures, but their emergence over time, inclusion of values and social status considerations, and reflection of such mores mean that the stability they provide may not be particularly advantageous. Still, it can nevertheless be hard to impossible to change them, especially in a short-term effort.

Avoiding competition to realize profits by capturing markets through the establishment of economic, political, or technological barriers is seen to lie in the interest of individual agents, but not the larger group, independent of the analytical approach chosen. Situations will, however, generally involve non-competitive aspects in relations. These are necessary to permit more complicated human interactions to unfold. Now, in your weekly supermarket run, that may not affect your transactions. Where smaller groups of agents are concerned, say in regional research cooperations, it does. How such relations are to be evaluated when we try to prevent distortions by smaller groups depends on the situation faced. Clear-cut answers can often not be offered. Situations are not neutral, and faced with alternative options, usually all scenarios will involve positive and negative aspects. Only when the system itself is endowed with characteristics that can check or even counter these dynamics to maintain socially desirable outcomes are these aspects not necessarily important.

The analytical frameworks shape the respective interpretation of the mentioned, and in principal shared, issues and factors, their embedding in the economic system, and policy proposals designed for dealing with them. When markets cannot be relied upon to guarantee a desirable outcome, a more involved approach and a clear definition of desirable trends are required. Still, in support of individual emancipation, a framework will also have to aim not to impose too many barriers and limitations, or get overly involved with planning. A core component of emancipation is the responsibility for one's decisions and their consequences. This cannot be taken away in attempts to cushion and improve everything, according to one's own vision of what should be. A balancing act will be required, and periodical adjustments will be an important aspect of the policy-making process. Avoiding difficult decisions by pretending that some impersonal correction mechanism could come to the rescue if only asked properly will not help most people very far either.

III

The top-down perspectives suggest letting the system do the work whenever possible, as it is presumably endowed with general characteristics that make it uniquely suited for this task. When it does not work properly, or at least not particularly well, policy makers will have to assess potential costs and benefits of actions in order to try to determine which is the least costly option to pursue in the situation under consideration.

Even when accepting perspectives that rely heavily on individual competition for generating socially desirable outcomes, a lot depends on beliefs, interests, and rhetoric. If you take the position that an economic sphere in general resembles that of the analytical framework closely, then regulations will bring fewer benefits and will likely be argued to be more costly by introducing more distortions relative to a scenario where a benchmark is accepted to structure the general thinking about economic issues only. Where distortions from within the economic sphere are assumed to be more prevalent, benefits of policy measures are likely to increase, while costs may be assumed to be reduced relative to the former interpretation. We may thus note that even a subscription to the same general framework of interpretation already opens the possibility for varied policy stances.

Two additional points to note for policy measures involve market structures and means for addressing distortions in the structure and functioning of markets. As pointed out, the concept of competition as it applies in the top-down approaches is somewhat ill-defined. A specific outcome is labeled competitive. That outcome relies on numerous supportive assumptions that are difficult to sustain when contrasted with structures and conditions in real economies. It will likewise be hard (to impossible) to measure, even if we accept the framework without real reservations. It lies in the eye of the beholder whether outcomes are judged to be proper or not.

Where they are not, the second issue applies, when turning to concrete proposals. The framework gives no general valid indication about what to actually do to improve outcomes. We saw that we could not gradually move the system to our preferred outcome if some necessary conditions are not fulfilled. It is a full shift or an open outcome. As the full shift of the system cannot be achieved, in all regularity, because of technological conditions, human issues, market volume, and so on, and may actually not be well-specified in the first place, the analytical framework does not leave us with much in terms of policy guidelines. We may of course resort to assuming that eventually, the outcomes of individual competition will always be better than possible alternatives.

IV

The different bottom-up perspectives cannot afford to put too much faith into the economic system itself. It works as well as the individuals in it make it work, and use it. These individual agents are limited by their capabilities and the embeddedness in a complex system that they cannot completely grasp, means unintended or undesirable consequences, at different levels of aggregation, are entirely possible outcomes. Dynamics in such situations can lead to outcomes that no single individual would have chosen, but that their individual actions nevertheless bring about. Policies that may seem counter-intuitive at first glance as some restriction to individual actions can enable more maneuverability for individuals once we start seeing these as members of groups and societies, and not solely as isolated individuals.

When an economic system is viewed under more open perspectives, typically, a process of ongoing change presents itself. With a view on the policy focus, this process will require a continuous adaptation of rules and regulations. The environments of technology, policy, and social conditions are not static, so that rules will be more or less suitable for attaining their objectives over time. Ways within as well as around the sets of rules are likely to be explored constantly as part of agents' strategic actions so that even within a momentarily stable environment, adaptations of rules may become necessary. Also, nobody can know everything at the outset. Fine-tunings and corrections can be expected to be normal, especially in a system in which change at different levels of aggregation is recognized as a possibility whether immediately discernible or not. The functioning of the system itself, emerging as the result of the ongoing individual interactions and their impact can change itself. Economic policy is part of the process of economic activity and has to be adapted to changing situations.

This leads to demands on policies that require short-, medium-, and long-run objectives, always as stepping stones toward later goals and intermediate markers, for determining a path to follow. Monitoring situations and creating structures for individual interactions beyond, however defined, competition, will have to be a part of the policy-making process, and the role of private agents cannot be only unidimensional. We see ongoing processes in which the roles of public and private agents are not antagonistic, but rely on one another in different coalitions, shapes, and forms, to collaborate, coordinate, compete, control, and so on, depending on the situation and the objectives formulated. For a fruitful path, involvement of different interests has to be guaranteed in the political system. A functioning political sphere in support of economic activity is needed. How that looks, at least over shorter periods of time, can differ, especially if economic expansion is our only focus. This has not been tied to any particular system of government. However, for individual emancipation of the overall objective, adequate political structures to that end will eventually be required.

An understanding of the system is required for gaining insights into possible changes of its state, such as phase transitions following which a system functions differently than before. There may be times when markets are governed by negative feedback, and others during which the same market may be governed by positive feedback cycles. Understanding the structure can then help determine how undesired developments can be avoided and desired ones supported. For financial markets, for instance, we saw that a buildup of individual and systemic risk exposure can go hand in hand with a dynamic of positive feedbacks. Preventing such a state, by restricting risk and leverage, for instance, can then help keep the financial system outside the areas where a dangerous accumulation of overall risk manifests.

There is no homogeneity of agents and interests in these frameworks. As an example, consider individual business versus social interests. If activities are technologically feasible, they can be undertaken. Businesses employing technology operate under constraints from the cost and potential revenue structures they face. Business decisions on a limited utilization of existing resources can be buffered, and under this perspective should be buffered, as, again, an automatic negative impact on private activity does not result.

The public sector can do a lot more here, fighting unemployment, without having to fear negative consequences. The same may be seen to be true for fostering technological development and change, as there are good reasons to suspect that socially desirable developments may not be forthcoming, or at least not nearly as quickly as would be possible, if research is left in private hands alone. Where the establishment of standards, in areas such as energy generation and utilization, for instance, are concerned, some focused regulatory structures may conceivably contribute to a more advantageous long-run path. That does not mean to completely undermine markets as social tools for aggregating individual decisions and value signals, but it does mean to not simply always accept their outcomes. Where individual consumption decision are concerned, insisting on a proper information base is also very much required.

Under heterogeneity of interests, private power being exercised in economic relations, and possibly needing a counterweight becomes an issue, as well. Market-based activity is not necessarily a tool for improving economic and broader outlooks. It is just as likely to cement existing structures and existing values, as the 'one-dollar-one-vote' rule may just as well lead agents who follow their prejudices, bigotry, or other, instead of permitting the desired openness to ongoing change, and, more importantly, improvements, of conditions. Where an analytical framework is chosen that offers a view on an emergent system with heterogeneous interests, no single sector or agent can be assumed nor expected to produce particularly good outcomes if left to their own devices.

Different interests require compromises among them for ongoing long-term activities and interactions. Acceptable benefit, cost, and risk distributions have to be found in all areas of concern. Overall, you cannot promote a neutral development, you will always shift influence factors and their respective weights. What policy has to determine is which ones to tinker with and which ones not; and, provide an answer to why those decisions have been taken, in a consistent, concise, and public manner.

V

When assessing an economy as a whole, we gain an overview of the conditions that the individuals in that economy face. Especially overall employment is of interest, but also the development of prices and the overall relations to other economies, for instance. These aspects give a first view of the conditions in the economy, in terms of job availability, price stability, or net investment positions abroad and their changes. When these indicators show results or suggest trends that are deemed undesirable, the question is what can be done to arrest the trend. Different interests may, of course, hold different positions regarding the signal that certain indicators are sending. An export surplus, for instance, may be seen as a sign of a good foundation for economic activity in an economy, it may be seen as a signal that spending in an economy is too low, it may be seen as a chance to build up investment positions abroad as insurance against future turmoil, or may be seen as a chance for private agents to move their resources out of the country, among others. This can change over time, and of course, the different possibilities are not mutually exclusive. A very pronounced export surplus is usually a sign of something being, at least, not quite right in an economy. In any case, it means that resources leave the economy in question, without a concurrent influx of resources from abroad; and the employment abroad that would signify. An import surplus may be seen as a problem of economic activity, by simply not having enough capacity to sell abroad, it may also be seen to signify an economy that can attract a lot of investment. Depending on whether and how different types of investments are distinguished, this may be interpreted more or less optimistically. The overview itself can thus be only a starting point, and will have to be complemented by further considerations and analyses.

We saw that we can again distinguish top-down perspectives and bottom-up perspectives in macroeconomics as well, with the economic system itself being endowed with certain characteristics, or with its characteristics emerging from the interactions of individuals, leading to different characteristics in different parts of the economic sphere. The top-down approaches are closely wedded to the top-down approaches to individual markets. Agents do what is best for them, and are constrained by the overall market outcome and prices that reflect the aggregation of individual wishes according to a 'one-dollar-one-vote' rule. The best way forward is to make sure that all agents can participate in the economic sphere in a way that lets them freely exercise their individual choices.

Overall, these are theories of economic harmony, where disturbances are introduced from outside the economic system. The potential for policies to change situations in a sustained manner is limited, at best, even though sometimes they may have to provide a kick-start to economic activity. This holds whether the system is constrained by an equilibrium, or whether it is assumed to follow the best possible path to reflect individual wants if functioning well.

Where we take the bottom-up perspectives, we have seen complementary structures and activities of private and public sectors. Public agents and private agents jointly shape their emerging system through their ongoing, active and passive, economic activities. Crises here can result from the normal economic activities of the agents in an economy, so that we may speak of crises theories. In terms of policy requirements, negative developments are to be prevented, and the system itself supported on a path toward predefined, consensual objectives and compromises. Policy space involves structure to dampen the impact of negative developments, for instance, by acting as employer of last resort, without crowding out private activity, but rather decreasing individual economic vulnerability, and increasing the stability of the economic sphere overall.

In a system that constantly moves, and potentially changes, there is no reason to suspect negative feedback to constantly constrain system and outcomes. On the contrary, there are good reasons to suspect that positive feedback will be a possibility in parts of the system's functioning, in response to the information that agents garner from others' actions, for instance, as expectations and mood matter, and others' activities as well. These shape the ongoing process and outcomes and let the economic system emerge.

Furthermore, in heterogeneous societies, different interests persist that need to compromise. Political structures serve this purpose. That 'one-dollar-one-vote' could lead to socially acceptable compromises is unlikely in a number of social spheres, and even economic areas once a static outlook has been abandoned. Furthermore, in such systems we have to contend with unintended consequences of actions and fallacy of composition problems – individualistically good-looking courses of action produce overall rather negative results, for individual and group – that, among others, manifest as changes in aggregate indicators that are signaling disadvantageous developments. An awareness of such issues – which a price mechanism cannot fix, as seen earlier – has to be maintained, for assessing situations, as well as the approach to policies. Interventions will definitely not always be desirable, but no one is served by excluding the option from the start. Again, admitting the potential for beneficial policies and structures beyond the necessary complementarity of private and public action does not mean that there would not be possible negative impacts of public activities. The potential for disadvantageous interferences is, in fact, given under all perspectives. An understanding of the situation is, likewise, paramount to the structured and directed success of measures. A voluntary absence of a presence is, however, a policy decision as well.

VI

Trade-offs will arise in the implementation of proposals. They range over a wide set of possibilities and can include such issues as the distribution of risks and costs, referring to single transaction arenas, as well as broader areas where systemic risk and its distribution is concerned, or, in general, questions of resource allocation and the distribution of the impact of activities. Other issues include technological change, where the advantage to be gained by the innovator, which may well rely on limited access to the technical specifics of the novelty, may be a major motivator for attempting to innovate in the first place. On the other hand, giving up that advantage for expanding the technological foundation for future innovation is the desirable course of action on the social level. The access of an individual to the social knowledge fund and its utilization, we might say, and the treatment of their potential contributions to it, have generally been contentious. Private ownership, and intellectual property, both directly derived from an embodying knowledge that has been gathered in society, and the need for spreading technological competence as the foundation for further change, represent different interests within the institutional structure that permits the private use of common structures. Giving up on social uses and permitting private individuals to lay claim may, on the other hand, be just the way to increase the general economic potential of societies, if technological progress is in fact strongly dependent on private agents' risk taking. Having said this, bear in mind that large parts of actual research are not undertaken or financed by private, but by public agents; its spread in terms of use and access is, however, often closely connected to its private economic utilization in modern economies. Patents are, of course, one way for addressing related issues. We may want to note, however, that in reaction to a patenting framework, some private companies have taken up hoarding patents, with the pursuit of supposed infringements as their business model, if we can call it that, or with the goal of upping their book value by stashing these patents away. Patents have also increasingly been taken out on basic research findings, not final products or processes, in a structure that may mean a potential hindrance to further research. Overall, there will likely be no clear-cut answer to which degree a protection of private usage, and especially intellectual property, may be necessary under an economic perspective, and where social uses have to take precedence, and are in fact required under a long-term perspective. This will in general be true for all areas where trade-offs between different interests are concerned, and will in part also depend on values and motivations of individual agents.

The changes that innovations bring mean that at the local, sectoral, market, or other lower levels, upheaval is a feature of economic activity and, at least potential instability its constant companion. At the macroeconomic level, the resulting potential instability might be interpreted as a negative development for the group. However, for continuous change and innovation, the upheaval appears necessary, so that macroeconomic stabilization and micro-level changes have to be balanced, as both are necessary ingredients to a continuation of an unfolding path of structural change. Policies have to be formulated deciding how to try to protect individual agents from the impact of disadvantageous outcomes of processes, without disrupting a process of generating improvements to their ability to live a full life. A critical aspect to consider in this area is that stability has generally led to stagnation in human societies, and a petrification of structures. Individual emancipation is not well served under such a dynamic. A certain degree of instability has been required to permit ongoing changes and potential improvements to gain a foothold throughout the history.

VII

Capitalist structures have always relied on inputs from the wider societal spheres to enable private profit. Machines embody knowledge amassed over time, training and education enable workforce participation, infrastructure allows organization and transport, legal systems stabilize exchanges and transactions, and so on. All private initiative is for naught if it were not for the enabling and complementing structures that society puts in place. None of these other aspects of human life and society, as well as nature, is naturally subservient to the economic sphere, even though current public discourse suggests that at the moment people might see things that way. The focus on economic performance and indicators can, however, lead to a shift in values, eventually even elevating economic considerations over other aspects of human life. In that case, we find an exclusion of individuals from areas, say health and education, that strengthen their potential and can foster their individual development and emancipation.

It may bear noting that human development is not generally fostered at the cost of economic performance, especially if we discard the importance of increasing short-term profits – for-profit education, for-profit health care, for-profit prisons, and the like may take a hit, but societies overall will be more healthy, stable, and economically sound, and do not condemn a number of their populations to positions where the development of their potential is severely limited from the get-go.

Therefore, beyond the different objectives in economic matters themselves, once policies are concerned, the embeddedness of economic activity into a wider social and environmental framework has to be remembered. Fostering a smooth functioning of economic relations is advanced under the much broader umbrella of enhancing individual emancipation. Decisions among issues, the weighing of trade-offs, involve values and objectives beyond a single focus in one perspective on an economic sphere.

References

For the full list of references, see the bibliography at the end of the text.

Adelman, Irma, Cynthia Taft Morris (1988) Comparative Patterns of Economic Development 1850-1914. The Johns Hopkins Press, Baltimore

The authors examine development processes to find underlying causes for the diverging experiences of different economies.

Akerlof, George A., and Robert Shiller (2015) Phishing for Phools: The Economics of Manipulation and Deception. Princeton University Press, Princeton et al.

The authors explore the consequences of the insight that market interactions do not necessarily lead to improvements for everyone involved in transactions, because our decision-making allows consumers to be deceived and manipulated by producers and sellers of goods.

Ariely, Dan (2008) Predictably Irrational: The Hidden Forces that Shape our Decisions. Harper Collins, Scranton.

The author shows that irrational behavior of humans shows discernible patterns that can be utilized by others to sway our decisions, and that should be taken into account when formulating policies.

Ayres, Clarence E (1944) The Theory of Economic Progress: A Study of the Fundamentals of Economic Development and Cultural Change. Chapel Hill, University of North Carolina Press

The author analyzes processes of change in economies and the influence that the formal and especially also informal rules and norms in a society have on the shape of the process.

Beinhocker, Eric (2006) The Origins of Wealth: Evolution, Complexity, and the Radical Remaking of Economics. Harvard Business School Press, Boston

The author integrates a large number of concepts and approaches to evolutionary and complexity economics to provide the foundation for rethinking what we thought we knew about economics.

Bell, Daniel (1976) The Cultural Contradictions of Capitalism. Basic Books, Inc., New York

The author argues that in capitalist societies, the cultural developments that have gone hand in hand with it, will eventually lead the system to break down.

Berle Adolf A., and Gardiner Means (1932) The Modern Corporation and Private Property. The Macmillan Company, New York

The authors analyze the structure of corporations and the impact that the separation of legal ownership and control of a company has had.

Bhagwati, Jagdish (2002) Free Trade Today. Princeton University Press, Princeton and Oxford.

The author presents an overview of arguments for free trade policies.

Chandler, Alfred (1977) The Visible Hand: The Managerial Revolution in American Business. The Belknap Press of Harvard University Press, Cambridge and London

The author analyzes the changes in the structure of economic activity, with a focus on the nineteenth century.

Chang, Ha-Joon (2007) Bad Samaritans: The Myth of Free Trade and Secret History of Capitalism. Bloomsbury Press, New York

The author shows that successful economic development processes have always relied on government interventions and support.

Chang, Ha-Joon (2002) Kicking Away the Ladder: Development Strategy in Historical Perspective. Anthem Press,

The author analyzes how the modern canon of trade and development policies undermine the potential for successful development processes in countries with more limited technological capabilities.

de Soto, Hernando (2000) The Mystery of Capital: Why Capitalism Triumphs in the West and Fails Everywhere Else. Basic Books New York

The author analyzes the importance of legal property rights for capitalist economic systems and their expansion.

Eichengreen, Barry (2003) Capital Flows and Crises. The MIT Press, Cambridge and London

The author addresses the issue of capital flows, and their potential for positive as well as negative effects on economies, from a number of vantage points.

Eichengreen, Barry (2007) The European Economy Since 1945: Co-ordinated Capitalism and Beyond. Princeton University Press, Princeton et al.

The author discusses the particular cultural and institutional background that has fostered economic development in postwar Europe.

Elsner, Wolfram, Torsten Heinrich, and Henning Schwardt (2014) Microeconomics of Complex Economies – Evolutionary, Institutional, Neoclassical, and Complexity Perspectives. Elsevier /Academic Press, Oxford et al.

The authors present a number of different perspectives on microeconomic issues.

Friedman, Benjamin (2005) The Moral Consequences of Economic Growth. Alfred A. Knopf, New York

The author analyzes how changes in the standard of living can affect openness, democratic structures, and political stability.

Friedman, Milton (1962) Capitalism and Freedom. University of Chicago Press, Chicago

The author argues that uninterfered economic activity is a necessary building block for political freedom.

Galbraith, James K (2008) The Predator State: How Conservatives Abandoned the Free Market and Why Liberals Should Too. Free Press, New York

The author argues that economic prosperity has always been achieved based on private initiative and public sector activities.

Galbraith, John K (1958) The Affluent Society. Houghton Mifflin Co., Boston

The author argues that in rich modern societies, the notion of scarcity is no longer the principle problem of economic activity to address, and analyzes the consequences that abundance has for economic activity.

Galbraith, John K (1967) The New Industrial State. Houghton Mifflin Co., Boston

The author analyzes the influence of large corporations in the economic sphere, and in society more in general.

Hall, Peter A, and David Soskice (eds.) (2001) Varieties of Capitalism: The Institutional Foundations of Comparative Advantage. Oxford University Press, Oxford

This edited volume offers a framework for understanding the differences in the specific forms the capitalist systems have taken, and a number of case studies to show these in more detail.

Hayek, Friedrich von (1944) The Road to Serfdom. Routledge Press, London

The author presents his views on the political dangers of public sector planning in the economic sphere.

Hazlitt, Henry (1946) Economics in One Lesson: The Shortest and Surest Way to Understand Basic Economics. Harper Brothers, New York

The author argues that, no matter how well-intended, economic policies that try to improve a situation for a selected group in economies will eventually make the situation worse for everyone.

Hirschman, Albert O. (1981) Essays in Trespassing: Economics to Politics and Beyond. Cambridge University Press, Cambridge et al.

This collection of essays brings together a number of the author's writings, many of them concerned with the relation between economic development and institutional environment.

Johnson, Chalmers (1982) MITI and the Japanese Miracle: The Growth of Industrial Policy, 1925–1975. Stanford University Press, Stanford

The authors analyze the prominent involvement of the Japanese Ministry of International Trade and Industry in the development of technological capacities in the Japanese economy.

Kahneman, Daniel (2011) Thinking, Fast and Slow. Farrar, Strauss, and Giroux, New York

The author discusses how our minds actually work, and the impact this has on our decision-making.

Keynes, John Maynard (1936) General Theory of Employment, Interest, and Money. Macmillan and Co, London

The author develops a framework for understanding an economy, which may not return to full employment out of its own dynamics.

Kindleberger, Charles P. (1978) Manias, Panics, and Crashes: A History of Financial Crises. Basic Books, New York

The author presents and analyzes financial crises over the centuries.

Lazonick, William (2009) Sustainable Prosperity in the New Economy? Business Organization and High-Tech Employment in the United States. W.E. Upjohn Institute for Employment Research, Kalamazoo

The author analyzes the impact of the changes in the structure of economic activity over the last few decades.

Marshall, Alfred (1890) Principles of Economics. Macmillan and Co., London

The author presents, systematizes, and expands, the state of economic analyses at the time.

Mazzucato, Mariana (2011) The Entrepreneurial State: Debunking Public vs. Private Sector Myths. Anthem Press, London

The book analyzes the importance of the public sector for economic activity.

Metcalfe, J Stanley (1998) Evolutionary Economics and Creative Destruction. Routledge, London and New York

The author discusses competition as leading to an ongoing process of change.

Milberg, William, and Deborah Winkler (2013) Outsourcing Economics: Global Value Chains in Capitalist Development. Cambridge University Press, Cambridge et al.

The authors analyze changes in the organization and structure of production processes, and the impact this has had on modern economies.

Minsky, Hyman (1975) John Maynard Keynes. Columbia University Press, New York

The author offers an interpretation of Keynes' work that integrates a number of aspects of that work which are frequently neglected.

Minsky, Hyman (1986) Stabilizing an Unstable Economy. Yale University Press, New Haven

The author analyzes how dynamics in the financial sector can lead to instability in these, and how that can spill over to productive economic activity.

Mokyr, Joel (2002) Gifts of Athena: Historical Origins of the Knowledge Economy. Princeton University Press, Princeton

The author analyzes how complementing technological developments and institutional structures have shaped economic development processes.

Myrdal, Gunnar (1953) The Political Element in the Development of Economic Theory. Routledge and Kegan Paul, London

The author analyzes the ways that ideological component enter economic analyses.

Nell, Edward (1998) The General Theory of Transformational Growth: Keynes After Sraffa. Cambridge University Press, Cmabridge et al.

The author analyzes how ongoing innovations in markets change the functioning of the economic system.

Nitzan, Jonathan, Shimshon Bichler (2009) Capital as Power: A Study of Order and Creorder. Routledge, London and New York

The authors analyze frequently used notions of the concept of capital, and offer a new definition to overcome flaws in existing concepts.

North, Douglass, and Robert P. Thomas (1973) The Rise of the Western World: A New Economic History. Cambridge University Press, New York

The authors analyze the role of property rights in the process of economic development in Europe.

North, Douglass (1990) Institutions, Institutional Change, and Economic Performance. Cambridge University Press, Cambridge et al.

The author develops how institutions and their change impact economic performance.

Olson, Mancur (1982) The Rise and Decline of Nations: Economic Growth, Stagflation, and Social Rigidities. Yale University Press, New Haven

The author analyzes how the increasing impact of special interests can hinder economic activity.

Pickett, Kate, and Richard G Wilkinson (2009) The Spirit Level: Why Greater Equality Makes Societies Stronger. Allen Lane, London

The authors analyze numerous studies on the impact of economic inequality on societies.

Polanyi, Karl (1944) The Great Transformation: The Political and Economic Origins of Our Time. Farrar and Rinehart, New York

The author analyzes the interplay of increasing economic turbulence and political developments.

Schumpeter, Joseph A (1934; first English edition) The Theory of Economic Development: An Inquiry into Profits, Capital, Credit, Interest, and the Business Cycle. Harvard University Press, Cambridge

The author analyzes how the drive for profit leads to ongoing changes in economic systems.

Sen, Amartya (1970) Collective Choice and Social Welfare. Holden-Day, San Francisco

The author studies group decision-making and what conflicts may arise, drawing on economic theory and a number of disciplines beyond that where required.

Sen, Amartya K (1999) Development as Freedom. Oxford University Press, New York

The author develops a broader concept of freedom than can be captured by increased average per capita income.

Sunstein, Cass, and Richard Thaler (2008) Nudge – Improving Decisions about Health, Wealth, and Happiness. Yale university Press, New Haven

The authors use insights form psychology and their reproduction in behavioral economics to consider policy options which follow from them.

Wray, L. Randall (2012) Modern Money Theory: A Primer on Macroeconomics for Sovereign Monetary Systems. Palgrave Macmillan, Basingstoke and New York

The author lays out how money is created in modern monetary systems, and what follows for our understanding of macroeconomic problems.

6

Final Considerations

I

All perspectives on economic systems have been developed with the goal of strengthening economic and social spheres, and fostering individual emancipation. They do, however, draw different pictures of how that economic sphere can be employed for reducing individual insecurity and vulnerability, enhancing societal well-being, and helping secure and increase personal freedom.

In part this is due to emphases in analyses that differ, focusing on specific aspects of the larger economic sphere, as well as static and dynamic, and short-term and long-term aspects of activity. More importantly, however, we find a fundamental difference in the basic assumptions in the distinct analytical frameworks. One group assumes a top-down perspective, making assumptions about the economic system itself, to then fill the resulting space with economic agents and their behavioral options to fit into their analytical system. The other group looks at how economic agents may interact, and asks what kind of system may result from these interactions. In tendency, the top-down perspectives arrive at a view of economic activity that stresses mutual interests and potential for harmony. While characteristics of goods and transactions that interfere with best

H. Schwardt, *The Path to a Modern Economics*,
DOI 10.1007/978-3-319-52785-7_6

possible outcomes play an important part in analyses, the reference frame against which these are formulated, and on which measures to counter their impact are developed, is a harmonious one. The bottom-up perspectives, on the other hand, integrate the potential for undesirable and even harmful developments from individual economic activity as a normal aspect of economic systems. Markets cannot necessarily be expected to foster particularly useful outcomes, and on the economic level, crises are a normal outcome of individual activities. The requirements formulated toward the public sector to correct misdevelopments and counter private power and misalignments are much more pronounced, and the approach to be taken for its integration in modern economies, more intricate.

A key point under the larger perspective on individual emancipation is to keep processes ongoing to permit continuous change in social and economic relations. Stable environments, unfortunately, have tended toward social and technological stagnation in the course of human history. The prevention of stagnant environments, and of consolidation and petrification of hierarchies, has been a central component of structures permitting individuals to develop and utilize their potential. Some degree of disturbance has always been necessary for advancing societies. At the same time, individuals value and require stability, which also provides the foundation for the pursuit of directed and systematic attempts at changes and improvements. Striking a balance between enough stability to permit ongoing activity and enough space for that activity to introduce changes is the overarching problem structure to address.

Independent of analytical perspectives, economic activities have been an important component to the processes of change. How to utilize underlying motivations and dynamics in service of successful societal developments is a necessary question to ask. Assessments of the most promising routes toward that end diverge. Such assessments can even diverge within a perspective, depending on more detailed emphases. No matter which foundation is chosen, there is no unequivocally best course of action and set of regulations that would result directly from an analytical framework. We can find an agreement on the necessity that private power has to be kept in check, just as a limitation to governmental power is required. Detailed emphases differ, and depend in part on the assumptions we formulate concerning the economic system itself.

II

Embedded in this larger, often implicit, area of concern are the analytical frameworks for approaching economic issues. We had distinguished top-down and bottom-up perspectives for making sense of interactions of individuals, their relation to their environment, and the impact of them on their environment and vice versa.

In the top-down perspectives, benchmark results describe the best possible faithful aggregation of all individual economic motivations and wishes. The economic system is characterized by negative feedback, between prices and quantities. Estimates of results, on equilibrium or path, provide a reference serving as a guidepost for the development, assessment, and implementation of measures. Obstacles may occur – we mentioned information problems, external effects, public goods, amongst others – but can be addressed, at least to some degree, and by making use of the presumed characteristics of the system itself, where certain regularities and influences are at work that cannot be undone. There is, however, no clear path toward determining economic structures that represent the best achievable outcome coming directly out of the analytical frameworks.

In the bottom-up perspectives, the economic environment emerges from individual interactions. It is not being pressed into one particular state of functioning from the outset. How agents behave shapes their economic environments. These environments' functioning can differ at different times, and for different objects of exchange, depending, among others, on the state of the economic environment itself at the time and the technological capacity available. The aggregate measures of economic activity may react differently to the same impulses or policies at different times and in different situations. Agents' social environment and their current context matters, as people act differently in different situations. Furthermore, there is the possibility of unintended, undesired, or unforeseen systemic effects that emerge from the sum of individual decisions and that feed back onto individual results. These may not be foreseeable. Positive feedback dynamics, amongst others, are possible within such a system. In short, overall outcomes may be difficult to foresee. No stable cause–effect relationships, as economic laws, can be presumed to exist.

The economic sphere, at least potentially, changes itself if given room, within larger environment, and as a function of that larger environment. Economic activity itself can thus change the economic potential in an economy once we allow a dynamic perspective. However, we cannot grasp such a process jumping from equilibrium to equilibrium.

III

All economic activity requires the creation of interaction arenas. Rules and norms are an integral part of the economic activity. Without any structure, the environment individuals' face would be too difficult to navigate. Top-down and bottom-up perspectives differ insofar, as top-down perspectives lead to an emphasis on trying to find rules that permit the functioning of the system in an undisturbed manner, whereas the bottom-up perspectives have to take a broader approach. Structuring the economic process in a way that allows to achieve the objectives formulated has to be the emphasis. How trade-offs between different objectives are approached also differs accordingly.

The assumptions that set up the top-down perspectives mean that prices will be the best possible mediators between different economic interests. Independent evaluations of goods by individuals shape price levels. People do not buy a good if the price is too high to reflect their preferences. Due to the independence of individual decisions, outcomes reflect individual wishes. In an undisturbed environment, they reflect individual wishes in the best possible way for societies. Getting the price mechanism to work, or setting rules to let people behave as if it worked, provides the framework for policies.

Competition in a framework of scarce resources drives the developments in economic activities and introduces stable behavior patterns and relations that we can draw on to support policy objectives. Of course, areas for which such 'one-dollar-one-vote' rules are considered inadequate for meeting societies wishes may be excluded from consideration. However, depending on how important scarcity is considered to be, and how suitable a monetary aggregation of voice over other possibilities is evaluated, opinions on the applicability of economic structures to societal problem areas differ.

If decisions and valuations are not independently taken, prices will not be enough to administer trade-offs between different interests. If the parties involved cannot participate on level grounds in shaping price levels, these will not be enough to offer a suitable representation of all interests either. At the very least on the theoretical level, there will be room for improvement. If or how that can be implemented in practice, may depend, so that prices still may be interpreted to be the best available option for assessing and balancing different interests. Whether societal interests are indeed best served by this aggregation rule can therefore not be asserted without additional considerations in specific cases.

As agents are assumed to interact and influence one another, possibly under uncertainty, the bottom-up perspectives cannot rely on a singular mechanism for informing decisions about trade-offs among differing interests. Given the limitations that price formations are subject to, additional considerations to inform decisions will have to be formulated and implemented. Shaping the processes that unfold based on individual motivations and actions becomes the task for policy makers and economic agents alike, and together. It becomes apparent that the strict separation of public and private agents is an artificial one. Market transactions alone are not unlikely to strengthen existing structures, rather than overcoming them, and to enhance positions of power, rather than diminishing them. There is no economic argument for a blanket reduction of public-sector involvement, just as there is none for its indiscriminate expansion.

Beyond competition for profits only, collaboration, cooperation, coordination, oversight, for-profit, nonprofit, short-term, long-term, and a plentitude of other states, motivations, and objectives play a part in social and, therefore, in economic activity. Competition itself can take many different forms and focuses. In important ways, such issues, relating to one another, influence economic performance. They can strengthen economic and innovative potential and ease operations, without colluding to harm customers or competitors through coordinated price policies for instance. For clues as to the structure of interaction arenas, systemic stabilization, and continued emancipation for individuals where this may be influenced by economic activity, single solution or aggregation mechanisms come up short. Not recognizing the importance of competition in modern societies would likewise, on the other hand, be very likely to lead to failure, as it provides a core component of modern social organizations, and motivations, as a main factor in the ongoing process of change that is required to prevent a petrification of structures. However, it is not the only one, nor can it be properly understood and addressed in isolation from other social structures and relations.

IV

The numerous issues that may be raised around it notwithstanding, an equilibrium-based approach has been adopted by most economists. It is seen as the appropriate way for communicating ideas in a manner that is deemed acceptable for discussions in the economics community. It serves as the best, if not only, way accessible for identifying economic laws. However, such laws may have to be recognized as man-made only, given our considerations; and not only man-made but made on, and to a good degree confined to, paper. Where they serve as pointers for the formulation of expectations, they may trigger behavior leading to self-fulfilling prophecies. That is not the same thing as a generally valid perspective on economic issues. At the same time, the view on economic problems and potential solutions is shaped by the assumptions informing it, noticeably concerning the economic system itself, and first and foremost the belief that an equilibrium would offer an appropriate foundation for economic analyses.

In this perspective, finding which model is most appropriate to the situation at hand, then, is the supposedly proper way of doing economics. However, this simply moves the level of discussion to questions regarding the applicability of one model over another. The 'it depends', is still there, just not in the actual model. That individual wants can be amended in every conceivable manner in model formulations compounds this, insofar as modifications to try to fit the current focus of observation may not be easily transferable to other situations, and introduce another rather arbitrary component into analyses. For policy-related questions, the application of said models relies on results from outside the analytical framework, even as data is studied through the prism of the reference perspective. An analysis of the environment is still required for selecting the proper model. This may appear more forced than forceful. At this point, that model may be seen as an attempt at a description, more appropriately, rather than an analysis, and a description of a specific situation. The description comes with a very specific view on an economic system attached to it, and will guide thoughts and suggestions for solutions in a very specific manner. At the very least, a general validity of results offered cannot be postulated.

That the definitions of terms in the top-down perspectives is not unproblematic, as the relation between mathematical construct and verbal translation is rather open, does not help matters of analyses or policy recommendation either. Where matters of innovation are concerned, the problem is more firmly related to the fact that the understandings of complex systems embedded in the top-down approaches have decided to abstract from a number of issues and aspects that we know can affect such systems. What we can take from the perspectives already lies in their assumptions – individual influence, or small influential groups may be expected to exploit the advantage they have for their own benefit, whether such an advantage is originally due to characteristics of the goods in question, or the technology employed for producing them. However, this assumption does not set any perspective apart from others.

Even where policy recommendations are more open to adapting to the situation in an economy, when drawing on equilibrium models for framing and communicating them, the reference shapes people's thinking; in ways that have no claim to superiority for assessing economic issues, much less correctness, but that have nevertheless established themselves as such. Insisting on this perspective to serve as the reference framework for tackling economic issues is like insisting on roaming the streets of Glasgow using a map of Rome, claiming that was better than nothing. We may know it is wrong, but everyone who is serious uses it, and so supposedly they understand each other when trying to get from A to B. A better guide there is someone with more experience to circumvent the restrictions and wrong information from the map concerning the present situation. How to work around those adverse issues while still making reference to said map eventually makes a great guide. Now, claiming that finding ways to describe a route through the city making reference to the map while working around its restrictions was a better use of time than trying to draw up a new map, even as sketches for such alternative drafts can already be found floating around, continues to be puzzling. But then, cui bono will apply here as well.

V

Left to their own devices, individual agents cannot be expected to move their economic systems along on particularly advantageous paths, even without taking into account a tendency toward concentration that comes from agents striving to control their exposure to systemic effects through increased control over their environment. Put differently, economic systems alone cannot guarantee the ongoing change that has proven to be the only way, so far found, to maintain an openness of the system for permitting individual development. Thus, economic policies do not only have to provide the stable structure for economic processes to unfold and correct developments that run counter the properly functioning system. They become part of the process of economic activity and cannot be separated from it, as they influence the behaviors of agents and thereby shape the emerging economic system. As there is no neutral reference point, they are part of the system, and the system cannot be conceived without them. And without the natural correction resulting from systemic characteristics, a functioning public sector is also required to counter or balance adverse outcomes of private activity. Where such a public sector balance is not given, it is unlikely that behavior in an economic system alone would continue to yield desirable results. Some informal rules and structures offer scope for improvement for sure, but as they mostly rely on personal relations, there is a natural limit to how far they can carry a system. At some point the formal and impersonal framework that a public sector sets becomes necessary.

Where agents' interactions shape the path that an economy follows, policy decisions get more involved. But they also become more necessary for fostering the potential that a society offers, as well as the potential that individual agents hold, as we can no longer count on a specific a-personal mechanism to lead societal processes. That is not to say that all decision-making should be centralized to avoid private power. Far from it. Decentralized private activities can and do serve as the grounds for experimentation and can see competition directed toward overall advantageous ends and, of course, as a principle outlet for individually autonomous lives in and of themselves. It is neither the one, nor the other, but the healthy mix of both that moves things forward.

However, a proactive public sector presence can help address systemic issues and stabilize an economic environment, to the benefit of the individuals involved. It can offer protection against systemic effects outside the sphere of influence of individuals, and it can support the development of options for improving future conditions, among others. The level of control that an individual agent has over their economic environment, and the protection she can afford herself against undesirable outcomes, are limited.

In a number of cases, a well-structured policy environment is the best, or even only way, that can hope to lay the foundation for improvements in outcomes. Even if there are some negative effects to be identified, that does not mean that there is only one alternative to a specific course of action, and that said alternative was automatically better. If the sky is not green, it is only red, if these are the only options you permit. But there is a broader spectrum for capturing economic, social, and other activities. There are, in fact, many alternatives.

Policy formulations are therefore difficult. Public agents accompany private agents' activity, complement it, and provide the framework for it. The contrarian fashion of relations in public and private sector that top-down perspectives easily suggest cannot be maintained. When adopting a process-based understanding of economic issues, we arrive at a view in which public and private agents are required to interact and jointly shape the potential of a group, and the ways and capacities for utilizing that potential. Relations of public and private agents are not antagonistic as a general rule, but can occur in a coordinated or even cooperative fashion. Where they may be made to appear as antagonistic, this may just as well refer to a conflict of interests of different private groups, for which public decision-making structures are chosen as mediators, such as in labor legislation. In a complex modern economy, public agents are as much a part of economic activity as are private ones, and a principal tool to effectively provide structure to balance, counter, or bar right away, private abuses of power. A reduction of a public agent presence may frequently mean that the ability of some private groups to exert influence over others increases. Furthermore, the insecurity and vulnerability of individual agents to systemic developments in modern economies, and the recognition that these can be ameliorated by collective measures, has increased the importance of a functioning public sector.

Where issues of long-term structural change and technological development are concerned, and equilibrium perspectives cannot be drawn upon for shedding light on potentially problematic issues, the involvement of government in related processes has so far been proven to be, in fact, necessary. Given the characteristics of technology, tendencies toward concentration, and slow change in markets without regulatory structures, and the effort required in research for laying the foundation for continuous innovation, it is difficult to envision that this could be any different.

An analytical framework may of course focus on one specific area of interest in economic matters and in fact may have to, for casting some light on aspects of a situation. However, once it is drawn on for policy recommendations, the focus that is chosen in the framework translates to the policy focus. Then, an enhancement of some goals over others results when such policies are put into practice. Different objectives, or, different areas of focus, rather, may well require different measures which can be at odds with each other. Trade-offs between different objectives are always a possibility, and for a proper policy formulation awareness and acknowledgement of such trade-offs will be desirable. A price mechanism to resolve potential conflicts in any particularly desirable manner cannot generally be relied on, as we have repeatedly seen. How to address potentially emerging issues has to be weighed carefully in policy formulations: that there is a potential problem, and an analytical potential for policies to address it, does not necessarily mean that active policy involvement could necessarily garner an improved outcome. More regulations, restrictions, or planning are not necessarily better, or better than a reduction of measures taken in that regard. Part of individual emancipation is the ability to make one's own decisions and live with the consequences. But for agents who are embedded in modern societies and economies, assuming that everything they faced was a result of their own decisions is a grossly simplistic view on matters, and outright discarding the partnership of public and private agents as a promising route to the betterment for the people can only play into the hands of powerful private interests. Results can be improved if we find a suitable political structure. We may still come to the conclusion that a limited involvement of public agents is the preferable route to choose, but a consideration of the role of public agents will be a necessary component of analyses.

Cautioning against an over-reliance on public agents is certainly merited. Erratic policy decisions and overreach by public agents, as well as beholden influence-taking, are of course a possibility and have a long history, just as well-intentioned decisions that may worsen a situation. The rather intricate problem structures in complex economic systems have long been a reason to argue for restraint and against active interventions, and for the creation of space for private agents to experiment, in order to be able to draw from the various potential solutions to problems that different private agents may develop. However, that is not the same as withdrawal of public structure, oversight and control, support and incentives. Rather, it may mean to support bottom-up developments by establishing diverse structures and potential solutions, in competitive, coordinated, or cooperative manners, depending. A simple reduction only opens the door for other influences. There is no neutral state in which no one can assert themselves over others. Doing away with economic policies cannot be the solution, as the modern economic system requires structures and rules for stabilizing it, and for allowing the innovative capacities of capitalist economies to actually come to fruition. How far potential is developed and employed is a product of the society the public sector serves.

A focus on participatory, truly democratic, political systems provides the foundation for inclusive political economic analyses. This contrasts with views of a suitably defined economic sphere which permit a retreat to rather technocratic considerations. Now, the integration of diverse interests will likely come at the price of slowing down the process of arriving at decisions. This aspect, however, appears to be the price that has to be paid for trying to prevent small interest groups from capturing decision-making processes, and to permit individual emancipation to proceed.

Economic analyses show potential for productive involvement and interactions, while political considerations may reveal the structures that can hopefully allow the integration of broad societal interests into required processes. That integration is always a key, as all incentives for representatives to be responsive to their constituents, cannot prevail in fostering inclusive policies, if the constituents do not show up and make themselves heard. Already Machiavelli pointed out that representatives can get away with more limited pursuits, the more their constituents sideline themselves.

Overall, while it is certainly true that policy interventions do not automatically improve results, and that they likewise stand in danger of serving particular interests too narrowly, or cause unintended trouble, that does not mean that doing nothing was automatically preferable. Criticisms against ill-conceived policies that tackle symptoms rather than causes remind us that there lie numerous problems and possibly even dangers with policy interventions, and relying on the public sector for fixing problems, for sure. Nevertheless, what economic analyses show is that there is no reason to suspect particularly good outcomes from individual interactions, either, once we move beyond perspectives in which the economic system forces such outcomes onto individuals. That someone complains about particular policies, through which society says 'no more', does not mean that policy interventions were bad. We may decide against more public sector involvement based on our personal assessment of likely political developments, but should also remember that a number of healthy societies have managed to establish stable systems of partnership to the benefit of their citizens. Where unhealthy ones fail in the political sector, it is difficult to see how an emphasis on private activity could remedy the situation.

VI

Whether economic activity, with its confinements and constraints, is in fact suitable for addressing a problem has to be considered as well.

Independent of the objective that a certain structure is supposed to primarily foster, the utilization of transactions to advance this objective means that specific constraints are in place for private agents, and monetary ones not the least among them. Such constraints can interfere with a socially desirable course. As seen, a profit-orientation by businesses does by no means have to guarantee employment and desirable production conditions and volumes, for instance. Concerning the utilization of markets, areas where broader considerations make individual access desirable, health and education to name but two, are restricted under for-profit provisions. Our perception of problems and potential solutions is influenced by the structures we choose, so that these structures influence our ways forward. This can affect social relations too, for instance. Family neglect may be re-branded as career advancement, depending on the circumstances. Such shifts are hard to account for, and the decision in one direction or another will grow out of the values held within a group, but will then also shape these values. Dynamics of change play out in various dimensions of human life, not just technology in a somewhat narrow sense.

VII

Our knowledge about complex systems does not justify stark assumptions about the economic system at the outset. The singular force of competition between individuals cannot stabilize a complex system, unless the system we choose for our analyses is so restricted that there is no other option in it. Trade-offs will have to be acknowledged and accepted between different interest groups, but also in matters such as the efficiency of production in which fewer large producers may be able to gain substantial cost advantages when compared to numerous smaller ones whose ability to tilt results in their favor is limited, for instance. The larger producers' increased influence over the market or niche they service may be the cost we may have to accept for improvements in the effectiveness of production processes. There is no market mechanism to remedy such problems. How we deal with them is a political decision.

As perspectives on economies that address the complexity of economic systems more openly by integrating emergent structure tend to offer different views than more narrowly formulated perspectives do, we cannot discard them outright. They do not offer the same view using more involved techniques, such as drawing on more elegant mathematical tools, or being willing to move beyond a mathematical formulation where necessary. They offer different perspectives on possibilities and pitfalls in utilizing the economic sphere for reaching desirable societal outcomes. They suggest that there is more to economies than the simplest perspectives can capture. Just as a two-dimensional view on a building can only do it so much justice, so can an analytical framework at best capture some aspects of a complex system. Assuming that any one of a number of simple models may be the proper one to apply in a situation, and trying to figure out which one it is, recognizes that fact implicitly. Removing the level of analyses to the decision process concerning model applications, however, opens the analytical structure to arbitrariness instead of soundness. A recognition of the validity of alternative perspectives on economic issues promises an improved foundation not only for economic research, but, more importantly, for economic policies.

Bibliography

This bibliography offers a commented list of the texts that the material in the book draws on. In part, these texts themselves are more specific overviews of areas and developments in economics. They thus provide a more detailed presentation of aspects addressed in this text, specific themes in economics, but some have also laid the foundation for entirely new perspectives on economics and economies, and have greatly enhanced our understanding of developments toward and in modern economies.

As you will see, a number of these texts rely on some variations of bottom-up perspectives. However, texts that lay the foundation for top-down perspectives and explore their implications further are, of course, included as well. For an overview of the basic mechanics in the reference framework, you can pick up pretty much any textbook that promises an introduction to microeconomics or macroeconomics.

Finally, you can find many scholarly articles by the authors whose works were used in this text, as well as the articles they themselves drew on, both not infrequently as free pdfs. A feature like scholar.google makes it very easy to see references as well as citations, and so establish

H. Schwardt, *The Path to a Modern Economics*,
DOI 10.1007/978-3-319-52785-7

an idea how different authors may relate. You can thus use this bibliography as a starting point to build a more comprehensive overview of economic thought, if you are interested.

Finally, the publication year in brackets refers to the first date of publication. A number of these texts have undergone various editions, and, of course, the latest ones are generally preferable.

Adelman, Irma, Cynthia Taft Morris (1988) Comparative Patterns of Economic Development 1850-1914. The Johns Hopkins Press, Baltimore

The authors examine development processes to find underlying causes for the diverging experiences of different economies.

Akerlof, George A., and Robert Shiller (2015) Phishing for Phools: The Economics of Manipulation and Deception. Princeton University Press, Princeton et al.

The authors explore the consequences of the insight that market interactions do not necessarily lead to improvements for everyone involved in transactions, because our decision-making allows consumers to be deceived and manipulated by producers and sellers of goods.

Ariely, Dan (2008) Predictably Irrational: The Hidden Forces that Shape our Decisions. Harper Collins, Scranton.

The author shows that irrational behavior of humans shows discernible patterns that can be utilized by others to sway our decisions, and that should be taken into account when formulating policies.

Arrow, Kenneth (1974) The Limits of Organization. W. W. Norton & Co, New York and London

The author addresses different ways to organize economic activity, including markets, governments, the internal planning of firms, and communal approaches.

Arthur, W Brian (2014) Complexity and the Economy. Oxford University Press, Oxford et al.

This book offers a collection of papers by one of the first economists to explore in a formalized manner the implications that an approach to economies as complex systems have.

Ayres, Clarence E (1944) The Theory of Economic Progress: A Study of the Fundamentals of Economic Development and Cultural Change. Chapel Hill, University of North Carolina Press

The author analyzes processes of change in economies and the influence that the formal and especially also informal rules and norms in a society have on the shape of the process.

Beinhocker, Eric (2006) The Origins of Wealth: Evolution, Complexity, and the Radical Remaking of Economics. Harvard Business School Press, Boston

The author integrates a large number of concepts and approaches to evolutionary and complexity economics to provide the foundation for rethinking what we thought we knew about economics.

Bell, Daniel (1976) The Cultural Contradictions of Capitalism. Basic Books, Inc., New York

The author argues that in capitalist societies the cultural developments that have gone hand in hand with it will eventually lead the system to break down.

Berle Adolf A., and Gardiner Means (1932) The Modern Corporation and Private Property. The Macmillan Company, New York

The authors analyze the structure of corporations and the impact that the separation of legal ownership and control of a company has had.

Bhagwati, Jagdish (2002) Free Trade Today. Princeton University Press, Princeton and Oxford.

The author presents an overview of arguments for free-trade policies.

Bowles, Samuel (2006) Microeconomics: Behavior, Institutions, and Evolution. Princeton University Press, Princeton et al.

The author analyzes how the interplay of individual preferences and economic environment shape the economic sphere and its ongoing change.

Chandler, Alfred (1977) The Visible Hand: The Managerial Revolution in American Business. The Belknap Press of Harvard University Press, Cambridge and London

The author analyzes the changes in the structure of economic activity, with a focus on the nineteenth century.

Chang, Ha-Joon (2007) Bad Samaritans: The Myth of Free Trade and Secret History of Capitalism. Bloomsbury Press, New York

The author shows that successful economic-development processes have always relied on government interventions and support.

Chang, Ha-Joon (2002) Kicking Away the Ladder: Development Strategy in Historical Perspective. Anthem Press,

The author analyzes how the modern canon of trade and development policies undermine the potential for successful development processes in countries with more limited technological capabilities.

de Soto, Hernando (2000) The Mystery of Capital: Why Capitalism Triumphs in the West and Fails Everywhere Else. Basic Books New York

The author analyzes the importance of legal property rights for capitalist economic systems and their expansion.

Dobb, Maurice (1973) Theories of Value and Distribution since Adam Smith. Cambridge University Press, London

The author presents a history of economic thought, stressing the importance of ideology for its development.

Eichengreen, Barry (2003) Capital Flows and Crises. The MIT Press, Cambridge and London

The author addresses the issue of capital flows, and their potential for positive as well as negative effects on economies, from a number of vantage points.

Eichengreen, Barry (2007) The European Economy Since 1945: Co-ordinated Capitalism and Beyond. Princeton University Press, Princeton et al.

The author discusses the particular cultural and institutional background that has fostered economic development in postwar Europe.

Elsner, Wolfram, Torsten Heinrich, and Henning Schwardt (2014) Microeconomics of Complex Economies – Evolutionary, Institutional, Neoclassical, and Complexity Perspectives. Elsevier /Academic Press, Oxford et al.

The authors present a number of different perspectives on microeconomic issues.

Friedman, Benjamin (2005) The Moral Consequences of Economic Growth. Alfred A. Knopf, New York

The author analyzes how changes in the standard of living can affect openness, democratic structures, and political stability.

Friedman, Milton (1962) Capitalism and Freedom. University of Chicago Press, Chicago

The author argues that uninterfered economic activity is a necessary building block for political freedom.

Galbraith, James K (2008) The Predator State: How Conservatives Abandoned the Free Market and Why Liberals Should Too. Free Press, New York

The author argues that economic prosperity has always been achieved based on private initiative and public-sector activities.

Galbraith, John K (1958) The Affluent Society. Houghton Mifflin Co., Boston

The author argues that in rich modern societies, the notion of scarcity is no longer the principle problem of economic activity to address, and analyze the consequences that abundance has for economic activity.

Galbraith, John K (1967) The New Industrial State. Houghton Mifflin Co., Boston

The author analyzes the influence of large corporations in the economic sphere in particular, and in society in general.

Gintis, Herbert (2009) The Bounds of Reason: Game Theory and the Unification of the Social Sciences. Princeton University Press, Princeton et al.

The author discusses how game theory has to be integrated with broader aspects of social theory to provide a meaningful tool for analyses.

Hall, Peter A, and David Soskice (eds.) (2001) Varieties of Capitalism: The Institutional Foundations of Comparative Advantage. Oxford University Press, Oxford

This edited volume offers a framework for understanding the differences in the specific forms the capitalist systems have taken, and a number of case studies to show these in more detail.

Harvey, David (2010) A Companion to Marx's Capital. Verso, London and New York

The author offers a post-crises, overview, guide, and interpretation of the first volume of Marx's Capital.

Hayek, Friedrich von (1944) The Road to Serfdom. Routledge Press, London

The author presents his views on the political dangers of public-sector planning in the economic sphere.

Hazlitt, Henry (1946) Economics in One Lesson: The Shortest and Surest Way to Understand Basic Economics. Harper Brothers, New York

The author argues that, no matter how well-intended, economic policies that try to improve a situation for a selected group in economies will eventually make the situation worse for everyone.

Heilbroner, Robert (1953) The Worldly Philosophers: The Lives, Times, and Ideas of the Great Economic Thinkers. Simon and Schuster, New York

The author presents and analyzes economic thought and ideas embedded in the times and circumstances of those who articulated them.

Hirschman, Albert O. (1981) Essays in Trespassing: Economics to Politics and Beyond. Cambridge University Press, Cambridge et al.

This collection of essays brings together a number of the author's writings, many of them concerned with the relation between economic development and institutional environment.

Hodgson, Geoffrey (2015) Conceptualizing Capitalism: Institutions, Evolution, Future. The University of Chicago Press, Chicago

The author analyzes the importance of the legal framework for the development of capitalist economic structures.

Hodgson, Geoffrey (2012) From Pleasure Machines to Moral Communities: An Evolutionary Economics Without Homo Economicus. The University of Chicago Press, Chicago

The author analyzes how a nuanced understanding of human beings as self-interested and moral individuals enhances our capacity to analyze pressing issues in economic environments and economic policies.

Johnson, Chalmers (1982) MITI and the Japanese Miracle: The Growth of Industrial Policy, 1925 – 1975. Stanford University Press, Stanford

The authors analyze the prominent involvement of the Japanese Ministry of International Trade and Industry in the development of technological capacities in the Japanese economy.

Kahneman, Daniel (2011) Thinking, Fast and Slow. Farrar, Strauss, and Giroux, New York

The author discusses how our minds actually work, and the impact this has on our decision-making.

Kahneman, Daniel, Paul Slovic and Amos Tversky (eds.) (1982) Judgment under Uncertainty: Heursitics and Biases. Cambridge University Press, Cambridge et al.

The authors present a collection of papers that examine biases in people's behavior, and the heuristics in decision-making that lead to them.

Kalecki, Michal (1971) Selected Essays on the Dynamics of the Capitalist Economy. Cambridge University Press, Cambridge et al.

The collection of essays analyzes aspects of economic systems from a vantage point of economic activity as an ongoing process.

Kapp, Karl W. (2011) The Foundations of Institutional Economics (eds. Sebastian Berger and Rolf Steppacher). Routledge, London and New York

The author analyzes the role of institutions in economic systems.

Keen, Steve (2001) Debunking Economics, The Naked Emperor of the Social Sciences. Zed Books, London

The author presents a detailed discussion of short-comings and inconsistencies of standard economic theory.

Keynes, John Maynard (1936) General Theory of Employment, Interest, and Money. Macmillan and Co, London

The author develops a framework for understanding an economy, which may not return to full employment out of its own dynamics.

Kindleberger, Charles P. (1978) Manias, Panics, and Crashes: A History of Financial Crises. Basic Books, New York

The author presents and analyzes financial crises over the centuries.

Lazonick, William (2009) Sustainable Prosperity in the New Economy? Business Organization and High-Tech Employment in the United States. W.E. Upjohn Institute for Employment Research, Kalamazoo

The author analyzes the impact of the changes in the structure of economic activity over the last few decades.

Maddison, Angus (2007) The Contours of the World Economy 1 – 2030 AD: Essays in Macroeconomic History. Oxford University Press, Oxford et al.

The author analyzes long-run trends and dynamics in economic activity to identify principal influence factors behind them.

Marshall, Alfred (1890) Principles of Economics. Macmillan and Co., London

The author presents, systematizes, and expands, the state of economic analyses at the time.

Mazzucato, Mariana (2011) The Entrepreneurial State: Debunking Public vs. Private Sector Myths. Anthem Press, London

The book analyzes the importance of the public sector for economic activity.

Metcalfe, J Stanley (1998) Evolutionary Economics and Creative Destruction. Routledge, London and New York

The author discusses competition as leading to an ongoing process of change.

Milberg, William, and Deborah Winkler (2013) Outsourcing Economics: Global Value Chains in Capitalist Development. Cambridge University Press, Cambridge et al.

The authors analyze changes in the organization and structure of production processes, and the impact this has had on modern economies.

Minsky, Hyman (1975) John Maynard Keynes. Columbia University Press, New York

The author offers an interpretation of Keynes' work that integrates a number of aspects of that work which are frequently neglected.

Minsky, Hyman (1986) Stabilizing an Unstable Economy. Yale University Press, New Haven

The author analyzes how dynamics in the financial sector can lead to instability in these, and how that can spill over to productive economic activity.

Mirowski, Philip (1989) More Heat than Light – Economics as Social Physics, Physics as Nature's Economics. Cambridge University Press, Cambridge et al.

The author discusses the influence of physics in the development of neoclassical economic theory.

Mokyr, Joel (2002) Gifts of Athena: Historical Origins of the Knowledge Economy. Princeton University Press, Princeton

The author analyzes how complementing technological developments and institutional structures have shaped economic development processes.

Myrdal, Gunnar (1953) The Political Element in the Development of Economic Theory. Routledge and Kegan Paul, London

The author analyzes the ways that ideological component enter economic analyses.

Nell, Edward (1998) The General Theory of Transformational Growth: Keynes After Sraffa. Cambridge University Press, Cambridge et al.

The author analyzes how ongoing innovations in markets change the functioning of the economic system.

Nitzan, Jonathan, Shimshon Bichler (2009) Capital as Power: A Study of Order and Creorder. Routledge, London and New York

The authors analyze frequently used notions of the concept of capital and offer a new definition to overcome flaws in existing concepts.

North, Douglass, and Robert P. Thomas (1973) The Rise of the Western World: A New Economic History. Cambridge University Press, New York

The authors analyze the role of property rights in the process of economic development in Europe.

North, Douglass (1990) Institutions, Institutional Change, and Economic Performance. Cambridge University Press, Cambridge et al.

The author develops how institutions and their change impact economic performance.

Olson, Mancur (1982) The Rise and Decline of Nations: Economic Growth, Stagflation, and Social Rigidities. Yale University Press, New Haven

The author analyzes how the increasing impact of special interests can hinder economic activity.

Ormerod, Paul (1994) The Death of Economics. St. Martin's Press, New York

The author assesses the state of economic theory and analyzes what a theory will have to include to successfully address current economic problems.

Ormerod, Paul (2005) Why Most Things Fail – Evolution, Extinction, and Economics. Pantheon Books, New York

The author analyzes why failure is common in complex systems, and what economics and economic policy can learn from this fact.

Penrose, Edith T. (1959) The Theory of the Growth of the Firm. Basil Blackwell, Oxford

The author analyzes internal structures and the performance of firms.

Perkins, John (2004) Confessions of an Economic Hitman. Berret-Koehler Publishers, San Francisco

The author describes how development policies and organizations are used to extract wealth from less developed countries.

Pickett, Kate, and Richard G Wilkinson (2009) The Spirit Level: Why Greater Equality Makes Societies Stronger. Allen Lane, London

The authors analyze numerous studies on the impact of economic inequality on societies.

Polanyi, Karl (1944) The Great Transformation: The Political and Economic Origins of Our Time. Farrar and Rinehart, New York

The author analyzes the interplay of increasing economic turbulence and political developments.

Potts, Jason (2000) The New Evolutionary Microeconomics – Complexity, Competence and Adaptive Behavior. Edward Elgar, Cheltenham

The author develops an approach to microeconomic analyses that draws on various economic schools of thought and combines them with the analytical tools of complexity science.

Prasch, Robert E (2008) How Markets Work: Supply, Demand, and the Real World. Edward Elgar, Cheltenham

The author presents approaches for making sense of market functioning in real-world settings.

Robinson, Joan (1956) The Accumulation of Capital. Macmillan, London

The author develops an analytical framework for addressing questions concerning developing economies.

Schelling, Thomas C (1978) Micromotives and Macrobehavior. W. W. Norton and Co., New York

The author shows how decisions by individuals can have large cumulative effects that were unintended by any one of them.

Schmookler, Andrew B (1993) The Illusion of Choice: How the Market Economy Shapes our Destiny. State University of New York Press, Albany

The author illustrates how a market-based approach to relations cannot provide good solutions in a number of areas of life, and how it affects our behavior where relations are organized using markets.

Schumpeter, Joseph A (1934; first English edition) The Theory of Economic Development: An Inquiry into Profits, Capital, Credit, Interest, and the Business Cycle. Harvard University Press, Cambridge

The author analyzes how the drive for profit leads to ongoing changes in economic systems.

Schumpeter, Joseph A (1954) History of Economic Analysis. Oxford University Press, New York

The author provides overview, interpretation, and analyses of a few millennia of economic thought.

Scitovsky, Tibor (1976) The Joyless Economy – The Psychology of Human Satisfaction. Oxford University Press, Oxford et al.

The author applies current psychological knowledge to analyses of consumer behavior.

Sen, Amartya (1970) Collective Choice and Social Welfare. Holden-Day, San Francisco

The author studies group decision-making and what conflicts may arise, drawing on economic theory and a number of disciplines beyond that where required.

Sen, Amartya K (1999) Development as Freedom. Oxford University Press, New York

The author develops a broader concept of freedom than can be captured by increased average per capita income.

Simon, Herbert A (1957) Models of Man – Social and Rational. Wiley and Sons, New York

The collection of essays presents analyses of the rational and non-rational aspects of human decision-making and behavior.

Sraffa, Piero (1960) Production of Commodities by Means of Commodities – Prelude to a Critique of Economic Theory. Cambridge University Press, Cambridge et al.

Relying on classical economists' view of economic activity leading to flows of commodities through economies, the author provides an alternative approach to determining the exchange value of goods and profit rates in their production.

Sunstein, Cass, and Richard Thaler (2008) Nudge – Improving Decisions about Health, Wealth, and Happiness. Yale university Press, New Haven

The authors use insights form psychology and their reproduction in behavioral economics to consider policy options which follow from them.

Surowiecki, James (2004) The Wisdom of Crowds: Why the Many are Smarter than the Few and how Collective Wisdom Shapes Business, Economies, Societies, and Nations. Doubelday, New York

The authors describe how large groups of people can make better forecasts than smaller ones, if the structures for aggregating their respective inputs are set up properly.

Sweezy, Paul M (1942) The Theory of Capitalist Development – Principles of Marxian Political Economy. Oxford University Press, Oxford et al.

The author examines Marxist theory and analyzes how far it can help to understanding the dynamics of capitalist systems.

Sweezy, Paul M, and Paul A Baran (1966) Monopoly Capital: An Essay on the American Economic and Social Order. Monthly Review Press, New York

The authors analyze the effects that the monopolization of markets in modern economies have.

Veblen, Thorstein B (1899) The Theory of the Leisure Class: An Economic Study of Institutions. Macmillan, London and New York

The author analyzes the impact of social and economic structures on individual behavior, and resulting dynamics of change in socioeconomic environments.

Veblen, Thorstein B (1904) The Theory of Business Enterprise. Charles Scribner's Sons, New York

The author analyzes the role of companies in modern economies.

Wray, L. Randall (2012) Modern Money Theory: A Primer on Macroeconomics for Sovereign Monetary Systems. Palgrave Macmillan, Basingstoke and New York

The author lays out how money is created in modern monetary systems, and what follows for our understanding of macroeconomic problems.

Index

H. Schwardt, *The Path to a Modern Economics*,
DOI 10.1007/978-3-319-52785-7

T

The manufacturer's authorised representative in the EU is Springer Nature Customer Service Centre GmbH, Europaplatz 3, 69115 Heidelberg, Germany. If you have any concerns regarding our products, please contact ProductSafety@springernature.com

Printed and bound by CPI Group (UK) Ltd, Croydon, CR0 4YY

30/09/2026

02225656-0018